# John Richardson
# of Saint John's in the Vale

*His life, poetry and prose, 1817–86*

EDITED AND INTRODUCED BY

— DAVID HILTON —

First published in 2025 by the author.

Edited and proofread by Natalie K. Watson. Typeset by Richard Rutherford Hilton.

**British Library Cataloguing-in-Publication Data**
A catalogue record for the book is available from the British Library

ISBN 978-1-0683272-0-9

*I often wonder at an author's need or wish to dedicate their book. So, to join the tradition, I do so to my mother, Mary Hilton (née Huggon) and her siblings for raising my awareness of John Richardson over many years; to John Huggon, another great-great-nephew of the poet, for providing me with material as a catalyst; and to the late Brian Wilkinson of Keswick and foremost member of the Lakeland Dialect Society for contributing more material, sharing his own considerable writings about Richardson and giving me the confidence and sense of the importance of such a book, to proceed with it.*

# CONTENTS

# ABOUT THE AUTHOR

David Hilton is a native of Carlisle and a true Carliol by way of education. Following on from Carlisle Grammar School, he attended Westminster College of Education, Oxford, and later, the University of Lancaster where he obtained a B.Ed. (Hons) in Education and Rural Studies. Fifty-one years later, he was awarded a B.A. by Incorporation from Oxford Brookes University for the time at Westminster! Throughout this training, his subject assignments and theses were based among the hill farms and rivers of Cumberland. Resident there until 1975, he has subsequently lived in Wolverhampton and now resides in Morpeth, Northumberland. He doesn't claim to be a specialist in Cumbrian dialect or poetry. This book is the culmination of years of casual interest in his family connection with the renowned poet and writer in that idiom: John Richadson of Saint John's in the Vale.

David's mother's side of the family hailed from Beaumont on the nearby Solway Plain and occasionally referred to the presence of a poet in their ancestry. Her brother was named John Richardson (Huggon) after their uncle, the author's great-uncle. Over the decades, this became a lazy, occasional interest for David and gained impetus after a piece of work for Westminster College resulted in a distinction, the subject matter being the compilation of a "Cumbrian" poetry anthology. It included two poems—his first acquaintance with John Richardson's output. Subsequent encouragement to publish this was ignored, but after more cogitation, David delved further into the poet's origins and writings, and—many years later—this book is the result.

Several separate volumes of Richardson's poetry and other writings are available in Carlisle Library and the Cumbria Records Office. Publications of the Lakeland Dialect Society regularly contain reference to, and extracts from, "J.R."'s poetry, and newspaper archives likewise. However, David believes that this book represents the first attempt at collating all of the master mason's, cum teacher's, cum poet and writer's output; it may still have omissions that he is unaware of and would welcome being made aware of such.

Enjoy browsing this book.

# ACKNOWLEDGEMENTS

First and foremost, I am indebted to the person who initially encouraged me to write this book, the late Brian Wilkinson of Keswick. He was generous with his time and resources and was the in-house expert about John Richardson for the dialect fraternity. Other members of the Lakeland Dialect Society (LDS) who have provided contacts and materials for this publication are Louise Green, the editor of the LDS magazine; and the writer and researcher of a variety of topics, including folk songs in the "Cumberland" dialect, Dr Sue Allan. Louise had the tenacity to walk across the fields to meet me at the church in the teeth of Storm Arwen! When we met, the power cables to the church and Diocesan Centre had been brought down, so there was little incentive to prolong our discussion. The road down the Vale was blocked and the lane to the church was flooded in parts and strewn with large branches which had to be cleared before vehicular access was feasible for the author. The Reverend Geoffrey Darrall, retired vicar of St John's in the Vale church and writer and publisher of several books about that community, has also been generous with his time and hospitality as well as with resources. He owns, and occupies, one of what I refer to as the Richardson properties. The staff at Cumbria County Archives, Keswick Museum and Carlisle Library have given full and professional help and advice. In this respect, I must mention Carla Richards at Carlisle Library, who has patiently supplied me with books and documents from the Jackson Collection and retained them as a discrete subset for at least three years. She has gone beyond her brief, undertaken searches off her own initiative and provided me with books that she has sought out on my behalf. Another relative, who like me is a great-grand-nephew of John Richardson, and a local historian in his own right, John Huggon, Carlisle, has shared unique tokens of detail about our great-great-uncle's funeral and other family connections with the poet.

I have received publishing advice from my son, Richard Rutherford Hilton, founder of Sacristy Press in Durham. My wife, Carolyn, at our home in Northumberland, has tolerated (mostly!) this writer's horizontal "filing" "system" in various rooms for weeks on end over a period of several years. She has endured countless "expressions of frustration", especially with my lack of competence with most matters relating to computer software, my repeated bouts of downtime because of deteriorating eyesight, and all this during the stringent restrictions of the Covid-19 pandemic. My brother, Martin, and friends in Carlisle have been the providers of accommodation on numerous sojourns to research and write the book. My thanks to Dr Natalie K. Watson for editing and proofreading.

My thanks to them all. And please accept my sincere apologies if I have offended you by omission or commission!

# LIST OF ILLUSTRATIONS

# PREFACE

Until I was in my fifties, I had three uncles, two of them had middle names which, as a child, I often found both perplexing and interesting. My mother's family name was Huggon and her brother's first and middle names were John Richardson. My mother and this uncle, John, "Uncle Jack" to me, and their sister, were Cumbrians from Beaumont near Carlisle. They eventually moved to Wigton, and then Carlisle, where my brother and I were born.

I came to understand that Richardson was the family name of a man who lived in the Lake District and had been a poet. Little or no mention was ever made of this John Richardson or of his poetry. I didn't find any of his prolific output on our bookshelves. All I knew was that he, or someone closely related to him, had married into the maternal branch of my family. I now realize that it was Richardson's sister, Isabella, who did so, and she is buried in the churchyard in Burgh-by-Sands, Cumbria. John Richardson is my great-great-uncle.

Just how Isabella came to meet and marry one William Huggon is unrecorded and not known within the current family. William originated from the Longtown/Arthuret district of Cumberland, the son of Edward, a husbandman. Isabella worked as a maid in Burgh-by-Sands on the Solway coast near Carlisle. It is speculated that William may have been assigned to a steading near her in the seasonal "Hirings" that were held throughout market towns. The 1841 Census shows him working at Longburgh, Burgh-by-Sands, before Isabella moved there, and before their marriage on 14 May 1842 at Burgh Parish Church. He was a bachelor husbandman and she a spinster. Their Marriage Notice in the *Carlisle Journal* has them both living at Boustead Hill. There is no evidence of the date of Isabella's move to Boustead Hill for her work before the wedding.

When we think of Stratford-upon-Avon, Shakespeare immediately comes to mind. For many Cumbrians, and others interested in poetry, the Wordsworths, Tennyson, and Coleridge rank high in their consciousness. How much more rarely would John Richardson, of St John's in the Vale, along with other "Lakes Poets", such as the Revd Josiah Relph, the renowned Dr Alexander Craig Gibson, Susanna Blamire, Miss Catherine Gilpin, Robert Anderson, Blind John Stagg, and Mark Lonsdale, get a mention, let alone a placename to be associated with them? Richardson gets close to this. These pre-twentieth-century poets represent what W. G. Collingwood referred to when he said: "We are proud in these parts of our native local poets; that Cumbria [Collingwood's word for the region in 1932] should have bred such a nest of singing birds, though so many of them are unknown abroad."[1]

It wasn't until 1967, when I was a College of Education student, that I discovered some of John Richardson's poetry. I had to compile a poetry anthology comprising 50 poems of my choice. I decided to assemble a Cumbrian collection and awaken some college tutors and fellow students to the fact that there were many poets beyond the "dreaming spires" of Oxford which Matthew Arnold had lauded and which were close to my college.[2] Such modesty! I was actually a biology and geography student, and this idea was a daunting challenge of unknown proportions. Many vacation days were spent in the reference rooms at the former Carlisle Library in Tullie House, delving through anthologies or the complete works of individual poets.

And so it was that I became, temporarily at least, familiar with the names and some of the poetry and prose of these renowned early Cumbrian authors. Ironically, the likes of the Wordsworths and Tennyson were relegated to the sidelines for this anthology. The upshot was that I included a couple of Richardson's poems, and the anthology gained a Distinction from my English tutor—my only such grade in any subject before or since. He was an enlightened critic! And a friendly typist deserved credit for coping with the dialectic idiosyncrasies of the poems, which were written out on a typewriter

---

[1]    G. Collingwood, *The Lake Counties* (London: Frederick Warne & Co. Ltd., 1932), p. 33.

[2]    And how appropriate is this when, much later, I learned that—at the head of Thirlmere at Wythburn's "modest house of prayer", near to where Richardson's wife was born—there is a stone seat to the memory of Arnold by Canon Rawnsley.

and occasionally illustrated by postcards or my photographs. This was before the onset of the universal computer age and domestic publishing software.

One or two family and friends suggested that I work towards publishing the anthology, but that fell on humble and deaf ears, and for 40 years my active interest in the matter lay dormant. The market gradually became saturated with illustrated anthologies and collections; many authors have excelled in such matters. This seemed to entice me to do something similar, but different. I am not, and never have been, "well-versed" in any form of literature, if you'll pardon the pun.

Ten years before seriously embarking on this publication, I met a well-respected and knowledgeable member of "the John Richardson fan club" and the Lakeland Dialect Society, who not only shared his resources but convinced, even encouraged, me to pursue a focus on the life and writings of poet John. I remain forever indebted to the late Brian Wilkinson of Keswick. Brian wrote many articles, usually in the magazines of the LDS and delivered talks about Richardson; Brian's contributions are best summarized in his biographical sketch and critique.[3] Along with a few other authors, I have drawn heavily on Brian's knowledge and articles.

In writing this book, it has been difficult to contribute original material. Others more skilful than myself have researched and written about Richardson's life and careers and critiqued his poetry. So, it is inevitable that I have drawn considerably on their efforts. I apologize if any of my contributions seem familiar or repetitive of theirs, which they are, or if I have mis-quoted or mis-represented them. Sincere apologies also if I have omitted any credits where they are due.

As a teenager in the 1960s, a few of my Anglican friends spoke of the Diocesan Youth Centre at St John's, to which they would go for weekend gatherings. (We) Methodists spoke of it, but to my knowledge none of us stayed there. Although I had travelled through the Vale, walked the flanks of High Rigg and climbed Clough Head several times, it was 40 years later that

---

[3]   Brian Wilkinson, "John Richardson (1817–1886) Waller, builder, schoolmaster and dialect poet 'A poet of the people'", in Elizabeth Foot and Patricia Howell (eds), *Keswick Characters*, Vol. 1 (Carlisle: Bookcase, 2006), pp. 48–9.

I was to call by to view the church and the graveyard, where I had been told John Richardson was buried. I took photographs and subsequently returned, usually getting saturated as I explored High Rigg and the Vale and vowed to delve into John's life—the dialect poet, not the Saint. Is it too wishful to think that some would regard them both as saints?

# JOHN RICHARDSON: HIS LIFE AND WORK

# St John's in the Vale and the landscape
## that inspired John Richardson

John Richardson was arguably the most able of poets in the Cumberland dialect after the days of Robert Anderson and Blind John Stagg. He was born, in 1817, raised, lived, worked and died, in 1886, in St John's in the Vale, but his work was widely read and appreciated, and he acquired a degree of modest eminence in Cumberland.

*1. Towards St John's in the Vale: Clough Head, Wanthwaite*
*Crags and Bramcrag to left of cleft and High Rigg opposite*

The Vale of St John takes its name from St John's Church which is located on the hause between this valley and that of the Naddle to the west. To the north of the church, across the A66, lies Threlkeld village and the hulk of Blencathra with its challenging slatey, south-facing truncated spurs. To the immediate east is the broad shoulder of Clough Head, with its westward facing crags and old quarry at Bramcrag. The hause lies between the knobbly Low Rigg to the north and High Rigg 3 km to the south, a largely wet area of very rough grazing, exposed rock and bogs. The valley road running south from Threlkeld down the eastern side of this rough area of volcanic rock meets the A591 just beyond Legburthwaite. The gated, minor road to the church has high hedges and walls and is barely wide enough for small to medium sized cars. To proceed westward and south past Piper House/Stone Cottage and emerge at the Old Vicarage, which Richardson built and which is now holiday rental accommodation and much extended, is best left to walkers, as the track has greatly deteriorated.

Many a contemporary visitor may consider the Vale to be the epitome of Lakeland scenery with its lowland pasture, stone or whitewashed residences and outbuildings, and enclosed improved grassland, some with flocks of pedigree herdwicks. However, William Gilpin on his Picturesque Tour of the Lakes was disappointed with the Vale on his 1772 visit, 45 years before John Richardson was born:

> It is esteemed one of the most celebrated scenes of beauty in the country: but it did not answer our expectations. The ground, consisting of patches of fenced meadow, adorned with farmhouses, and clumps of trees, was beautifully tumbled about in many parts: but the whole was rich, rather than picturesque; and on this account, I suppose, it hath obtained its celebrity. Its circular form, everywhere within the scope of the eye, wanted that variety, which the winding vale affords.[1]

Walter Scott, on the other hand, in *The Bridal of Triermain*, thought the valley so romantic that he saw Castle Rock as an enchanted castle fit for tales of Arthurian romance.

---

[1]   Grevel Lindop, *A Literary Guide to the Lake District* (Wilmslow, Cheshire: Sigma Leisure, 2005), quoting Gilpin's *Observations, relative chiefly to picturesque beauty, made in the year 1772, on several parts of England; particularly the mountains, and lakes of Cumberland, and Westmoreland* (1786).

John Richardson was born on 20 August 1817, in Stone Cottage off the Naddle Fell road, almost equidistant between the current A591 Ambleside road and the church in which he was baptized by the Revd Edward Wilson on 6 October 1817.

The Revd Geoffrey Darrall, who is now (2022) the owner-occupier of the properties and probably the most thorough researcher about all matters relating to the church's and Vale's history, feels that Richardson moved into Piper House after his marriage.

It was in 1855, on the death certificate of his father Daniel, that both of the dwellings are for the first time referred to as "Piper Houses" (plural, inclusive of Stone Cottage; see below). Its name had reverted to the singular 22 years later. Prior to that, and from 1603 when "Stone" is first recorded, Stone, or Stone in Naddle, were inclusive of both properties.

A story goes that at one time a Scottish piper was living at the house (as a guest of the Richardsons) and used to gladden the hearts of the local community with his music. Rawnsley wrote in *Chapters in The English Lakes* that the piper "skirled his pipes and played his reels … to wile away with tunes his long imprisonment by snow and storms".[2] And in another volume, he writes "a man who was good with the chanter and drones once lived there … for some years gave shelter to a character who refused to have anything to do with drones; this same Richardson, the poet-schoolteacher."[3] He reputedly played in the then much smaller west-facing window. In return, it was decided to rename the cottages. But the new name lasted only briefly and was later attached only to the present Piper House. The author has discussed this with Geoff Darrall who has found no substantive evidence for the existence of a piper and is most sceptical of the legend. Yet he wonders why, if the evidence is so scanty, the property is called Piper House. And if Rawnsley knew John so well, would he have any reason to invent the story?

More authentically, there are tales of a long tradition of cock fighting taking place in a pit on the hill behind the school and many of the protagonists

---

[2]  Rev. Canon H. D. Rawnsley, *Chapters at the English Lakes* (Glasgow: MacLehose & Sons, 1913), pp. 149–51.

[3]  Rev. Canon H. D. Rawnsley, *A Coachdrive at the Lakes* (Keswick: T. Bakewell, 1902). p. 78.

are purported to be buried in the churchyard "with no twinge of conscience for the suffering they had caused … and were no doubt surprised when the sport was banned". The commentator, "Whiteoak", reckons that Richardson could not have been a supporter because he was so critical of it "as being like pitting two men to fight each other with daggers strapped to their toes". Other contemporary sports were otter and badger bating.[4]

*2. Stone Cottage and Piper House, the Richardsons' home*

Canon H. D. Rawnsley wrote: "There stands beside the bank beneath the hill a very simple Cumberland Cottage, four eyes, a nose and a mouth upon its white face in the shape of dark windows, porch and open door. That cottage has sent forth songs that will not die—songs born of sympathy with simple

---

4    "Whiteoak", "An Epitome of Lakeland", *Workington Times & Star*, 1 November 1991.

men and solemn nature."[5] This description of Stone Cottage hints at its locally famous resident, who was, as just mentioned, a friend of Rawnsley, meeting him on many occasions.

A former resident of Piper House wrote more pragmatically of it during the early twentieth century:

> I don't think it has been altered at all since John Richardson was born there. At the rear, facing the fell, it has a huge, whitewashed porch and four small windows. At the front, facing west, the house has had new, up to date, windows much larger than they were in the old days. It had a very large living room with an uneven flagged floor; much-recessed walls, an old-fashioned chimney neuk with its quaint Ranel bokes ... a queer winding staircase, now wood. In the Richardsons' time, the staircase would most likely have been of stone.[6]

In its early days, and indeed until quite recently, Piper House, for instance, was probably "nowt but a hovel"—as another former resident, Anne Edgar, had commented in the early twentieth century.[7] It had an outside, deep-pit, closet, stone-flagged floors, and no mains electricity or generator. Water was obtained from Willy Gill or William's Beck 100m away. In present times, water is piped from there to the property.

Piper House was certainly crowded. The means of heating isn't specified, but coal was probably available from the rail depots along the Keswick–Penrith line, the nearest being Threlkeld village. The incumbent was a friend of Richardson and a source of material for a poem. Notwithstanding the Richardson family's good reputation as builders and masons, there is nothing to suggest their standard of living was at variance with the other locals.

---

[5] Rev. Canon H. D. Rawnsley, *Rambler's Notebook. At the English Lakes* (Glasgow: MacLehose & Sons, 1902).

[6] Brian Wilkinson, Handwritten notes to the author, based on various sources including a later resident of Piper House, John Bainbridge, *c.*1904.

[7] Geoffrey and Pat Darrall, "Stone Cottage and Piper House", in Geoffrey Darrall (ed.), *Rediscovering our Past—A History of the Houses in the Parish of St. John's in the Vale, Castlerigg and Wythburn* (Naddle, Carlisle: Piper Publications, 2012).

The following photograph hints at the standard of living of residents and schoolchildren.

*3. The school that John built, St John's in the Vale*

Indeed, Daniel and his wife Mary were neither wealthy nor proud, receiving gifts (perhaps the forerunner of what in some denominations today are referred to as "Poor Funds?") from the parish charities, distributed twice a year. In records of Charitable Distributions from Parish Funds, and commencing in 1817, and for several years thereafter, Daniel received variously sums of 2s.6d, 1s.0d, 4s.2d, 6d and 3s.9d out of a total annual fund of £1.2s.6d (in 1828). The last evidence of such payments was in 1835. In 1832, William Richardson received 4s.6d. As you will read later, the Richardson children, along with others, were also recipients of the Book of Common Prayer. Mary, Daniel's daughter, received three loaves distributed at the altar table to "the undermentioned poor persons".[8]

St John's Church seems to have supported several charities for the benefit of the poor, often distributing either cash or bread, veal or mutton. However, this "food bank" donation to the Richardsons, among others, seems eventually to

---

[8]    Cumbria County Council Archives, Carlisle: Ref. PR/153/1/31.

have become a historical legacy, more of custom and practice—which is described in his paper Old Customs and Usages—and not related to absolute poverty.

The vicar, Charles Dowding, wrote some 13 years after John died, in the Minutes in the churchwardens' book of Whitsunday, 1899:

> The vicar and churchwardens distribute these loaves [to the recipients], but from habit, not from need. The loaves have to be given away and recipients are needed, but as marking the improved condition of "the poor", since the time this Charity was left, it may be stated without fear that no man, woman, or child goes short of food from year's end to year's end in his parish unless it be from gross incompetence on the part of the wife.[9]

Of course, it couldn't have been the man's fault!—Political correctness and sensitivities were perhaps not part of the Revd Dowding's repertoire of social concern. It was during Dowding's tenure that the size of the parsonage was doubled on account of his large family!

John's mother, Mary Faulder, who had been christened in Watermillock, married Daniel Richardson on 27 May 1804 in Patterdale. Their first child, Elizabeth, was born there in 1805. Their second child, Daniel, was born in 1810 at Stone Cottage in St John's in the Vale. Mary was born in 1813, John four years later in 1817. Other children followed: Isabella was born in 1820, Timothy in 1823, and Jane in 1829. Home conditions were very primitive and were probably exacerbated by the cottage being at an elevation of about 165m.

The couple lived at Stone Cottage throughout the 49 years of their married life, except for the first few years. Mary died on 26 October 1853, aged 70, and was buried in St John's in the Vale where she was to be joined two years later by Daniel on 17 June 1855.

John received his education up in the school at the hands of the Curate, the Revd Edward Wilson, who was buried in the church graveyard a year after Mary Richardson, in 1855. With the school almost literally on his doorstep, and later working locally throughout the valleys and in Keswick, John would

---

9    Cumbria County Council Archives, Carlisle: Ref. PR/153/1/31.

have been immersed in the life of the fells and soaked up the rural culture, speaking the dialect and observing his father at work as a "wa'er". On John's baptism certificate, Daniel is described as a husbandman; later, in *The Trades Directory* of 1847 and on the Census Return of 1848, Daniel is a mason, the term used to describe a "wa'er". John progressed to be a master craftsman building many properties in the Vale and in Keswick, taking on work in his own right and gaining an outstanding reputation for his work.

# John Richardson's early career

John probably left school at the age of 12 and was to spend the early years of his working life following in Daniel's footsteps. John soon branched out on his own, having a hand in many farmsteads and houses in both the locality of Piper House and in the Keswick area. Buildings at or near Saint John's in the Vale in which he had a skilled hand include the church rebuilding in 1845, which cost £98, the school in 1848, and the vicarage at Dale Bottom in 1856, for which he was paid £185. Other contractors brought the total cost to £332.10s.0d. This must have been one of his last significant buildings as he became the schoolmaster two years later. He had worked for 25 years as a waller and builder.

Describing the scenery of the area on his journey from Windermere to Keswick, Canon H. D. Rawnsley writes from the main road:

> … nothing now but roses … till, facing one of the oldest mossiest dry walls in the country, the humble little parsonage of St. John's Vale greets us, standing close to the turn that takes us … to Naddle Fell. Yonder the little road on Naddle Fellslopes upward to the most picturesquely placed church in the Lake District.[10]

Of the many houses he and his father built in and around Keswick, the magnificent frontages of St John's Terrace on Derwentwater Place, are tribute to the craftsmanship of father and son. The popular writer William Smith lived in 3 Derwentwater Place. He describes one room as being a "light, pleasant, three-windowed room with peeps of lake and mountains, fresh from the hands of mason-poet Richardson of Saint John's in the Vale".

---

[10]  Rawnsley, *A Coachdrive at the Lakes*, pp. 75–7.

*4. Some of the houses that John built, Derwentwater Terrace, Keswick*

During the early years as a waller, John courted his future wife, one Miss Grace Birkett, who was born and baptized in Withburn (as it was then spelled) and who lived at City Farm, near Wythburn (which is now under Thirlmere). Their courtship is described in one of his best-known and most frequently re-printed poems, "It's Nobbut Me". Cunningly, in this poem, he writes from his girlfriend's perspective.

It is said that he used to walk to City from St John's for what little social life he could create. The return trip must have been about ten miles. Perhaps he resorted to pony or horse occasionally? The author of *Lore of the Lake Country*, journalist Frank Carruthers, wrote; "It's a long way to City House Wythburn … and since social gatherings, at which meetings were possible and where courtships began, were few and far between, it seems that John had taken a sort of shy initiative."[11]

It must have worked! They were married on 8 July 1841, when John was 24 years old. The press notice read: "At St. John's Church, Keswick, on Thursday last. Mr. John Richardson, waller, to Miss Grace Birkett, of St. John's". Grace's home had been in the parish of St John's, Keswick. The 1841 Census lists a Grace Birkett, aged 20, a dressmaker, living at Low Nest, which is just across the valley within sight from Piper House. Grace may have moved to lodge at the Nest some time prior to her marriage. This would save him the tedious journey to Wythburn to see her.

The reference to two "St. John's" in the marriage notice is explained by Geoff Darrall:

> Grace ... was born at City, Wythburn and it would have been certain that in those days, she would have been married there ... At the time John and Grace were married, Low Nest was not in the parish of St. John's in the Vale, but in the parish of St John's, Keswick. The parish boundaries were later changed, and the area round Low Nest was moved into St John's in the Vale parish. At first, I thought there was a confusion between the two St. John's churches, but I then realised the truth of the situation! They were married at St. John's Keswick because this was now her parish.
>
> In the 1841 Census, I came across the name of Grace Birkett, aged 20, dressmaker living at Low Nest, which is just across the valley from Piper House, within sight, in fact. This seemed to me to indicate that she had moved to lodge at the Nest some time recently, to be near John at Piper House! This would save him the tedious journey to Wythburn to see her. Thirty years later, under John and Grace's residence at Bridge House, there is the same information: she was a dressmaker and teaching sewing. Surely this must be the same Grace?

Wythburn Chapelry and joint township with St John contained a small hamlet called "The City" near the head of Thirlmere Lake, eight miles SSE

---

[11]  F. J. Carruthers, *Lore of the Lake Country* (London: Robert Hale & Co., 1975), p. 147.

of Keswick. The Chapelry extends from five to ten miles south by east of the same town to the confines of Westmoreland, where the boundaries of the two counties are marked by the Dunmail Raise Stones.

The map shows the area before the building of the dam, started in 1886, to raise the level of the lake(s) to provide water for the residents of Manchester. The water to the north of the isthmus used to be called Leathes Water and that to the south, Wythburn Water. It was all deemed good farmland in the area. Certainly, by the turn of the century, City was under the new Mere level. Some writers had referred to the dwellings as The City of Wythburn and were confused by the various nomenclatures. The 1847 *Trade Directory* and the earlier National Census of 1841 record that one City dweller was a John Birkett, Shoemaker, aged 76 by the former listing, and his wife Mary. Other residents were son, George, aged 30, a John, aged five, so not a son of Grace and John Richardson of the same name, but born in 1848. There is no mention of daughter Grace at that time. However, another inhabitant with the Birketts was a tailor called Jonathan Kendal. Could it be that this is where Grace received her foundation training as a seamstress and later teacher of sewing? A second dwelling in City had, by 1851, become occupied by John Birkett, son of the aforementioned John Birkett and a 51-year-old farmer. His youngest sister was Grace Birkett who had married John Richardson in 1841.

It was from his mother-in-law, Mary Birkett, that Richardson derived the background for many of his stories which were eventually published as the "Stwories Ganny used To Tell" in the *West Cumberland Times* in 1879–80. Grace's family would not have been flattered by the comments of one Edward Baines in 1834 who felt "that ancient hamlet … called the City of Wythburn … a hamlet of rude architecture, and the citizens as unpolished as their habitations".[12]

---

[12]   Geoffrey Darrall, *The Valley of Thirlmere—Rediscovering our Past*, Part 2 (Piper House, Naddle, Keswick: Piper Publications, 2018), p. 26.

# The "new" Richardson family

Along with John's parents, there were eventually 12 mouths to feed and people to sleep in Stone Cottage! Grace and John had ten children, two of whom died in infancy. Their eldest, born the year after their marriage, was Daniel. He died, aged 27, in 1869, in Woolwich in London. Mary, who became a servant at the parsonage in the vale, was born in 1844 and Sarah in 1846. John, Grace and Birkett were born at two-year intervals before their last two children; Jeffrey and Elizabeth were born in 1855 and 1857 respectively. There were two others who died in infancy, so between them John and Grace raised eight of their ten children. All their sons had good careers in many parts of the country, and one emigrated to New Zealand to work in bank management.

John's own parents, who had been living with them, had died before Elizabeth was born; his mother in 1853, and his father on 15 June 1855. John and his family continued to live in Piper/Stone for another three years until he was appointed schoolmaster in 1858 and he and his family moved to Bridge House.

# The church and Chapel House

The church was first mentioned in 1554 when it was bequeathed money for repairs. The site later came to be used by the Knights Hospitaller of St John of Jerusalem and was reputedly a refuge, or hostelry, for travellers along the well-trodden, though rough, route from the Eden Valley via Penrith to Keswick. "Chappell" House is first recorded in the "Indenture of 1623" shared between several tenants and their Lord of the Manor. In due course, it became an inn-cum-farm.

Over a century later, in 1787, James Clarke wrote in his *Survey of the Lakes*:

> On the Sunday after Easter, all the inhabitants of the parish, old and young, men and women, repair to the Ale House after Evening Prayer; they then collect a penny from each person, male or female, but not promiscuously, as the women pay separately; this money is spent on liquor, and at one of these meetings (or penny fairs as they are called) the sum amounted to three pounds, so there must have been 720 persons present.[13]

According to John Richardson, the use of the churchyard for burials was established about 1710. It would have been 20 or so years after the original chapel and churchyard were established before anyone was buried there, on account of the superstition that the devil was waiting to claim the first person to be buried therein. Worshippers came from both sides of Naddle. In the days before St John's was a Chapelry, it was served by curates of Crosthwaite. There was no vicarage, and the curate lived at various houses in the parish, including, for instance, Yew Tree, Piet Nest and Bridge House.

In early November 1844, at a meeting of ratepayers of St John's Chapelry for the purposes of considering the best mode of repairing the now dilapidated chapel, it was unanimously agreed that it would not be advisable to attempt any repairs. A future meeting later in the month would decide the way

---

[13]    James Clarke, *A Survey of the Lakes of Cumberland, Westmorland and Lancashire* (London. Printed for the Author, 1787).

forward, including the rebuilding of the said chapel. Any moneys were to be raised by public subscription. It was from this parlous state of the buildings that John Richardson was commissioned to build the new church.

*5. St John's Church, St John's in the Vale*

The contract required the work to be completed by the beginning of August in the following year:

> The Contracts are to be entered into with the Committee and the works to be commenced with immediately and the whole to be finished on or before the first day of August 1845.
>
> Payments will be made as follows—viz one half when the building is covered in and the remainder when completed, examined and approved of by the Committee, and Chapel Wardens.

This is the Specification referred to in our Agreement for building St.
Johns Chapel as (through our) this fourth day of (January) 1845.

(Witness) to the signing, Joseph Wilkinson

[Signed by—] John Richardson Miles (Storey)

Thomas Tyson Henry (Rowley)[14]

In January 1846, John Richardson was paid £4.13s.0d "for walling and new
work round the (enlarged) chapel yard".

*6. Date stone on north wall of the church*

The church census of *c.*1848 notes the last recorded occupation of Chapel
House, after which both it and the farm seem to have fallen into disrepair.
It was probably plundered for its stone for both the school's rebuilding in
1848–9 and the construction of the hearse house in 1865, the year in which
St John's ceased to be a chapel of ease. Alongside was a chapel and churchyard,
which was also founded there, the latter possibly as long ago as the very early
1700s. The chapel, as it was before the church was built, doubled as an early
school; the Reader was also a teacher.

---

14   Cumbria County Council Archives, Carlisle: Ref. PR/153/1/31.

There is a note in the Chapel Wardens' minutes for May 1855, that The Revd Chas. A Perring appointed John Richardson, Master Mason, to act as Clerk in St John's Chapel in the Vale.

The present church is a plain low and small building. It was "a dales chapel rebuilt by a dalesman". F. J. Carruthers maintains that

> [n]o church in the diocese has a more dramatic setting; more spectacular surroundings. No church in the county holds better the shape and the spirit of the church which it replaced. The chapel which John Richardson rebuilt was erected at a time when new churches were being built in towns and cities across the land with soaring steeples and graceful aisles. Not so for John Richardson. His new chapel was plain, low and small with a miniature tower at the west that is not much bigger than a chimney. It is a delight to see, and fitted perfectly in its situation among the rugged crags and extensive views of the northern Lakes scenery. If anything, it was a reflection of John.[15]

St John's had been a chapel of ease, one of five with the mother church of St Kentigern at Crosthwaite, Keswick and serving the farming community of the Vale of St John. In 1863, it united with Wythburn, where there were only four services a year, to form a separate Parish which included Thirlmere, separate from that of Crosthwaite. This is recorded in *The London Gazette* on 28 July 1863:

> The SCHEDULE to which the foregoing Representation has reference.
>
> The District Chapelry of Saint John in the Vale, being:
>
> All that part of the parish of Crosthwaite, in the County of Cumberland, and in the diocese of Carlisle, which is comprised within, and is co-extensive with all that portion of the parochial chapelry of Saint John in the Vale, which is not included within the limits of the particular district of Saint John, Keswick, in the county and diocese aforesaid.
>
> Her Majesty having taken the said representation, together with the map or plan thereunto annexed, into consideration, was pleased, by and with the advice of Her Privy Council, to approve thereof, and to order, and it is hereby

---

[15]  F. J. Carruthers, *Lore of the Lake Country* (London: Robert Hale & Co., 1975).

ordered, that the proposed assignment of a District Chapelry to the consecrated church of Saint John, situate in the Vale, in the Parish of Crosthwaite, in the county of Cumberland, to be called "The District Chapelry of Saint John in the Vale," be accordingly made; and that the recommendations of the said Commissioners, with reference to the publication of banns of matrimony and the solemnisation or performance of marriages, baptisms, churchings, and burials, in the said church; and with reference to the fees to be received in respect of the publication of such banns and the solemnisation or performance of the said offices, be carried into effect agreeably to the provisions of the said Acts: and Her Majesty is further pleased to direct that this Order be forthwith registered by the Registrar of the diocese of Carlisle.

Edmund Harrison.[16]

The small graveyard was full by about 1880 when an ultimatum was issued on public health grounds for the parish to either close or extend the churchyard. This resulted in the demise of the inn which, as already mentioned, was part of the buildings which became "Chappell" House. What may have been a barn was attached to a farmhouse and it, in turn, to a dairy, perhaps, and other outbuildings. These were enclosed in land which conforms to the shape of the "new" graveyard. The land was conveyed to church ownership in 1884 and the original, now insanitary, churchyard was extended into it. I am grateful to the late Brian Wilkinson for commenting (as have others before him) on Richardson's inspection of the completed drystone wall of the extended graveyard, when the latter declared it "as fine a bit of work in that line as I ever saw—even on the fells". In this context, the poet enjoyed quoting Defoe:

Wherever God erects a house of prayer,
The devil always builds a chapel there;
And 'twill be found upon examination,
The latter has the largest congregation.

---

[16]  Cumbria County Council Archives, PR/153/1/20.

# John's second career and life at Bridge House

Canon Rawnsley suggests that John Richardson became the village school master for reasons of ill health: "Too delicate in health for the hard work of a waller, he became the dominie of St John's in the Vale school."[17] He would hold the post for 27 years. The *Carlisle Patriot*, 7 May 1886, in its obituary to him, describes it thus:

> A lingering spell of indifferent health first suggested the idea of his trying for the situation of teacher at St. John's school. Having been of a studious thoughtful and observant turn of mind from boyhood he managed by degrees to adapt himself to the various duties of his new undertaking.

A handwritten note found in the Cumbria County Archives relates to his appointment:

> Public Notice:    A meeting of the inhabitants of St John's in the Vale will be held in the schoolroom on Thursday the 15th Inst. at 5 o'clock in the afternoon for the purpose of appointing a Schoolmaster and also to make arrangements respecting the allotment of land belonging to the school.
>
> John Taylor, Incumbent    John Scott    John Fleming John Hawkings.    April 3rd 1858.[18]

Thereafter, John and his wife Grace moved to the other side of Naddle, east of the church and school, to live in Bridge House, alongside St John's Beck. The Richardsons continued to live there after John's retirement. The 1881 Census mentions John and his daughter Sarah as residents, but there is no mention of Grace, although she did not die until 1908 whilst a resident of Penrith.

---

17  Rawnsley, *Chapters at the English Lakes*, pp. 149–50.
18  Cumbria County Council Archives, PR/153/1/48.

*7. Bridge House and St John's Beck from the roadside near the church*

*8. Bridge House from the footbridge*

*9. Bridge House from the south*

John Richardson seems to have "laboured (at the school) with untiring energy and "remarkable success".[19] The School Rules required that (the teacher) worked seven hours a day there, delivering The Sacred Scriptures, the "3-Rs"—Reading Writing and Arithmetic—in addition to Mathematics, Book-keeping, Land Surveying, Geography, English Grammar and History; and also attend Sunday worship.[20][21]

In the Minutes of the School Trustees for 19 September 1855, three years before he was appointed teacher, "on the motion of Mr Fisher of Seatoller, the Deed requiring the Minister to pay the annual sum of five pounds to (the Schoolmaster), was unanimously voted (for)".[22]

---

[19] Sydney Lee (ed.), *Dictionary of National Biography*, Vol. 48 (London: Smith Elder & Co., 1896), pp. 235–6.

[20] Cumbria County Council Archives, PR/153/1/42.

[21] Alan Hankinson, *Writers in the Lakes* (Carlisle: Bookcase, 2008), p. 123.

[22] Cumbria County Council Archives, PR/153/1/42.

I wonder if John found teaching an easier occupation and whether he was subjected to the "barren' oot" that he and his peers inflicted on their schoolmaster, and which is described vividly in the poem of that title? Did he keep his hand-in, working with the stones from time to time, or was it a "once-and-for-all" lifestyle change? He may have found it hard, especially in the summer months, and more challenging in different respects, making the transition from outdoors in most if not all weathers as a waller and stonemason, to the classroom, and no mention is made of him undergoing any kind of training for his new role. I wouldn't mind surmising that he had something of an outdoor slant to the curriculum—a pioneer teacher of environmental studies, perhaps, for all the children at the school?

As a teacher, John still found time to write his poetry and pursue his own continued education, to write prose and deliver talks to learned societies. Apart from one reference, in an obituary, to his regular attendance, there is almost nothing that I have seen in the records that reflects the job description's requirement for his church attendance, other than by implication. His family may provide evidence of his encouragement of the role of the church and Sunday School. Son George, when 16, received a copy of *Pilgrim's Progress*; Daniel, a copy of the *Life of Columbus*; in 1856 Jacob and Mary were given a gilt-edged Bible and John a *Testament of Life*. Six years later, Grace Richardson received a book of *Pictures of Hindoo Life*. And there are other (illegible, mainly) references up to 1874.[23]

However, perhaps in contradiction of his "remarkable success", the school's Logbook contains transcribed copies of Inspectors' Reports, which reveal that not all was well with standards of delivery and achievement. The following paragraphs are verbatim copies of Inspectors' Reports from some of the school's Logbooks which also have more mundane daily entries.

A Report of 12 December 1875, reads:

> Higher classes have been taught very intelligently but lower classes are not
> sufficiently well grounded … Reading is fluent in all classes. Handwriting
> needs to be larger and more formal … was much pleased with answers given

---

23   Cumbria County Council Archives, PR/153/1/42.

me in history, geography and grammar. Sewing is required to be taught and a suitable table should be purchased.

The 1876 Diocesan Inspection Report, in March, was much longer. It revealed

a good state of discipline but handwriting is too cramped and angular and ... they are behind in their attainment. Reading is very creditable ... Arithmetic is bad throughout the school ... 1st and 3rd Standards are quite ignorant of notation ... the Infants are extremely backward ... The entries in the Logbook are meagre. The reading books are too difficult for lower Standards ... Maps of Scotland and Ireland are required ... An Admissions and a Summary Registers should be supplied without delay ... and kept in accordance with the instructions in ... Circular 65. The floor of the schoolroom should be washed periodically ... The Needlework is deserving of praise and the older girls should now be pressed forward ...

My Lords cannot entertain the school's claim to a grant under Article 19D until the Report is more favourable. The Inspector's suggestions should meet with immediate attention ... I have to state that Article 32(b) will have to be enforced next year unless decided progress is visible in the writing and Arithmetic of the older children, and the Grant for the presentation of the Infants will not be renewed until the Inspectors can report that they are properly instructed (Article 19(B) 1(a).

The notes in the Logbook are signed by John Richardson, Teacher. Grace Richardson, Teacher of Sewing, and John Taylor.

Despite the shortcomings of the school, a half-day holiday went ahead! From January 1878, the subsequent Reports reflect:

some improvements in Arithmetic, though not in the lower Standards, (which are) altogether inferior and it is clear that sufficient endeavour has not been made to stem the defects of instruction in this point made last year. The reading is well advanced, the spelling on the whole moderate ... if better results in Geography and Grammar cannot be attained, they had better be dropped. Sewing is very creditably taught ... Partitions and lights should be made in the Office ... The warming should be made more effective ... Discipline is satisfactory ... My Lords regret to make a deduction of one-tenth from the Grant under Article 32(b) for defective instruction in Mathematics, especially in the lower standards.

(Signed: John Richardson, Teacher. Grace Richardson, Teacher of sewing. John Taylor, Correspondent of Managers.)

The Report of summer 1882 reads:

On the whole, advance has been made, though in some respects the attainments are below par. The reading is creditable, and the spelling of the lower Standards is satisfactory. The arithmetic however is still rather weak, especially in the lower Standards, and spelling and composition of the higher Standards is hardly up to the mark. The handwriting should be better formed. The Infants continue fairly well advanced. Distinct improvement has been made in Geography, but the Grammar of the boys is weak. Needlework as usual much deserves commendation. The discipline appears to be satisfactory. Historical Readers should be supplied. Better results in Arithmetic will be looked for next year as a condition of an unreduced Grant (Article 115 New Code for 1882).

(Signed: John Richardson, Teacher. John Taylor, Correspondent.)[24]

There are many hundreds of entries in the School Logbook for the time John served there. These relate to visits of the Attendance Officer, pupil attendances, and the effects of weather on these. There are frequent references to storms, floods and snow. On one occasion, two-thirds of pupils were absent; on others the school was closed. The children of some families were absent for the whole of tatie gathering.

It is written of John:

Simply bred, he lived to the end in sturdy independence of spirit but with absolute modesty both of manner and of wants and having things—home,

---

24   Cumbria County Council Archives, PR/153/1/42.

work, wife and bairns, a bit of garden ground, a good conscience, the exquisite beauty of the Vale to quicken and inspire, with a few good books close at hand, was there with him all content. Of him it might be truly said, "remote from towns, he ran his Godly race nor 'ere had changed, nor wished to change his place."

*10. John Richardson in the attire and pose of a "statesman"*

John Richardson, a man of whom it might be said that the Vale of St John's had laid strong hold of his affections and was to him a pleasurable feeling of blind love, the pleasure there is in life itself. Apparently, there was nothing he loved more than the quiet reflection of the dedicated fisherman as he cast his hook into the local St John's Beck:

> Mr. Richardson was a quiet, estimable man, slow to speak, but to the purpose when he did speak, and always working either with his hands or his head.[25]

Elsewhere, Richardson is described as strong and well-built:

> His face was the face of an elderly man who has found the peace that is bred from adversity, a fine open forehead he has lined with care but mostly with thought; grey "Viking" eyes that have a dreamy far-away look about them. A face solid and reposeful enough but filled with soul and Benevolence, a mouth that is closely set and, except by a twinkle in the eye, you feel the man has laughter at his heart. He is a true son of Isaac Walton and has been fishing all the way up the River Bure [now St. John's Beck] from his home, Bridge House, that's shaded in green trees there in its shelter't neuk ... . He loves playing with the trout and has "put on time" with a bit of "prickly bass fishing and aw." And he has fallen into a reverie, as was not infrequent with him there by Thirlmere side.
>
> After patiently trying various baits, he shoves his rod into the ground and describes at length what a privilege it is to be amongst such peaceful surroundings, oblivious to, but aware of, the predatorial nature of urban business folk out to make a living. He employs metaphors with the natural world that he is sharing there and then with typical insightfulness. After all his musings and metaphors, he attends to his rod and line to find that he has missed his catch and an eel or pike has taken its bait, hook, line and floater.

John was exceptionally proud of Cumberland folk and wouldn't hear a word spoken against them, writing: "What! Cumberlan' fwok let them gang whar

---

25    Darrall, *The Valley of Thirlmere*.

they will, we're allus respected and weel thowt on still; and to say that they're wicked, it's aw just a farce, ye'll fend them in Croziers from the Riddings ... and Lunnon a hundred times warse."

# Retirement and funeral

When he stopped work, his health was failing. Not long after he retired, John had a stroke, and it is reputed that the Bishop of Carlisle and Stafford Howard of Greystoke attempted to obtain a Literary Pension for him. After another year of failing health, following this "paralytic seizure", John collapsed, or fell, as he walked down to his home by the Bure. Another commentary suggests that he was rushing to catch the Windermere coach. He died, some sources say, on the hillside; another implies "at home", on 30 April 1886 and was buried the following Tuesday, 4 May.

*11. The much older John Richardson*

# In memoriam

The entire valley turned out to pay their last respects and were joined by many others from further afield. Mourners included representatives of the Cumberland Association for the Advancement of Literature and Science, to whom John had lectured; the Wilsons from the Keswick Hotel; the Brunskills from Threlkeld Vicarage; the Croziers from the Riddings, where John Crozier was both the founder and Master of the Blencathra Hunt for 64 years. Richardson wrote about him in the poem set to music by the Carlisle Cathedral organist, William Coward. The sombre procession followed his coffin which was borne on a single-horse-drawn hearse as it wound its way up the fellside road from Bridge House, where he continued to reside after retirement, to the little churchyard beside the church (which he had built 40 years earlier) and the school which he had served so well.

The gravestone makes no remark of his impact on the fabric and culture of the area. The inscription merely reads:

> In loving memory of John Richardson of Bridge House, St. John's in the Vale,
> who died on the 30th April, 1886 aged 68 years' and 'Also of Grace, his wife
> who died February 11th, 1908, aged 90 years.

Here was a man skilled in addressing diverse manual and intellectual challenges.

*In Memoriam.*

To be interred at St. John's-in-the-Vale Church, on Tuesday, 4th May.

The interment will take place at 2 p.m.

In Loving Remembrance of

# JOHN RICHARDSON,

Of Bridge House, St. John's-in-the-Vale,

WHO DIED ON THE 30TH APRIL, 1886,

AGED 68 YEARS.

"Blessed are the dead that die in the Lord, for they
rest from their labours."

*12. Funeral card*

*13. Richardson's gravestone*

*14. John Richardson Huggon, great-grandson of*
*John Richardson, at the poet's gravestone*

*15. Gravestone inscription*

As we stand by Richardson's grave, we feel that we are standing by the resting place of one who was the creature of the very scene we look upon. As long as for the baptismal font, for the thirsty wayfarer or use of village child, the churchyard spring shall flow from the rock hard by, there must flow from this man's tomb in the Naddle rock, a sense of what mountains can do to "Make and keep hearts gentle and inspire with lofty thought the lowliest of men."[26]

Here he lies buried a man whose poems show him to have been a man of racy shrewdness and deep feeling for the realities of life; a man that Cumbrian literature will never forget; a natural product of the scene we are travelling through; a genius St. John's Vale may be proud of.[27]

John Richardson is remembered frequently in the church services which the Lakeland Dialect Society holds annually, and the following is an example:

> John Richardson died following a stroke in 1886 aged 68 efter he'd bin 27 years scheul maister, reader here. He' 'n' his wife Grace lie buried ootside near t' east end, its nut surprisen th't et his funeral its sed th't aw t' valley turned oot, 'n menny mair aside.
>
> Earlier on we heard t' words, let us praise famous men, 'n oor fathers afwore us, 'n seah we remember ta-day John Richardson in particular, for his whole entire life here in St. Johns, his buildin' in steane, his buildin' ev young lives through larnen, his lively interest in aw things connected wid t' country side, 'n' nut least his knowledge ev dialect, he reat quite a bit aboot dialect, and in dialect, things th't were published in his life time, 'n its fray these writin's that we git a picture ev the kind ev man he war, f'r instance he reat a poem cawed, "Wat ah wish for": But first ah wish f'r a peaceful mind, wid conscience free fra' aw' that's wrang, 'n' then wat ivver comes amiss ah couldn't be unhappy lang. He wishes for a snug cottage wid a rustic porch, a bit o' garden grun, some shelves f'r beuks, lang neets ta cheer, a newspaper twice a week, 'n a beck where he could gaan fish, eneugh brass just ta pay his way, a wife ta love 'n trust 'n barns th't he wad help ta be industrious, sober, free fra' pride, upreet 'n' oppen hearted still. His wife Grace war a Miss

---

[26]   Rawnsley, *Rambler's Notebook At the English Lakes.*

[27]   Rawnsley, *A Coachdrive at the Lakes*, p. 78.

Birkett, fra' Wythburn, they had ten children, two of which died in infancy, and he gives us such a delightful glimpse of their courtship in that piece we heard Margaret say "It's nobbut me" ... ... et that time when young fellers wad walk miles through' t neet ta steal a cuddle or just merely catch a glimpse of their intended. He talks a deal in his writings aboot Ganny, 'n tales she used to tell, this is thowt ta be his wife's mother who died in 1870 aged 96. John was a local man through and through, he leuked f'r his inspiration neah farther th'n his own village, hereat aboot things he really did know aboot.

Seah we praise God ta-day for this canny Cumbrian Christian.[28]

---

[28] Transcript of a tribute to John Richardson, read at an annual church service of the Lakeland Dialect Society and with dialect inflections as printed by the reader.

# John Richardson's probate award

There was a probate award which is indicative of Richardson having assets, but he died intestate. Presumably, as, or if, he owned his own land it was as a "Manorial Tenant".

**Letter of Administration**

Transcription:

On the twelfth day of July, 1886, Letters of Administration of the personal Estate of John Richardson, late of Bridge House, Saint John's in the Vale, in the Parish of Crosthwaite in the County of Cumberland, deceased who died on the thirtieth of April, 1886 at Bridge House aforesaid, was granted by Her Majesty's High Court of Justice in the District Registry attached to the Probate Division thereof at Carlisle to Grace Richardson of Bridge House aforesaid the lawful widow and relict of the said deceased, she having been first sworn duly to administer.

33rd Section

Sureties, Robert ***** of Keswick in the said family ********and Mary Richardson of Bridge House aforesaid, spinster.

******** of effects £281-9-6 Extracted by ******** [29]

---

[29]    Cumbria County Council Archives, (Probate Award) PROB/1886/A137.

# Attempted impersonation by plagiarism

The *West Cumberland Times* played a significant role in printing John Richardson's writings and poetry for public appreciation. It seems that another contributor to the paper's poetry section was keen to exploit Richardson's poetic reputation, as it happens damaging his own reputation if the subsequent public response was anything to go by. In 1888, about two years after the poet's death, one Mr. J. R. Suddert from Wilton, near Egremont, Cumberland, dared to submit the poem "Auld Will Rutson's Machine" and the newspaper published it, complete with pre-amble.[30] (Rutson was a Wasdale farmer.) The following week the newspaper responded thus as readers wrote in:

> J.R. Suddert, whoever that individual may be, would be able to find something to edify him in the letters and post-cards that have reached this office, bearing on his theft, last week, of "Auld Will Rutson's Machine." The verses which the aspiring Suddert sent as his own production were pilfered from "Cummerland Talk," one of the pleasing volumes which the late Mr. John Richardson of St. John's Vale, gave to the world, through Messrs. Coward, publishers, of Carlisle, as pointed out by (these) gentlemen in a letter printed on another page. "However, have you allowed yourself to be thus imposed upon?" asks one of the numerous correspondents who have kindly acted as detectives in the case.

Suddert responded:

> Sir,—
> Some folks are rater impudent, when they want a glass;
> But I'll act rater modest, for wanting a bit o' brass;
> I'm a Cumberland lad, and I love my country dear;
> For I often climb up onto Scaw Fell, where the air is bright and clear

---

[30]  *West Cumberland Times*, 10 March 1888, p. 7.

And I admire the surrounding country, both far and wide and near;

I 've got a love of composing poetry and song, and my mind is always in that way;

I'll send you a few selections, if you tell me how you pay;

I needen trouble my mind, but I only need suggest;

You'll give the most money for the song that is the best.[31]

Well, might it be asked how it came to pass that the fraud was not detected, especially when the manuscript copy of Mr. Richardson's artistic verses was accompanied by another crude sample of the Wilton "poet's" own workmanship. One reader's letter said:

> Mr. Suddert's scrawl is reproduced without alteration of a letter or comma. The "poet," like others of his craft, including the present Laureate, has evidently a keen eye for business. As remuneration for his thievish enterprise, he says, he is "wanting a bit o' brass." He may continue to want it. This week he has sent another production, on "Auld Will and his Pack," which he describes as "a newly composed song." It consists of eight verses, duly numbered, with a hunting chorus attached to each. It is, however, such a shocking attempt, even as a hunting ditty, that I cannot find four presentable lines. Whatever may be the punishment due to him for this appropriation of "Will Rutson's Capper," he ought at the least, to be scourged with a whin bush for his baby outrage on "Auld Will and his Pack."' [32]

I trust the author of this book is spared a similar accusation and suggested punishment!

---

[31] *West Cumberland Times*, 17 March 1888, p. 3.

[32] *West Cumberland Times*, 17 March 1888, p. 4.

# Obituaries

Many of the contemporary tributes to John are still available in newspaper archives, though sections of many of them have become illegible over the years. There is an inevitability about some of their content being repetitive, and so this book may be regarded not just as a biographical snapshot of the poet but also an archive of at least partially transcribed documents that represent the substance of most obituaries. Words that are illegible are shown in this book by ***** and "likely" words are in brackets. The following are decipherable:

### Sudden Death of Mr. John Richardson of St. John's in the Vale
*West Cumberland Times*, 1 May 1886, p. 5

Yesterday (Friday) morning the sad news reached Keswick of the sudden death of Mr. John Richardson of Bridge House, St. John's In The Vale, who had expired about midway on the road between his residence and the Keswick and Grasmere turnpike road, towards which he was walking, accompanied by Mrs. Richardson in order to catch the mail coach which leaves Keswick about six o'clock, for the purpose of spending the day with some friends in Wythburn. Mr. Richardson, it is conjectured, had heated himself with walking, and this had brought on the fatal consequences which often accompany heart disease. About twelve months ago the deceased gentleman had a severe palsy attack, which affected his right side, and since then he has not had the full use of his limbs. Older readers of our paper will remember that Mr. Richardson was the contributor of many racy and popular sketches and stories written in the Cumberland dialect, which we published some years ago, and he has also produced two or three volumes, mostly in the dialect.

His works, both in poetry and prose, were received by the public with marked favour. They form attractive reading, being enlivened with frequent genuine touches of humour. In his early manhood, Mr. Richardson was a builder; but retiring altogether from that trade nearly forty years ago, he became the schoolmaster at the school in St. John's Vale, which post he filled till within the past two or three years. A native of the vale, he was greatly respected by his neighbours, and by everyone in the district, and his quiet inoffensive manor gained for him the friendship of all who came in contact with him. Mr Richardson was in his 70th year.

### Death of Mr. J. Richardson.
*English Lakes Visitor and Keswick Guardian*, 1 May 1886, p. 4

This estimable gentleman, who for over thirty years was schoolmaster at St. John's Vale, died suddenly yesterday (Friday) morning on the road. He and Mrs. Richardson were hurrying to catch the Windermere coach at the time. About twelve months ago he was stricken with paralysis, which invalided him and necessitated his retirement. He recovered so far as from his advanced years could be hoped and was as mentally bright as ever, and his sudden departure will be deeply regretted by a wide circle of friends. Mr. Richardson was the author of "Cummerlan' Mak o' Talk" and took a deep interest in the dialect of the county, upon which subject he has read several valuable papers before the Keswick Literary Society.

### The Late Mr. John Richardson.
*West Cumberland Times*, 8 May 1886. p. 2

The remains of Mr. John Richardson, of Bridge House, in the Vale of St. John, whose sudden death was recorded in last Saturday's paper, were interred on Tuesday afternoon, in the churchyard of St. John's in the Vale, which occupies a sequestered position amongst the mountains about three miles to the east of Keswick. The mournful occasion brought a considerable concourse of people– the friends and neighbours of the venerable deceased—into "the narrow valley of Saint John," celebrated by Sir Walter Scott in his "Bridal of Triermain." The eight surviving sons and daughters of the deceased, seven of whom are married, and for the most part located at considerable distance from the paternal home, were all enabled to be present—with the exception

of the eldest son, who is in New Zealand—to take part in the last sad act
of filial duty. The funeral was also attended by many other of the numerous
relatives of Mr. Richardson, or of his estimable widow; by representatives
of the scattered population of the valley, and of neighbouring dales; and by
friends from Keswick and elsewhere in the neighbourhood. Amongst the
assemblage we observed Rev J Brunskill and Mrs Brunskill, of Threlkeld
Vicarage; Mr J Crozier and Mrs Crozier, The Riddings, Threlkeld; Mr J
Fisher, Crosthwaite; Mr Joseph Hall, Mrs Wilkinson, Fisher Place, Keswick;
Mr and Mrs Wilson, Keswick; Mr and Miss Coward, Carlisle … Mrs Hind,
Waterhead House, Wythburn … (and many more).

Bridge House, from whence the funeral cortege proceeded, stands within
a stone's throw of the little rivulet known as St. John's Beck, which meanders
down the valley on its way to join the Greta at Threlkeld. From the residence
of the deceased to the church the route is all up-hill. The sacred building is
erected on a peculiarly isolated site amongst precipitous hills between St.
John's Vale and the Vale of Naddle. The church is a plain structure, and
all its surroundings are wholly unpretentious; but if unassuming in itself
it is encompassed by soaring heights, huge, scattered protuberances, to
which a very little effort of the imagination will give the appearance of vast
cathedrals. Nearby is the schoolhouse, where Mr. Richardson was engaged,
during about twenty-seven years of his useful life, in teaching the children
of the neighbourhood's dales people. Most of the high-backed pews of the
little church were filled, on Tuesday, with a sorrowing congregation, as the
vicar, the Rev J. Taylor, read the service for the dead, while the coffin, with
its covering of floral wreaths, lay in the midst, upon trestles. Years ago, when
the now (unconscious form) was the habitation of vigorous (life) and of far
exploring thought this mountain scenery was made the subject of a graceful
little poem by Mr. Richardson, which, for the accuracy of the portrayal and
the contemplative spirit may be appropriately quoted here:

By these*******Lakeland oe'r,
Its hills to climb, its glens and peaks explore,
If chance should lead them through that lovely vale,
So well directed to Earth's romantic tale,

On a low hill, two higher hills between,

A house of prayer ** *** tower is seen,

By (pious dalesmen) those who*******

Mr Richardson was born on August 20th, 1817, and was consequently well advanced in his 69th year. ... He was brought up in the same trade as his father, this of a mason, of which we may be sure he would make himself a proficient master, and be able to turn his hand to any of its various branches with all the general aptitude that is so frequently required of country masons, among whom there is less division of labour than with their brother craftsmen in the towns. Early in his life he began to take building contracts on his own account, and many houses, cottages, and farm buildings in his own neighbourhood and in the town of Keswick testify to the (volume) and substantial character of his work. His operations in the building line included the church, the parsonage, and the schoolhouse in St. John's in the Vale; Derwent Place in Keswick; and other houses and clusters of houses in the town and district. In this work he continued about a quarter of a century ...

The obituary continues, mainly illegibly, and includes his poem "It's Nobbut Me". It goes on:

Ten children were born to them. Four sons and four daughters grew up to manhood and womanhood, and all are married, with the exception of conduct and success in life one daughter, who remains under the parental roof. [It details the occupations and locations only of the sons.] Doubtless the rearing of so large a family would be a matter of frequent (worry) to the worthy couple; but their old age would be gratified by the knowledge that exemplary conduct and success in life were among the rewards of the unremitting care that had been bestowed in the training of their offspring.

Mr Richardson seems to have early exhibited the poetic faculty. At irregular periods, often widely separated, his thoughts were given form and expression in measured and rhymed lines and usually in the dialect of his native county. On taking the office of teacher at St. John's School he would have more leisure to respond to the poetic (tendencies). Some few of his productions appeared, at scattered intervals, in the county newspapers, or were printed on leaflets for private circulation amongst his friends. It was not until 1871, when he had traversed the half-century, and four years beyond it, that his first book was issued to the public (realm). A second (volume) of his 'Cummerland Talk' followed in 1876. The volumes were both published by Mr. George Coward of Carlisle and met with genuine success on their own inherent merit. The late Dr. Gibson, who is admitted to have been the most skilful writer in the county vernacular, will be an authority on the subject, and about the time of the publication of the first series of "Cummerland Talk" he addressed a couple of letters to the author, in which he refers to the work in terms of emphatic communication. Through the mediation of a common friend we have been enabled to obtain copies of the letters from Mr. Richardson's family, and though otherwise of no public significance they are here reproduced, in the belief that they will interest a large number of our readers:

Bebington, Birkenhead, Nov.23rd.

My dear Sir,—I have been for some time thinking of writing to Mr. Coward to ask if your work was yet published; for I have been looking out for it with much interest since he sent me the first draft before I went abroad at the beginning of the present year. I suppose he is not aware of my return, as I have neglected writing to him since I got home. It is doubly gratifying, however, to receive a copy of the book direct from the author, whose autograph would have added to the value of the gift. I thank you heartily for the (compliment implied) and assure you I shall continue to value it as an excellent addition to the literature of our grand old dialect. I began to read the volume as soon as I received it yesterday, and read it through without laying it down, a pretty clear proof that I was interested in it. I was greatly pleased with the anecdotes of the ... , [Gibson's blank] whose name you very properly hid under that of "Stubbs". I know John ... well and "Bob" slightly; the story is very characteristic of the family, especially the father's exhortation to 'mix(this)(talk)', which I have good reason to think would be needed. Did you know that these ... s [Gibson's blank space] were the last people who **(sh..'t(?)*** the Bull ring at Keswick? I have little doubt but your book will meet with success. It well deserves it, as an able exposition of the most (distinct) dialect in the kingdom and as (abounding?**** favourable (illustrations) of the life and manners of a fascinating people.

Do you happen to have a photograph of yourself to spare? If so, I should like to have it and should be glad to return the compliment, should you wish it.

By (offering) my thanks, I remain yours very heartily,

A. Craig Gibson.

Bebington, Birkenhead, Feb. 23rd.

My dear sir:—I have much pleasure in sending you a photo, taken in Constantinople last April, by an artist said to be "the best in Europe". It is thought a good likeness, and is certainly a good photograph. In one respect it differs from my usual self, namely, in having a moustache, which I don't generally exhibit. I hope you will not be long in getting yourself well (taken). I have been so much interested in your book that I long to see what you are like in the flesh. I am very glad to learn from Mr. Coward that your volume is going out at a satisfactory rate. I have often suggested to Mr. Coward the idea of getting the likenesses of all Cumberland writers of rhyme arranged in a group, with Miss Blamire in the centre. I am sure such a picture, well photographed, would be in great demand and engraved would make a most attractive frontispiece to the new edition of his "Songs and Ballads of Cumberland."[33]

I suppose you know my old and very clever friend, Dr. (Dixon)? I have had some verses this morning from him about the Queen and Prince, written, I fancy, by himself, to the tune of "Johnny comes marching Home". They are hardly worthy of his power; though, I dare say they may sing well. I am rather tired of the subject. I don't think much of a loyalty that requires a Prince to be sick nigh unto death to develop it. Nobody had a good word for that poor lad before his illness, yet I have little doubt he was as good before as now.

---

[33] It seems that Gibson didn't achieve this group photograph of "Cumberland Rhymers" as he proposed it to Richardson. The frontispiece of *Songs and Ballads of Cumberland* had a picture of Susannah Blamire on her own. Gibson had his photo commissioned in Constantinople. At best, it was an incomplete gathering.

I have got **** portraits of all our Cumberland rhymers of late date, except you and John Rayson. Do you think you could put me in the way of getting one of him? I believe he (lived/died) at Penrith. There surely must be some likeness of him there. Have you got any friends there for you to set about finding out?

I hope you will be coming to Liverpool this year; in which case you must not fail to give me a call. It is a very pleasant two-penny sail from the Landing Stage to New Ferry, which is very near to me. I wish I could see my way to a visit to your district; but the state of my health precludes me to hope of that. I shall always be very glad to hear from you, Yours heartily,

A.Craig Gibson.


In addition to his deservedly popular volumes of "Cummerland talk" Mr Richardson contributed several useful and interesting papers to the local Literary and Scientific Societies, some of which have been published in the "Transactions" of the County Association. In the records of the Keswick library, seven papers are catalogued as having been read by him … [and those that have been published are transcribed herein. All seven are listed at the end of this book.]

Six or seven years ago Mr Richardson contributed to our columns, under the appropriate title of "Stwories 'at Ganny used to tell," a series of sketches and anecdotes illustrative of life in the Cumberland dales in the time of the grandfathers of the present generation. The scenes and incidents he described, we have since been informed, were of actual occurrence, and were given in nearly the same language used by the original narrator, the mother of Mrs [Grace] Richardson, who died in the teens of years ago, at the age of ninety-five. These, we are regretfully obliged to confess, were almost the sole products of Mr Richardson's pen with which we had acquaintances until the present week, when his published volumes have fallen temporarily into our hands. Some of his "Cummerland Talk" both in prose and verse, we have read in other local publications, and some of his musical productions, such as "John Crozier's Tally-ho" and "Laal Isaac"—both shining ballads of the chase—we recognise s constant favourites at festive gatherings of hunters. We purpose to take an early opportunity of returning to these volumes, and making such extracts as may illustrate their character and interest to those of our readers to whom they may be unfamiliar. The present imperfect notice of Mr. Richardson's useful and honourable career may be fittingly closed with his little poem, "What I'd wish for", not because of any particular merit it possesses as a piece of versification, but because, written in his youth, it so truly exemplifies his early disposition and aspirations, and because he lived to realise to the full the "wishes" to which he thus gives expression.

This obituary is followed by:

**In Memoriam,**
**John Richardson,**
**The Cumberland Poet and Village Schoolmaster,**

Obit St. John's Vale, April 30, 1886.
Oh, never clad in Academic gown,
To wisdom led the simpler cottage way;
By nature tended till thy hairs were grey,
The heart of nature grew into thine own;
And, whether neath Helvellyn's moorland brown,
Or, as by glittering Bure thy steps would stray,
A poet angler; or, on market day,
Mixed with the yeomen of our village town,

Above thy estate thy soul did ever soar—
Beyond thy mortal sight thine eyes could see
And the poor scholars at their upland school
Learned of thee this— the Poet's golden rule—
That eyes and heart were given to man, to be
On earth the gatherers of a heavenly lore.

H.D. RAWNSLEY, Crosthwaite Vicarage

**Parish Notes St. John's-in-the-Vale**

*English Lakes Visitor and Keswick Guardian*, 15 May 1886

THE LATE MR. RICHARDSON.

In his sermon at St. John's Vale Church, on Sunday morning last, the Rev. J. Taylor, M.A., vicar, made a brief reference to the late Mr. Richardson. In speaking of death, the preparation for death, and the results, he pointed to an example in the late Mr. John Richardson, who had lived for many years among the people of St. John's Vale; whose form had been recognised at church each succeeding Sabbath, mingling his prayers and praise with them; and whose sudden death had been deeply lamented by his friends and acquaintances. As they were assured that "Blessed are the dead which die in the Lord," so they might hope and trust that his spirit was now with his blessed Redeemer, joining in everlasting praises in the mansions of the blest.

Much of the remaining obituary repeats notes in my biographical section, about teaching and Grace, "a truly suitable yokemate." It then prints "It's Nobbut Me" before summarizing the contemporary occupations and places of residency of their nine married progeny.

# John Richardson's poetry

Read for yourself the prose and poetry in this volume to explore and experience Richardson's humour; he even disparages the exaggerated accounts of social events as recounted by earlier poets, considering them to be on the bawdy or crude side of what was being described. Hence, John himself is at pains to point out in his introduction to *Cummerland Talk* that his readers would not find "descriptions of rude or riotous scenes, similar to those described by Anderson and Stagg [dialect writers of an earlier era] or some others of the Cumberland bards … and the half century which has passed away since they wrote has brought a great and beneficial change in the manners and customs of the Cumberland rural population".

Richardson has consequently attracted a following well beyond his native Cumberland. John knew every inch of the area and many, if not all, of the characters he writes about. This shines through his words; as does humour, philosophical thought and a critique of gossip. For Richardson's account of this trait, read "Somebody sed Seah".

> We can trace the Cumbrian poets down in almost unbroken succession from the year 1700 until the present time. It is an advantage to them in their representative character that they have sprung from almost every class, and filled almost every rank in their native county. We have the quiet and retiring country clergyman and school master leaving his pupils at the end of a hard day's teaching, to go and muse in his church or on the banks of the quiet streamlet, and then committing his musings to writing, to be found, and published, long after his early death … We have schoolmasters of almost every class—Lonsdale, Rayson, Clark and Richardson—giving expression in the poetry of the district to their intimate acquaintance with the scenes and doings of their native county.[34]

---

[34] Rev. T. Ellwood, B.A. "The Poets and Poetry of Cumberland including the Cumbrian Border", in J. G. Goodchild, F.G.S., F.Z.S. (ed.), *Transactions of the Cumberland Association for the Advancement of Literature and Science, 1883 – 1884*, Pt. 9 (Carlisle: G. & T. Coward, Printers, 1885), pp. 146–7.

Writing about Gibson, Ellwood continues: "For years he certainly occupied the very first place as a writer in the dialect of Cumberland, and his death made a gap in the ranks of its literati which will not be easily filled", adding as a footnote that because he (Ellwood) has a rule not to write about living writers, he is precluded from writing about John Richardson. "Some future chronicler of the poets and prose writers of Cumberland will be able to show that he has as faithfully portrayed in prose and verse the dialect of doings in our county in our own times as have any of our former poets in the era to which they belonged."

Dr Alexander Craig Gibson, who was even in Richardson's time recognized as the ultimate authority on dialect writing, bestowed unstinted praise on the schoolmaster of St John's:

> [He was] one of our best writers in the vernacular ... who in song and story depicted for us the manner and customs, tragedies and humours in the lives of his fellow dalesmen and women ... ' said Gibson, who was perhaps more popular; Richardson's writings were 'more racy of the soil and his characters true to type ... His idiom ... is more authentic.

Apparently, Gibson would write the "drafts" of his poetry in standard English before translating it into Cumbrian, whereas Richardson's writing reveals that he thought in dialect and reflected the idioms of the locals. As a result, many critics believe his writings express a more "convincing realism".

John Richardson's lifelong interest in poetry was only reflected in print as late as his fifty-fourth year. Like many writers, poets and artists, his written work reflects his life experiences. Carruthers wrote:

> The most famous person of the parish, he achieved fame without ever leaving the place. His work, when studied, is characteristic of all that is known about the author, quiet, resolute and self-effacing, the product of a thoughtful mind and a sympathetic heart.[35]

---

[35]   Carruthers, *Lore of the Lake Country*, p. 144.

John's first publication, and the basis of this publication, was *Cummerland Talk; being short tales and rhymes in the dialect of that County*, in 1871. Critics claim he achieved the unique outcome of "romantic dialect poetry". There are three volumes or Series in this work; subsequent ones being 1876 and 1886, differing slightly in content, especially the third one. Some of his poetry and other writings appeared in Cumberland's newspapers at various intervals, societal journals or as leaflets for private consumption among his friends. The publication of Series One was well received and not only well praised by Dr A.C. Gibson but, according to John Walker, a former pupil of John Richardson,

> was so popular as to appear on the shelves of most dalesmen and "statesmen" in the county ... All educated fellsiders could quote from it; it is treasured by them and regarded as a rival to the poems of the one and only Robert Burns. He was a general favourite ... and I have had the privilege of attending his school for some little time and am therefore entitled to add my own personal testimony as to his kindness, generosity and truthfulness ... His poetry has the magnetism of nature very strongly developed ... with its irresistible and indescribable appeal.[36]

In his book, *Companion into Lakeland*, Maxwell Fraser writes:

> Much has been made of the "difficulty" of understanding his dialect poems, but the difficulty is largely imaginary and the context is sufficient to give the meaning of the occasional unfamiliar words, whilst there is a wealth of detail about the old Cumberland ways, and the "auld fashint weddins and buryins" and other quaint customs and local beliefs which have long died out, but which he got first hand from his mother-in-law, Mrs. Birkett of "Wythburn City", who lived to the age of ninety-five. (His) "Cummerland Talk" and

---

[36] John Walker, "John Richardson", in William Andrews, FRHS (ed.), *North Country Poets: Poems and Biographies of Natives or Residents of Northumberland, Cumberland, Westmorland, Durham, Lancashire and Yorkshire* (London: Simpkin, Marshall & Co., 1888), pp. 97–8.

"Thowts by Thirlmere" should be read by all who are not content with a merely superficial knowledge of Lakeland.[37]

Typical characteristics of his [Richardson's] writing are a wry sense of humour and a down-to-earth realism, which are essentially Cumbrian, and which seem to be suited by the dialect he uses. He did not always write in dialect, and the introduction to *Cummerland Talk* is in prose rather than dialect or verse—remember that he was a teacher of English. Richardson valued the dialect for its expressive honesty and straight-forwardness, as reflected in his poem, "Auld Jwohnny Hoose", in which he pokes gentle fun at others:

fine refinet language I know laal aboot; The'r sooth country accent wi' t' "H's" left oot. Fwok tell me 'at meani' on't 's baddish to know; 'At white oft means black, an' aye sometimes no. Bit Cummerland dialect issent that way, fwok say what they mean, an' they mean what they say. It's raider auld-fashin't, an' broadish a' aw, bit plain as a pike-staff, an' easy to know.

Despite the contemporary relevance of much of his observational prose, it certainly is his poems which have attracted most attention—full of insight, sensitivity, and tenderness—as well as that delightful sense of humour I've just alluded to. The best known, and most repeated, is probably "It's Nobbut Me", which is said to be based on his courting of his future wife, Grace Birkett. It is claimed by plaudits to be one of the best poems in the Cumbrian dialect.

Of Richardson's writings and poetry, Collingwood states:

To strangers, the unnecessarily uncouth spelling of his songs is repulsive, but nobody better painted the later dales-folk—not the statesmen of the fine old days, but their already degenerate progeny in the nineteenth century. His old farmer, like Tennyson's, is all for "t'brass" and a good match for Sarah. He dreams that the bank has broken and what then?—

---

[37]   Maxwell Fraser, *Companion into Lakeland* (Bourne End, Bucks.: Spur Books Ltd. 1973), pp. 145–6.

Theer three clips o' woo up i' t' woo-loft;

Them Kendal chaps bad me elebben;

I thowt I sud hev twelve an' sixpence,

And noo, dang't, it's com't doon to sebben …


I's rayder sleepy; bit mappen

I'll dream that ill dream ageàn:—

But what! hang them Wakefields[38]—they'll brek nin

If I nobbut let them aleànn![39]

In his poem called "Blencathra", he pictures himself standing on the lofty summit of this mountain which he would see from his home every day:

I stood on the summit of lofty Blencathra,

And gazed with rapture on mountain and vale;

As far as the eye could reach endless variety

Of hills intermixed with streamlet and dale!


Beyond is the verdant Saint John's in the valley,

Spread out like a picture of beautiful sheen,

Still more to the south, lies the clear lake of Thirlmere

Like a sheet of pure crystal with emerald framed round;

And beyond, in the distance the valley of Wythburn.

---

[38]  Wakefields was a long-established local bank
[39]  Collingwood, *The Lake Counties*, p. 156.

*16. Blencathra (Saddleback)*

John, in common with many others, loved every inch of the area he knew so well. The song, "John Crozier's Tally Ho!" is about another local inhabitant, born five years later than Richardson, in 1822, who loved and knew every inch of, and foxes' lair on, Blencathra. He was well known as a keen sportsman by the time he was 18. Richardson immortalized "Squire" Crozier who was fond of wrestling and as adept with a fishing rod as he was with the hounds, which were originally under the mastership of his father, Joseph, who settled in the vale around the beginning of the nineteenth century, eventually moving into The Riddings. The "old squire" (John Crozier) was Master of the Blencathra Hunt for 64 years and whose "position as … squire and friend placed him … above all in the regard and affection of the countryside … he was the perfect ideal of a Cumberland "Statesman" ... and no man (was) so sincerely respected and beloved ... who have left behind them a record of quiet usefulness, thoughtful neighbourly kindness and help to all in trouble." He and the locals, rich or poor, addressed each other by fist names, from school days onwards. Crozier's hounds were a regular feature at Keswick marketplace on Boxing Day. His stature is reflected in the following photograph.[40]

*17. Squire John Crozier*

John Crozier, received his education at the school under the tuition of Priest Wilson where "no social distinction was or is recognised, all were brought up together in perfect equality, forming life-long friendships, squire and

---

[40]  Albert Nicholson, "John Crozier, of Riddings, Master of Hounds", *The Manchester Quarterly* (January 1906).

peasant, labourer and landlord … At this school he met playfellow John Richardson, a man whose true poetic spirit, … and whose friendship, no doubt, did much to cultivate that love of poetry in John Crozier which was one of the most marked characteristics of the old Squire." Little did either of them then realize that a rousing song would materialize as a result of their acquaintance and that some years after, a poet of more than local fame (John Richardson) became schoolmaster there. When Crozier relinquished control of the hounds he entrusted it to Isaac Todhunter—"Laal Isaac" of one of Richardson's poems.[41]

"What I'd Wish For" reveals much of Richardson's philosophy of life, while, as previously mentioned, "Somebody Sed Seah" reflects on the hazards of listening to gossip.

There was Jemmy Stubbs and his family, who lived at the foot of Skiddaw, and won notoriety for their foul language; there was Willie Cooband, of Patterdale, who earned his odd nickname when he borrowed Tom Wilson's mare and lost both it and his cart in Ullswater by Stybarrow Crag! Billy Spedding, who, along with John Crozier, was at school with John Richardson and worked as a porter at Penrith Station, told him the story of throwing a stone at Joe and Mally Gill's game cock and killing it—and letting "a laal nasty terrier" take the blame.

Geordie Tarlton, the tailor, used to sew for a week at a time at Waterend, Lord William Gordon's house on Derwentwater. On one occasion, Tarlton joined the footman and the butler to patronize a merry neet at Rosthwaite: the guinea Lord William had given them was more than enough to get them drunk twice over … of course they promised to come home cold sober. A final glass of whisky for the road after a riotous night of merry making proved too much. They struggled back to Waterend ("oft eneuf two on us war liggin in t' gutter togidder"), only to find his lordship was not abed. A series of accidents revealed their condition to Lord William: they expected "at ivvery man-jack on us wad git t'seck next mwornin", but fortunately they never heard another word.

Priest Wilson, the Master at the school, was, in common with other school

---

staff in the County, "barred oot" of his school by the pupils using various robust, dirty and/or wet tactics before declaring their demands.

Richardson describes at great length the tour of the Lakes undertaken by Tommy Dobson in scenes reminiscent of recent decades in terms of "crowd perceptions" and much more. I won't spoil the interest by disclosing the detail.

If you get the chance to go to the little church at St John's in the Vale, do make the trip. It's a special place and perfect for a quiet sit; somewhere for easily imagining the life of a nineteenth-century Lakelander with a keen understanding of the human condition. Walk down the fairly steep path to Bridge House (unless you've reached the church from it; see below), respecting its privacy, note the view of Blencathra and relax by the river and bridge with this volume at hand. Alternatively, there's space to park two or three vehicles at the junction of the lane to Yew Tree Farm with the minor road, west of where the latter leaves the main road through the Vale (Grid Ref: 313231 on Explorer OL5). Then walk up to the farm and either continue on tarmac to the church or go across the fields following the finger-post sign via Bridge House and up the aforementioned path. Adjacent to the parking spot is a fingerpost and style leading to the direct track to the modern footbridge, affording a lovely view of Bridge House.

For all this seems a thousand miles from the bustle of civilization, and a million from our digital age, John Richardson's poems feel as relevant today as when he first penned those delightful portraits of life, love and the landscape he so obviously enjoyed.

I have copies of the programmes for "Cummerlan' Neet Celebrations" for 1934–35–36 at the long-since-gone Silver Grill restaurant in Lowther Street, Carlisle. The 1934 programme has printed a poem by Dr Gibson, and Richardson's "It's Nobbut Me". In 1934, the menu was for afternoon tea: "What ther's T'eat an' Drink". Those for 1935 and 1936 have improved to that of full mains and sweet courses, with identical menus, reflecting the best of traditional local produce à la Silver Grill. After a verse by poet John Stagg, the invitation reads "noo lads an' lasses mek' yersels at heame, mek' a lang arm, reach forrad an' help yersels; divvent be bleate" (shy). These cordial gatherings included dialect poetry and story competitions, recitations, toasts and music, some of which was set to dialect poetry by the late Dr F. W.

Wadely, organist of Carlisle Cathedral.

In compiling this collection of John Richardson's poetry and prose, I have observed that numerous contemporaries and critics additionally refer to Richardson's "songs". Yet, with the exception of "Auld Jobby Dixon", "Laal Isaac" and "John Croziers Tally Ho", I haven't found any. However, the Cumbrian writer and researcher, Sue Allan, has come across "It's Nobbut Me" being sung in the Westmorland Festival Folk Song competition in Kendal 1902.

The competition was judged by Frank Kidson and published in a festival song book in 1903—but only the text, no tune. It was also sung by Linda Adams on the Fellside 1979 recording *Canny Cumberlan*, set to a tune by a lady in Workington. "Auld Jobby Dixon" is a composition, and an arrangement thereof, by Carlisle-born composer Jeffrey Mark, of four dialect songs for Carlisle Male Voice Choir in the late 1920s. "Laal Isaac" and "John Crozier's Tally Ho" may have been sung. The 1888 book *North Country Poets* refers to it as being sung by huntsmen. However, I've never come across any references to either being sung in hunting circles myself, nor do they appear in *Songs of the Fell Packs* or the Hunting Memories website, which features many Lakeland hunting songs. I infer from this that it has not been used as a song in living memory.

Certainly, John Richardson's uncle Joseph was a musician, being the inventor of the huge slate xylophone that is now in the keeping of Keswick Museum and which he and his band took to gigs all round Britain and abroad. But as for John, I have yet to succeed on this score. "John Crozier's Tally ho!" and "Laal Isaac" were undoubtedly popular ballads and, as affirmed by Sue Allan, favourites with the hunting fraternity. "Songs" was a term used broadly and often just referred to lyrical poetry.

The vast majority of his poems are not reprinted in more recent journals, which understandably have focused on the favourite few. At the time of this publication, the definitive extent of John Richardson's output is still uncertain, and the author would welcome authentic, additional material. The more I read of his wordsmanship in both prose and poetry, dialect and "English", the more I am impressed and humled. I hope you, the reader, will be.

In the following collection, I have endeavoured to use punctuation and accents as written by the poet, there being great variance in the use, or not, of the latter, especially by printers! Perhaps I'll be inadvertently guilty of doing likewise?

# JOHN RICHARDSON: HIS WRITINGS IN POETRY AND PROSE

## Cummerland Talk; Being Short Tales And Rhymes In The Dialect of That County, Together With A Few Miscellaneous Pieces in Verse

*Look out for the subtle mocking of the tensions between the spoken dialect and the poet's craving for accuracy of sentiment and feelings compared with the "proper", respectable, "fine" talk of southerners. This is also repeated in Richardson's "Introduction" that follows this poem. Even as a teacher of English in his later life, he writes mainly in the local idiom. Ed.*

# SERIES 1 (1871)

Efter meùsin' an' thinken for ivver sa lang,
I thowt I wad mak a few Cummerland sangs;
An' I sed to mesel, befwore writin' a line,
My sangs sall be true if t' words urrent sa fine.

It issent by t' dress iv a thing yan can judge,
For t' finest o' language is sometimes aw fudge;
An' Cummerland talk, 'at's as rough as git oot,
Hes sense, aye, an' treuth 'at some fine talk's withoot.

Yan oft sees a chap wi' a good-leken feàce,
Quite bonny eneùf to put in a glass keàse;
Bit if ye just quiz him aboot this an' that,
Ye'll finnd him as thin, barn, as t' lug iv a cat.

An' than theer some lasses sa 'ticen indeed,
'At t' young chaps aboot them ga wrang i' their heids;
Bit fine as they ur, when they're fleein aboot,
They're worth varra laal bit to leùk at, I doot.

The'r fine refinet language I know laal aboot,
The'r sooth country accent wi' t' "H's" left oot;
Fwok tell me 'at meanin' on't 's baddish to know,
'At "white" oft means "black," an' "aye" sometimes means "no."

Bit Cummerland dialect issent that way,

Fwok say what they mean, an' they mean what they say;

It's rayder auld-fashin't, an' broadish, an' aw,

Bit plain as a pike-staff an' easy to know.


Noo, sometimes when t' treuth's nat sa sweet an' sa good,

Fwok willent know t' meanin' when mebby they mud;

They'll say it' s daft bodder, it's this, an' it's that,

Bit treuth 'll be treuth, barn, na matter for that.


# Introduction

In submitting these sketches to the public, the author begs to inform his readers that they will not find among them any descriptions of rude and riotous scenes, similar to those so graphically described by Anderson, Stagg, and some others of the Cumberland bards. Such gatherings as "T' Worton Weddin'," "T' Bridewain," and many more described by them, have long been things of the past; and the half-century which has passed away since they wrote, has brought a great and beneficial change in the manners and customs of the Cumberland rural population.

Indeed, the author himself can remember the time when any local gathering, such as a fair or merry-night, had taken place, the first question asked the next morning by one person of another who had attended it, would have been, "What, was t'er owts o' feightin' yesterneet; or aw was middlin' whiet? and in nine cases out of ten, the other would have some "feightin'" to give account of. In Anderson's time, bull-baiting, badger-baiting, and cock-fighting would be in full swing; and one may imagine the scenes that would often be associated with such brutalizing amusements, and can easily believe that his descriptions are not much, if at all, exaggerated.

There are persons yet living who can remember a large stone in the pavement, near the centre of the market-place in the town of Keswick, to which was attached a strong iron ring, called the "bull-ring". To this ring the poor bull was fastened, with a rope or chain attached to its nose, and baited by dogs till completely exhausted, when it was taken away and killed; and it frequently happened that during the exhibition there would be several fights among the spectators respecting the merits and prowess of the different dogs engaged in the contest. I have been told that the ring remained in the market-place for many years after bull-baiting was discontinued, and that to "shak t' bull-ring" was reckoned an act of uncommon daring, for it was the same as throwing down the glove and amounted to a challenge to anyone in the town at the time. To put a stop to these frequent quarrels and uproars, the late Mr. Dixon, (who was then agent for the Commissioners of Greenwich Hospital,) had it taken away; and as a proof of the improved taste of the present day, an elegant fountain has lately been erected on its site.

During the last sixty or seventy years there has been a complete transformation among the rural population of Cumberland, in their diet, dress, and manners. Instead of the oatmeal porridge, oatmeal bread, salt beef, and home-brewed ale, which were then almost their sole living; wheat bread, tea, coffee, sugar, and other articles, which were then thought great luxuries, may be now found in the poorest cottage. Instead of the coarse Skiddaw-grey coats, and the linsey-woolsey gowns and petticoats, which were then universally worn by old and young; the finest broadcloths, merinos, alpacas and even silks, are common in every dwelling. Instead of the roystering merry-nights, weddings, bridewains, and other gatherings, described by Anderson and Stagg, the annual gatherings at the inns about Christmas are designated "balls," and are generally as well conducted, and as free from anything blameable or objectionable, as the balls and assemblies among the higher classes. The weddings, though sometimes gay enough, are almost invariably well conducted, and free from drunkenness and roystering, while the bridewains have long been obsolete.

At the sheep-shearings, or "clippings," as they are called, which are attended almost exclusively by country people, although the proceedings are characterized by the utmost hospitality, cheerfulness, and good-fellowship, they are now conducted with the strictest propriety. The author can remember being at "clippings" where the proceedings were of the most brutal and indecent description; when persons were compelled to drink, even against their wills, till they became totally helpless; and when the songs sung were of the most obscene and disgusting kind. Indeed, in those days, a song was no song at all at a "clipping," if it had not, as they used to call it, "a strip o' blue in 't." But at the present day, although song-singing is a favourite part of the entertainment at all "clippings", there is very rarely anything sung that the most modest female need blush to hear.

It will be evident to the reader from the foregoing remarks, that anyone attempting to write in the Cumberland dialect at the present time, will have to draw his incidents from far less exciting scenes than those described by Anderson and Stagg. But notwithstanding the changes which have taken place in Cumberland, as respects the manners, customs, and ways of living of its inhabitants, its dialect has undergone little or no change. In writing the specimens in the present volume, it has been the author's endeavour to give the dialect as nearly as possible as it is spoken; but it will be found by anyone who will take the trouble to compare the two together, that the dialect pieces written by Relph of Sebergham, one hundred and forty years since, contain almost the very same words and phrases as are in use at present. Indeed, if we are to have a dialect at all, we could not have one that would be more expressive, or better adapted for the interchange of ideas and feelings among country people. Anyone will admit this who has heard rustics talking together in a free and unconstrained manner; but the fact is, that very few well educated persons ever do hear them converse so, because a great many of them try to polish their talk a bit when the clergyman or the doctor, or any person of that description, goes among them, and the result is a mixture that is neither dialect nor ordinary English. There are, however, some exceptions to this. There are some sturdy old dalesmen who would not modify a syllable if they were talking to the queen; and there are many amusing anecdotes illustrating this characteristic. One will suffice.

A Cumbrian gentleman, lately deceased, had an old tenant named Matthew, whom he valued highly for his sterling honesty and straight-forward character, and had one day ridden over to assist him in planning some drainage, or other improvements on his farm. Having completed their survey, and arrived at the farmstead just as the family were going in to dinner, Matthew said to him, "What, ye may's weel come in an' hev a bit o' dinner afwore ye gang. Ye're varra welcome to sec as we hev." The old gentleman, partly from his great urbanity, and partly no doubt for the joke of the thing, accepted his invitation, and entered the kitchen, where was a large table which reached almost the whole length of the room, and at which were seated all his family, sons, daughters, servants, and labourers, to the number of nearly twenty. Near to each end of the table was placed a large hot-pot, which is a dish consisting of beef or mutton, cut into pieces, and put into a large dish along with potatoes, onions, pepper, salt, etc., and then baked in the oven, and is called in Cumberland a "taty- pot." Old Matthew placed a chair for his landlord next to his own at the head of the table, and, after loading his own plate, shoved the "taty-pot" towards him, and said, "Noo, ye mun help yer-sel, an' howk in. Theer 'ill be meat eneùf at t' boddom; but it's rayder het." Now, that was what we may call unadulterated Cumberland; and who will say that it was not far more expressive than any of the half-and-half which we so often hear?

With these few remarks, I send my promiscuous pieces to the publisher, trusting that they may afford some amusement to those who take an interest in the time-honoured dialect of "auld Cummerland."

J. R., Saint John's.

## "Cummerland Mak O' Talk"

### *A Cummerland Dream*

I'd a dream t' tudder neet 'at bodder't me sair,
I thowt I'd just been at a Martinmas fair;
An' bein' varra tir't, an' nut varra thrang,
Next mwornin' I slummer't an' laid rayder lang.

I thowt i' me dream, when at last I gat up,
An' Sally wi' coffee was fullen me cup;
'At yan o' thur pharisee fellows com in,
An' sed 'at I'd deùn a meast terrible sin.

I knew nowt I'd deùn, an' I axt when an' where:—
Ses he, "What, ye been at this Martinmas fair;
An' I may 's weel tell ye, 'at fwok 'at ga theer,
'Ill ga tull a war pleàce when they ga fra here.

"It's awful to think o'sek horrible wark
Theer is wi' thur fairs an' this coddlin' i' t' dark;
An' here, doon i' Cummerland,—issent it sad?—
Theer hofe o' fwok basterts, an' t' rest nar as bad.

"If 't wassent for me an' aboot udder ten,
Like Sodom it wad ha' been burn't up lang sen;
An' that 'ill be t' end on't, wi'oot ye repent!"—
I thowt when he'd sed that he gat up an' went.

I thowt i' my dream, 'twas a terrible thing,
Sek a judgment sud ower auld Cummerland hing;
An' as I knew nowt 'at wad deù enny good,
I'd better git oot on 't as fast as I cud.

Seeàh, I pack't up me duds, an' set off at yance,
An' thowt I wad tak off to Lunnen or France;
I thowt 'twas laal matter what way I sud gang,
If I gat oot o' t' coonty I cuddent be wrang.

I thowt I trudg't on till I leet iv a man,
An' I venter't to 'im what way he was gaan:
"To Lunnen," ses he, as he stop't an' leuk't roond:
"I hear 't ye're Cummerland; whoar ur ye boond?"

"To Lunnen," ses I, "if I nobbut kent t' way,
I've trudg't on afeùt for this menny a day;"—
An' than, I just telt him what sent me fra heàmm:
Ses he, "Oh! Ye're silly an' sadly to bleàme.

"What, Cummerland fwok, let them gang whoar they will,
Ur all'as respectit an' weel thowt on still;
An' to say they're wicked, it's aw just a farce,
Ye'll finnd them i' Lunnen a hundred times warse.

"Just leùk into t' papers, theer nivver a day
Bit barns ur fund murder't, an' put oot o' t' way;
An' than theer men leeven wi' udder fwok's wives,
An' plenty 'at dew nowt bit thieve aw their lives.

"Theer thoosands o' wimmen 'at walken on t' street,
'Ill sell their sels off to t' best bidders at neet;
An' t' best o' them thoosands is warse, I'll be bund,
Nor t' warst theer can be iv aw Cummerland fund."

I was that sair suppris't when I hard what he sed,
'At I gev a girt rowl an' tummel't off t' bed;
That waken't me up, an' me ankle was leàmm,
Bit reet fain I was when I turn't up at heàmm.

### *Robin Redbreast*

When winter winds blow strang and keen,
    An' neets are lang an' cauld,
An' flocks o' burds, wi' famine teàm't,
    Come flutteren into t'fauld;
I hev a casement, just ya pane,
    'At Robin kens reet weel,
An' pops in menny a time i' t'day,
    A crumb or two to steal.

At furst he's shy an' easy flay't.

    Bit seùnn he bolder gits,

An' picks aboot quite unconsarn't,

    Or here an theer he flits.

An' when he gits his belly full,

    An' 's tir't o' playin' pranks,

He'll sit quite still, on t'auld chair back,

    An' sing his simple thanks.


Bit when breet spring comes back ageànn,

    An' fields ur growen green,

He bids good day, an' flees away,

    An' than na mair he's seen;

Till winter comes ageànn wi' frost,

    An' driften snow, an' rain,

An' than he venters back ageànn,

    To leùk for t' oppen pane.


Noo, burds an' fwok ur mickle t' seàmm,

    If they be i' hard need;

An' yan hes owt to give, they'll come,

    An' be girt frinds indeed.

Bit when theer nowt they want to hev,

    It's nut sa lang they'll stay,

Bit just as Robin does i' t' spring,

    They'll seùn aw flee away.

## *It's Nobbut Me*

Ya winter neet, I mind it weel,
    Oor lads 'ed been at t' fell,
An, bein' tir't, went seun to bed,
    An' I sat be mesel.
I hard a jike on t' window pane,
    An' deftly went to see;
Bit when I ax't, "Who's jiken theer?"
    Says t'chap, "It's nobbut me!"

"Who's me?" says I, "What want ye here?
    Oor fwok ur aw i' bed;"—
"I dunnet want your fwok at aw,
    It's thee I want," he sed.
"What cant'e want wi' me," says I;
    "An' who, the deuce, can't be?
Just tell me who it is, an' than"—
    Says he, "It's nobbut me."

"I want a sweetheart, an' I thowt
    Thoo mebby wad an' aw;
I'd been a bit down t' deàl to-neet,
    An' thowt 'at I wad caw;
What, cant'e like me, dus t'e think?
    I think I wad like thee"—
"I dunnet know who 't is," says I,
    Says he, "It's nobbut me."

We pestit on a canny while,
 I thowt his voice I kent;
An' than I steàll quite whisht away,
 An' oot at t' door I went.
I creàpp, an' gat 'im be t' cwoat laps,
 'Twas dark, he cuddent see;
He startit roond, an' said, "Who's that?"
 Says I, "It's nobbut me."

An' menny a time he com ageànn,
 An' menny a time I went,
An' sed, "Who's that 'at's jiken theer?"
 When gaily weel I kent:
An' mainly what t' seàmm answer com,
 Frae back o' t' laylick tree;
He sed, "I think thoo knows who't is:
 Thoo knows it's nobbut me."

It's twenty year an' mair sen than,
 An' ups and doons we've hed;
An' six fine bairns hev blest us beàth,
 Sen Jim an' me war wed.
An' menny a time I've known 'im steal,
 When I'd yan on me knee,
To mak me start, an' than wad laugh—
 Ha! Ha! "It's nobbut me."

### *T'barrin' oot*

*Barrin' out was practiced in schools other than at St. John's in the Vale. For example, in the early 1700s at Carlisle Grammar School, where Statute 29 is aimed at outlawing "taking violent possession of the school and coming armed with swords and pistols and shooting with guns and pistols." This was also a Church School! Barrin' oot was traditionally enacted on the first fine Thursday after the school meadow had been cut. Ed.*

When I went to t' scheùll—oh! man, but theer hes been a deal o' ups an' doons sen that—I's abeùn sebbenty noo, an' seeah it 'ill be mair ner fifty year sen than. Bit i' them days, fwok use' to gang far langer to t' scheùll ner they deù noo. They hev to start wark noo-a-days ameàst be they're peat-hee; while fifty year sen they dud nowte bit gang till they war girt lumps o' fellows, gaily nar as big as I is noo.

Well, as I was gaan to tell ye, I went to St. Jwohn's schel when Preest Wilson was t' maister. He was racken't a varra good maister, teù. Sartenly, he was parlish sharp on us at times; an' some o' t' laal uns war nar aboot freetent to deith on 'im. Bit theer was on tull a scwore o' us girt fellows varra nar up tull men; an' we yan egg'd anudder on into aw maks o' mischieves, till he was fworc't owder to be gaily sharp on us, or else we wad ha' gitten t' maister on 'im awtogidder.

By jing! Hedn't we rare barrin's oot i' them days! Theer nowte et mak noo, for fwok hes gitten sa mickle pride, an' sa menny new-fanglet ways, 'at them auld customs ur aw deùn away wi'. It use' to be than when t' time com for brekkin' up for t' Cursmas er Midsummer hellidays, 'at when t' maister went heàmm tull his dinner, we use to bar up aw t' dooers an' windows, an' waddent let 'im in ageàn. An' than we wreàtt on a bit o' paper, 'at we wantit seeah menny week helliday, an' neah tasks, an' pot it through t' kaywholl. If we could nobbut manish to keep 'im oot, we gat oor helliday, an' neah tasks owder; bit if he contriv't enny way to git in, we use' to hev to slenk off to oor seats gayly sharply, hingen oor lugs. An' than we gat ivvery yan on us a gay lang task to git off i' t' hellidays, an' a lock o' t' warst on us, mebby, a good hiden to be gaan on wi.'

Wy, theer was ya midsummer—I can think on 't as weel as if it hed nobbut been yesterday—'at we war varra detarmin't, an' we contriv't aw to hev oor dinners wi' us that day, an' as seùn as ivver t' maister hed geàn tull his dinner, we began to prepare. We hed three or fower girt tubs riddy, an' we browt them into t' scheùll an' than we fetch't watter oot o' t' scheùll dem till they war as full as they cud hod; an' we warrant varra partickler aboot gitten varra clean nowder. An' than we hed swirts meàde o' kesks to swirt watter at 'im, if he try't to git in at t' windows.

We next bar't t' dooer, an' nailt t' window casements, an' meàde aw as secure as we cud, an' than we waitit till he com. As seùn as he com, an' fand 'at he cuddent git in, he shootit varra illnatur't like, 'at we mud oppen't dooer; bit asteed o' that, we pot oor bit o' paper through t' kaywholl demanden a month helliday, 'an neah tasks. When he saw that, he was madder ner ivver, an' he sed 'at he wad owder be in or know he cuddent git in.

Efter that, we hard neah mair on 'im for a canny bit, an' we began to think 'at he'd gone awtogidder bit we war ower auld to oppen t' dooer, teù. We keep't watchen, an' peepin' oot for a while, an' efter a bit, when dud we see bit greet Joe Thompson, at Sykes', an' their sarvent man, Isaac Todd, an' t' maister, aw cummen togidder, an' they hed geàvlecks an' hammers ower their shooders, to brek t' dooer in wi'. We war gaily flate than. This Joe Thompson was a girt fellow, a gay bit abeun two yerds lang, an' he was as strang as a cuddy, bit as num as a coo; an' a job o' that mak just suitit 'im. He wad ha' gone hofe a duzzen mile for a bit fun, enny time. Poor Joe! He was neah bad fellow, wassent Joe, bit he's deid an' geàn abeùn twenty year sen.

Bit, awivver, we consultit togidder, an' we thowt 'at as we'd begun, theer was neah way bit feightin't oot; an' seah, as seùn as ivver enny o' them com nar t' window, we aw let flee wi' oor swirts, an' hofe droon't them wi' durty watter. We dreàve them back i' that way a gay lock o' times, bit they all'as come on ageàn, an' at last they brack t' casement in wid a greet hammer. For aw that they cuddent git in when they'd deùn. We ram't furms an' things into t' wholl, an' dash't watter at them, till we fairly dreàve them back ageàn.

Efter that, aw was whiet for a while, an' we began to think 'at we'd banish't them awtogidder; bit we fand it oot efter, they war nobbut waitin' till Isaac Todd hed gone to late some tin-cans. It wassent lang till they began to throw watter through t' window, ya canful efter anudder, that fast, 'at we war gaan to be fairly droon't oot. We duddent know what to deù than for a laal bit, bit oor mettle was fairly up, an' we detarmin't to mak what t' soldiers caw a sortie. Seeah, we aw rush't oot pell-mell, an' sed we wad put aw three in t' scheùl dem. Two or three o' t' biggest gat hoald o' Isaac Todd, an' dud throw 'im in heid fwormost, an' telt 'im to git oot ageàn t' best way he could.

Theer was aboot a scwore on us buckle't greit Joe, bit he mannish't to git hoald o' t' dial post, an' he was that strang 'at we aw cuddent aw stur 'im. We mud as weel ha' try'd to trail Skiddaw, as Joe an' t' dial post, an seeah we left 'im, an' aw teùk efter t' Preest, like a pack o' hoonds i' full cry; bit he was a young lish fellow than, an' cud keep up a rattlin' pace for menny a lang mile. He teuk reet away on to t' Lowrigg, an' we seùnn lost 'im; an' I dar say if t' treuth was known, we war pleas't eneùff 'at we duddent catch 'im.

Bit, awivver, we'd won t' day, an' ye may be seùr 'at we meàdd neeah laal noise aboot it, when theer was atween thirty an' forty on us aw talken togidder, an' tellin' what girt feats we'd deùn.

It was mid-efterneun than, bit we set to wark an' sidit t' scheùll up as weel as we could. An' than we meàdd a collection amang oorsels, an' hed spworts, sek as russelin', an' lowpin', an' feùt-reàcin'; an' t' maister an' Joe Thompson com back an' join't us, an' aw was as reet as could be.

We saw neah mair o' Isaac Todd. We thowt 'at he'd mebby geànn heàmm, an' to bed till his cleàss gat dry.

### *"Git ower me 'at can"*

WHEN I was a bit hofe groun lad,
    To Threlket fair I went;
Sek lots o' fwok an' sheep I saw,
    Bit varra few I kent.
An' some theer war meàdd noise eneùff,
    Bit meàst I nwotish't yan,
'At still keep't shooten, as he talk't,
    "Git ower me 'at can."


I ax't me fadder who he was,
    Says he, "A statesman's son;
His fadder was a seàvven man,
    Bit noo he's deid an' gone:
An' that's his eldest son an' heir,
    'At's gitten aw his land;
He thinks he's summet when he says,—
    "Git ower me 'at can."


"That chap ageànn I nivver saw
    For ten lang years or mair;
An' aw 'ed slip't me memory quite,
    I'd hard at Threlket fair:
When yance a helliday I hed,
    An' doon to Kessick ran,
An' theer I hard a voice 'at said,—
    "Git ower me 'at can."

Thinks I, that mun be t' statesman's son,
    An' ax't a chap, 'at sed,
"Aye, that was t' statesman's son an' heir,
    'At land an' money hed;
Bit t' money's mainly gone, I think,
    An' noo he's selt his land;
"Just than he stacker't in, an' sed,
      "Git ower me 'at can."


Some hofe a duzzen year slip't ower,
    An' t' heir ageànn I sees:
His cwoat was oot at t' elbows, an'
    His brutches oot at t' knees;
His shoon war wholl't, beàth nebs an' heels;
    Bit still his ower-teùnn ran,
As lood as when I saw 'im furst,—
      "Git ower me 'at can."


Thinks I, it's queer, an' ax't a man
    If t' reason he could tell:
"Aye, weel eneùff I can," says he,
    "He's gitten ower his-sel;
He's swallow'd aw his fadder left,
    Beàth hooses, brass, an' land,
An' twenty scwore o' sheep beside;
    Git ower that 'at can!"

## *What use to be lang sen*

I's grou'en feckless, auld, an' leàmm,
Me legs an' arms ur far fra t' seàmm,
   As what they use to be:
Me back oft warks, an' 's seldom reet;
I've sceàrse a teùth to chow me meat,
   An' I can hardly see.

Bit yance I cud ha' plew't or sown,
Or shworn me rigg, or thick gurse mown,
   Wi' enny man alive:
An' yance, when in t' Crowpark we ran,
(An' theer war some 'at cud run than,)
   I com in t' furst o' five.

At russelin', if I say't mesel,
Theer wassent menny cud me fell,
   An' theer war gooduns than:
I've russel't oft wi' Gwordie Urn,
An' still cud fell 'im in me turn,
   An' he was neah bad man.

An' who wi' me cud follow t' hoonds?
I've travel't Skiddaw roond an' roond;
   An' theer war hunters than:
Bit I was gayly oft wi' t' furst,
An' went whoar nobbut odduns durst,
   An' nin noo leeven can.

An' than at fair or merry-neet,
Nin like me cud ha' us't their feet;
   An' theer war dancers than:
What, noo they fidge an' run aboot,
Theer nowder jig, theer reel, nor nowt,
   An' steps they hevvent yan.

When I was young, lads us't to larn
To dance, an' run, an' russel, barn,
   'Twas few 'at larn't to read;
Fwok thowt their barns war sharp an' reet.
If they cud use their hands an' feet;
   'Twas laal they car't for t' heid.

Fwok use' to drink good heàmm brew't yal,
It steùd on t' teàble ivvery meàll,
   An' ye mud swig ye're fill:
Bit noo theer nowt bit swashy tea,
Na wonder fwok sud warsent be,
   Fair snafflins they'll be still.

This warld an' me are beàth alike,
We're beàth on t' shady side o' t' dyke,
   An' tumlen fast doon t' broo:
Theer nowt 'at ivver yan can see,
'At's hofe like what it use' to be;
   Aw things ur feckless noo!

## *Auld Jobby Dixon*

Auld Jobby Dixon lik't his beer;
    An' oft he santer't on
O' market days, an' smeuk't a' sup't,
    Till t' meast o' fwok war gone:
Bit jolly neets mak sworry mworns,
    Yan's sometimes hard it sed;
An' yance I cawt, nut varra seùnn,
    An' Jobby was abed.

At last he turn't oot, bit hang't like,
    He geàp't an' rub't his heid:
Says I, "Wy, Jobby, what's to deù?"
    Says he, "I's var' nar deid."
"I seàvv't thee poddish," Betty sed,
    "Thoo'd better snap them up."
Says Jobby, "They may ga t' pig,
    I cuddent touch a sup."

Ses she, "I mass't a cup o' tea,
    Theer t' pot on t' yubben top."
Ses Jobby, "Thoo may drink't theesel,
    I cuddent tak a drop."
I'd better mak a posset, than,
    O' milk an' good wheat bread."
"I cuddent swallow bite or sup
    Iv owt thoo hes," he sed.

Auld Betty steùd a bit, an' than
She gev a wink at me:
An' than she sed, "I dunnet know,
I doot thoo' s gan to dee;
What, cant'e tak a glass o' rum?"
Thoo'll mannish that, I's warn."
"Wy fetch me yan," auld Jobby sed,
I mun hev summet, barn."

### Willie Cooband an' his Lawsuit

*Willie Cooband, of Patterdale, earned his odd nickname when he borrowed Tom Wilson's mare and lost both it and his cart in Ullswater by Stybarrow Crag. Ed.*

Dud ye ivver hear tell iv auld Willie Cooband? He use' to leeve up at t' hee end o' Patterdal' aboot sixty year sen, I've hard them say; an' use to git a leevin' be makkin' coobands, an' hoops, an' gurds for tubs an' furkins, an' sec like. That was t' way 'at he gat t' neàmm o' Willie Cooband.

"What, he was likely a smith," ye say. Nay, nay, nowt o' t' mak. Aw t' coobands, an' hoops, an' gurds, an' things o' that mak, war meàdd o' wood i' them days; an' a deal o' mair things 'at ur meàdd o' iron, noo. Bit, awivver, I was gaan to tell ye 'at Willie use to mak thur bands, an' hoops, an' things, an' carry them to Peerath to sell ivvery Tuesday, wi' an auld leàmm meer 'at he hed. Noo, it happen't ya week 'at t' auld meer was leàmer ner common, an' Willie thowt 'at she wad nivver git to Peerath an' back, an' seeàh he borrow't anudder auld meer iv a nebbor body 'at they caw't Tom Wilson.

I' them days t' rwoad fra Patterdale to Peerath was sent as it is noo, like a turnpike, wi' carridges an' things gaan back an' forret on't ivvery day, bit a rough shakky rwoad as cud be; an' iv a deal o' pleàces theer was nobbut just room for a car o gang. Theer was ya spot i' partickler, whoar t' rwoad went through a pleàce 'at they caw't Stybarrow cragg, 'at was varra dangerous. Theer was nobbut just t' brenth of a car hack't oot o' t' cragg feàce; an' if owt went ower t' edge it wad gang reet doon into Ullswater, an' waddent be worth laten oot ageàn.

Wy, this time I's tellen ye aboot, auld Willie set off wi' his hoops an' his bands, an' when he gat to Stybarrow cragg summet went wrang wi' t' auld meer 'at he'd borrow't; an' she began yellin', an' kickin', an' backin', an' threw hersel an' t' car doon t' cragg into t' watter, an' was droon't.

What, Tom Wilson threeten't 'at he wad mak Willie pay for t' auld meer; bit Willie thowt 'at Tom Wilson was liker to pay him for his car, an' his bands, an' hoops, an' things 'at hed gone to t' boddom o' t' watter, if theer was to be enny payin' aboot it. It pot on i' that way a laal bit, an' than somebody telt Willie 'at Tom Wilson was ganto put 'im into t' law to mak 'im pay for t' auld meer; bit Willie thowt he wad hev t' furst word, an' off he set to Peerath as hard as he could gang. When he gat to Peerath he inquir't o' somebody whoar t' Justice o' peace leev't; an', when they telt 'im, he bang't reet up to t' dooer, an' knock't, an', as it happen't, t' Mistress com' to t' dooer.

"Dus Mr. Justice leeve here?" ses Willie.

What, t' lady saw in a minute what kind iv a customer he was, an' rayder smil't, an' sed, "Yes, he does."

"Is he at heàmm?" ses Willie.

"No," sed t' lady.

"Wy," ses Willie, "ur ye Mrs. Justice, than?"

"Well," she sed, "I suppose I am."

"Wy, than," ses Willie, "suppwose ye war Tom Wilson' auld meer, an' I was to borrow ye to carry me bands, an' me hoops, an' me gurds to Peerath, to sell; an' when ye gat to Stybarrow cragg ye began o' yellin', an' kickin', an' backin', as enny auld wicked bitch iv a meer mud deù, an' was to throw yer-sel doon t' cragg an' breck yer neck, was I to pay for ye? Was I, be d----d!" An' away Willie set off heàmm ageànn wi' oot anudder word.

An' that was t' end o' Willie Cooband Lawsuit.

## *Fwok all'as know the'r awn know best*

FWOK all'as know ther awn know best;
  For aw theer some 'ill preach,
As if aw t' rest o' fwok war feùls,
  An' they war bworn to teach.
A man may deù what leùks bit daft:
  'Bit hoo ur we to tell,
What motives or what reasons for 't,
  That man may hev his-sel?'


Fwok all'as know ther awn know best,
  Hooivver some may bleàmm;
If them 'at bleàmms war in their shoon,
  They'd mebby deù just t' seàmm.
We howk wholls in anudder's cwoat,
  An' than shoot oot auld rags;
Bit oft he'll hev t' meàst wholls i' his,
  'At loodest talks an' brags.


Fwok all'as know ther awn know best;
  Bit theer 'ill wise uns be,
'At think they ivvery thing can know,
  An' through a millstone see.
Bit oft I've nwotish't i' me time,
  'At them 'at talk't sa fast,
An' thowt they hed aw t'sense theirsels,
  Hev turn't oot feùls at last.

## *Auld Pincher*

Me poor auld Pincher's deid at last,
    He's been a good un teù;
I'll nivver git anudder dog
    To deù as he wad deù.

For twelve lang years o' clood an' shine,
    He's been a treùthful frind;
A better nor I ivver else
    'Mang dogs or fwok cud finnd.

If I'd a crust he wag't his tail,
    An' thankful teùk his share;
An' if I'd nowt he wag't his tail,
    An' nivver seem't to care.

If I drest i' me Sunday cleàs,
    He frisk't, an' still wad gang;
If I pot on me jerkin rag't,
    He nivver thowt it wrang.

If I me plad or cwoat laid doon,
    He'd watch 't for a lang day;
An' ill betide that sneaken kneàve
    'At try't to tak 't away.

When I was merry Pincher bark't,
    An' frisk't aboot wi' glee:
When I was dull he hung 'is tail,
    An' leùk't as dull as me.

Bit what, he's geàn—it's nonsense noo,
    To tell what Pincher was;
It's wake to freet for a poor dog,
    An' seeàh we'll let it pass.

## *Sly Sally*

Young Simon an' his partner Jane,
    War thick as thick could be;
An' oft they cwortit bits on t' sly,
    An' thowt 'at nin wad see:
Bit Sally wi' her glancen een,
    Wad watch them like a hawk;
She thowt she saw love in their leùks,
    An' hard it in their talk.

They 'greed to hev a whiet walk,
    Ya Sunday efterneùn;
An' nin wad know what way they'd been,
    Or judge what they'd been deùn:
Bit Sally wi' her oppen ears,
    Hed hard that bargin meàdd;
An' when they just war gan to start,
    She slip't oot furst an' heàdd.

They santer't on reet lovenly,
    When oot o' seet they gat;
They walk't awhile, an' steùd awhile,
    An' than awhile they sat:
Bit Sally wi' her leetsome step,
    Still clwose at hand wad keep;
An' when they sat an' bill't an' coo't,
    She through t' thorn dyke wad peep.

An' when they santer't heàm ageàn,
　　They went in yan by yan;
As if they'd nut teànn tudder seen,
　　Sen oot o' t' hoose they'd geàn:
Bit Sally kent a bainer way,
　　An' heàm afwore them gat;
An' when they com in fra their walk,
　　Quite unconsarn't she sat.


They seùn war talken merrily,
　　O' what they'd hard an' seen;
As if they'd beàth gone different ways,
　　An' nut togidder been:
Bit Sally sed, "Ha! Ha! ye're sly,
　　Bit cannot ower me git;
Ye went to leùk at t' 'Druid steànns,'
　　Bit nivver saw them yet."


They blush't an' at teànn tudder leùkt,
　　Reet sheepishly, na doot;
An' wonder't what sly Sally knew,
　　An' hoo she'd fund it oot:
Bit Sally sed, "A laal wee burd
　　Com flutteren oot o' t' wood
Just noo, an' telt me whoar ye'd been.
　　An' aw ye sed an' dud."

### *Auld fwok an' auld Times*

We sometimes meet with an old stager,—though the race is fast dying out,—
who will tell us that there is nothing in the world now that is anything like
as good as things were when he was young; and after all it is a pardonable
prejudice, for we are all apt to look back to the days of our youth with an
affection and an enthusiasm which attach themselves to no other period of our
lives. Not long since the writer heard an old man who was fast approaching
fourscore, give his opinion of things, past and present, as nearly as he can
remember in the following words:—

I dunnet know what this warld's gaan to git teù efter a bit, I's seùrr, for
they gitten mowin' machines, an' reapin' machines, an' threshin' machines,
an' sheep-dippin' things, a I dunnet know what beside. Enny body 'at leeves
a few years langer 'ill see 'at theer 'ill nowder be mowers, nor shearers, nor
soavers, nor owt else 'at's good for owt. Thur machine things come oot yan
efter anudder 'at yan gits amakily teànn to them be degrees, or else I've oft
thowt 'at if yan o' them auld fellows 'at deet aboot three scwore year sen
could come back noo he wad gang clean crazy.

I wonder what Tim Crostet o' Wanthet wad think if he was to pop up
some day, an' could see enny bit snafflen thing drivin' away an' whusselen
an' mowin' sebben or eight yacker in a day. Tim was yan o' t' best mowers 'at
ivver was i' this country. He use to mow wi' a sye 'at hed two yerds o' edge,
an' he could fell fower square yerds ivvery stroke. He use to tak fower yerds
o' breed an' a yerd forret ivvery bat. Bit, what, theer neàh sek fellows as Tim
noo-a-days! He was abeùn sixteen steànn weight, aw beànn an' sinny, an' as
lish as a buck. He could ha' hitch't ower a five bar't yat wi' just liggen ya hand
on t' top on 't, an' theer nut sa menny sixteen steànn chaps 'at could deù that.

Bit i' them days theer war men 'at war worth cawin' men. Theer was Tom
Nicholson o' Threlket, 'at gat t' russelin' at Carel three year runnen,—an' it
teùk a man 'at was a man to git it i' them days. Theer was mebby laal else
bit a belt to russel for, an' they aw try't their best to git it. Theer was nin o'
this blackleggin' an' barginnin', an' liggin' doon to yan anudder, as theer is
noo. I've oft thowt 'at if three or fower sek fellows as Tom Nicholson, an'
Will Rutson o' Codbeck, an' Gwordie Stamper o' Millbeck, war to step intul

a ring some day they wad mak a bonnie scail o' thur scrafflen things 'at git silver cups, an' ten pund prizes, noo-a-days.

Bit, loavins me! It's nut ya thing—it's ivverything. When I was young, yan mud ha' gitten a bit o' Skiddaw grey cleàth for a cwoat; or a bit o' good heàmm meàdd linn for a sark 'at wad ha' worn fower or five year, an' nivver ha' hed a wholl in't; bit noo, yan 'ill be varra lucky if yan gits owder a cwoat or a sark to keep heàll for three or fower week.

If yan happens to gang intul a hoose noo-a-days, yan hardly dar set yan's feet doon for fear o' durtyen on 't. Aw fwok mun hev their fenders an' their bits o' carpet spread afwore t' fire, an' their fine grates brush't an' polish't, an' their cheeny cats an' dogs on t' chimley pieces; till t' hooses noo-a-days ur liker babby hooses nor owte else. When I was young fwok hed nowder grates nor chimley pieces. They use to hev girt oppen chimleys whoar they could hing hofe a duzzen flicks o' bacon, an' as menny hams to dry an' smeùk; an' than their fire-pleàces war on t' grund wi'oot owder grates or owt else. What wad ha' been t' use o' sek grates as they hev noo, when they use to put on a girt lump o' wood as mickle as yan o' them could lift; an' than mebby two or three armful o' peats, (they hed nin o' thur nasty seùty cwoals i' them days,) bit they hed fires 't war worth cawin' fires.

I've hard them say 'at sometimes at Lenceùnn, aboot Cursmas, they wad ha' yok't a nag tull a heàll tree an' snig't it into t' hoose, an' than rowl't it on to t' fire; an' theer wad ha' been yan or two o' t' barns sittin' astride iv ayder end while it was burnin' at middle.

Fwok burn't nowt than bit wood an' peats, an' a fine peat time was iv as mickle accoont as a fine haytime or harvest. They use to git t' main part o' them off t' tops o' t' hee fells; an' it was a gay job to git them heàmm efter they war grovven an' wrout dry. They use to mainly-what tak a nag up to trail them to t' edge, an' than they had to sled them doon t' breest be hand; an' it was middlin' hard wark bringin' a sledful o' peats doon, an' beerin' t' empty sled up ageànn ivvery time. Bit, what, they car't nowt aboot a bit o' wark i' them days. Fwok wad aw be kilt reet oot if they hed sek things to deù noo.

They mun aw hev new-fashin't ways o' mannishin' their land an' aw. They're howkin', an' drainin', an' prowin' in 't forivver; an' mebby they deù mak't grow rayder mair sometimes; bit than if they put twice as mickle in 't as ivver they git oot ageànn, what good does 't deù? I dar say they think theirsels varra clever wi' their fine farmin'. Noo, for my part, I dunnet see 'at it shews sa varra mickle gumpshin to lig oot eighteen pence an' git aboot a shillin' or fifteen pence in ageànn.

When I was young neah body ivver thowt o' sek a thing as cuttin'a bit o' drain, or takkin' a cobble steànn oot o' t'grund, or owt o' that mak. They use to just mend t' gaps up as they tummel't, an' teùk what God sent, an' war thankful for 't; an' I dar say they dud as weel as a deal o' t' fine farmers deù noo, an' mebby better.

Yan nivver sees a good lang horn't coo noo-a-days, sek as aw fwok use to hev lang sen. They're aw thur girt lang-leg't slape-hair't beggars. An' what ur they good for? They can nowder bide heat nor coald.

Shaff on't! it's neah use talken—it's neah use talken at aw, barn. Fwok ur aw gitten to be sa wise 'at yan dussent know who's t'wisest or who knows t' meàst. For aw that, it caps me if a lock o' them wiseacres dussent finnd oot what's what afooar they're much aulder: tak my word for 't.

### *"Somebody sed seah"*

"SOMEBODY sed seah." Who could it be?
What somebody sed mainly turns oot a lee;
I'd rayder gang supperless reet off to bed,
Nor lissen to "they say" an' "somebody sed."

For enny bit scandal 'at's fleean aboot,
'At somebody sed it theer varra laal doot;
Bit when yan wad fain know what's wrang an' what's reet,
Somebody 'at sed it still sneaks oot o' seet.

Auld Betty o' Trootbeck hes gitten quite fat,
An' "somebody sed" theer war reasons for that;
They say" 'at she likes summet stranger nor tea,—
That summet means rum; bit it's mappen a lee.

When laal Betty-Sally was pleenen last year,
"They sed" her complent wad turn oot summet queer;
 An' "somebody sed" 'at she'd been amang t' men,
Bit that was aw bodder – she's mendit lang sen.

"They sed" 'at laal Watson was back wi' his rent,
An' "somebody sed" 'at a nwotish was sent;
Bit that's been aw nonsense; he's rammen away,
An' gev eighteen pund for a coo tudder day.

Yan's oft hard fwok wish 'at "neahbody" was hang't,
An' what for deùnn mischieves he cannot be hang't;
Bit if he sud ivver on t' gallows tree hing,
"Somebody" an' "They say" mun be i' t' seàmm string.

## *Bonnie Spring Time*

It cheers yan up when winter's ower,
    An' fields ur springen green;
It maks yan seùn forgit aw t' coald,
    An' frost an' snow theer been:
Noo trees ur brusten into leaf,
    An' pomes on t' withe trees hing;
An' bees roos't fra their winter sleep,
    Amang them work an' sing.


Theer t' blackburd whisselen on t' thorn-bush,
    An' t' throssel on t' esh sings;
An' butterflees turn oot ageànn,
    An' spreed their gaudy wings.
An' than theer t' lambs i' t' paster field,
    Sa full o' spwort an' fun;
They'll aw draw up to some bit hill,
    An' than they'll reàces run.


In t' woods theer bonnie primroses,
    An' daffies in t'field neùk;
An' daisies wi' their breet gold een,
    Up fra t' fresh pasters leùk.
Theer crocuses on t' garden bed,
    An' snowdrops i' full blow;
An' menny mair just peepen oot,
    Beside some shelteren wo.

Whativver way yan turns yan's eyes,
    Theer summet still to please;
Some chirpen burd, some bonnie flooer,
    Or brusten bud yan sees.
An', best iv aw, beàth rich an' poor,
    Beàth beggars, lwords, an' kings,
Ur free alike to leùk at aw
    'At bonnie spring time brings.


### What laal Jenny' say was when she sed it

Thoo needent come smirken an' leuken sa pleas't:
Bit noo, as thoo hes cum't, I'll git me mind eas't;
I cuddent ha' sleep't mickle, up or abed,
Till I'd seen the', an' telt the', an' hed me say sed.


I've hard aw aboot the'; aye, weel thoo may glower;
Thoo'll nut wind me up as thoo's oft deùn befwore:
Oh! what hev I hard? What, I suddent believ't,—
Bit quite lang eneùf, I've been blinn'd an' deceiv't.


I' that fair feàce o' thine, nowt bit truth I cud see;
Bit noo theer nowt in't, bit deceit an' a lee:
An' them whiskers sa fine, 'at me fancy yance teùk,
They're nobbut to hide thee ill sinister leùk.


Thoo needn't deny't, for thoo's guilty, na doot;
Thoo needn't mak't strange, an' ax what it's aboot:
For thoo knows weel eneùf, what a taistrel thoo's been;
Theer issent a warse here an' Carel atween.

Thoo gangs slenken off, furst to yan, than anudder;
It matters nut much, whether t' dowter or t' mudder:
It's furst 'at comes handy, 'at's reet still for thee;
Bit thoo needn't come smirken an' kneppen at me.

It's aw stuff an' nonsense! Aye, mebby it may;
Bit I'll tak the'contrary to what thoo may say:
Thoo's meàdd it thee brag, 'at thoo welcome cud gang,
To enny i' t' deàll, bit thoo'll finnd theesel wrang.

Thoo thinks 'at thoo's cunnin, an' lang i' bein' catch't;
Bit when thoo gits weddit, I whop thoo'll be match't
Wi' an ill scoalden wife, 'at 'ill gi' the' thee pay,
An' cwoam the' thee toppin oot ten times a day.

Thoo'd better be gaan, for I've noo sed me say;
Thoo's nut welcome here, sa thoo'd best bide away:
An' next when thoo brags o' thee sweethearts sa menny,
An' neàms them aw ower, thoo may leave oot laal Jenny.

### *Oor Joe*

Ye say ye dunnet ken oor Joe?
    Wy, that caps t'cutlugs, teù:
I thowt aw t' wardle kent oor Joe,—
    I's seùr t' main o' them deù.

He's all'as selt oor sheep an' beese
    Sen Jemmy went sa queer;
An' when we'd ivver owt to deù,
    Oor Joe was all'as theer.

An' when we've ivver owt ga's wrang,
    Or owt we dunnet know, -
We nivver need be at a loss,—
    We all'as fetch oor Joe.

He's meàdd trustee, an' assignee,
    For fwok beàth far an' near;
An' seàlls wad nut be seàlls at aw,
    Wi' oot oor Joe was theer.

At weddin's, clippings, an'sec like,
    He's furst an' fwormost still;
Na matter who may be left oot,
    Oor Joe's invitit still.

Aw t' wummen fwok for miles an' miles,
    Hev cock't their caps at Joe;
Bit, what, he'll nut be catch't wi' caff,
    An' that I'd hev them know.

They say oor Queen 'ill wed na mair;
    Bit, faith, I dunnet know.
She'd mappen change her mind ageàn,
    If she sud see oor Joe.

Bit, what, ye'll git to ken oor Joe;
    For owt 'at I can tell
Is nobbut like a fleabite, barn,
    To what ye'll see yersell.

### *Jemmy Stubbs' Grunstane*

*Jemmy Stubbs and his family lived at the foot of Skiddaw and won notoriety for their foul language. Ed.*

A GAY lock o' years sen theer leev't doon at t' boddom o' Skiddaw an auld roysteren farmer 'at they caw't Jemmy Stubbs. He hed six sons, aw girt londeren chaps, nut yan o' them under six feùt; an' they war aw regular rapscallions for drinkin', an' feightin', an' mischief iv aw kinds. Theer was nivver a week end bit somebody's yats war thrown oot o' creùks, or their dooers tied, or their nags rudden off three or fower mile, or summet o' t' mak, an' thur Stubbs lads all'as gat t' bleàmm on't; an' I dar say they warrent oft bleàm't wrang.

This auld Jemmy was sek a fellow for sweerin' as wassent i' o' t' country side. He cuddent ha' oppen't his mooth to say owt bit theer hed to be two or three girt oaths amang't; an' as it mainly what happens 'at "as t' auld cock crows t' young un larns," thur lads hed grown up to be as bad or warse for sweerin' nor their fadder. I've hard them say, 'at yance when they'd some o' them fawn oot, an' war rippen an' sweeren varra nar ivvery word, 'at auld Jemmy went up to them, an' sed,—"lads, mix yer talk; ye deù nowt bit sweer."

Noo, this teàll aboot t' grunstane 'at I was gaan to tell ye, happen't i' this way. Theer war two o' t' younger end o' thur lads 'at war twins, caw't Isaac an' Jacob, an' they war all'as racken't t' warst for mischief iv aw t' lot; bit this grunstane job happen't when they war nobbut lads, an' Isaac telt me his-sel menny a year efter.

Sed he to me: Theer was ya Setterday me fadder hed geànn to Kessick,—he all'as dud o' t' Setterdays, an' it suitit us lads weel eneùf, for we gat a gay bit mair iv oor awn way when he was off, nor we dud when he was at heàmm. He use to give us menny a good hidin' when he was at heàmm; bit I think indeed it dud mair hurt than good, for it meàdd us warse i'steed o' better.

Bit, awivver, a while efter he was geàn that Setterday, oor Jacob com to me an' sed, "Will t'e turn us t' grunstane a bit, Isaac? I want to grun me knife." What, Jacob an' me war terrible girt cronies still. We hardly ivver fell oot as t' tudder lads use to deù; an' I was riddy eneùf to gang an' turn him t' grunstane. Noo, when we gat to grunding we nwotish't 'at t' grunstane wabblet back an' forret an' hed neàh stiddiness in 't. Efter he'd deùn grundin' his knife we began to examin 't ower, an we fand 'at it hed gitten quite lowse i' t' asseltree, an' we sed to teànn tudder 'at if we hed t' axe an' some wood wedges, we could easy mend it. Seah, what Jacob went an' gat t' axe an' t' saw, an' I laitit up some bits o' wood, an' we meàdd some wedges an' dreàve them in, an' gat it fassen't gaily weel, as we thowt; bit theer was ya pleàce 'at we thowt wad be o' t' better for just anudder wedge. Well, we meàdd yan, an' I was driven't in middlin' tight, when, 'ods wons! T' grunstane splat ebben i' two! We duddent know what to deù than. Oor Jacob an' me hed been i' menny a hobble, bit that was t' warst job 'at ivver we'd hed, an' we thowt me fadder wad hofe kill us when he fand it oot.

What, we war stannen an' leuken I dar say as silly as a hopeth o' treacle in a two gallon jug, when oor Bob happen't to come that way. Bob was a gay bit elder nor us, an' when he saw what was up, he brast oot wi' a girt horse laugh, an' sed, "My song! bit ye'll drop in for 't to-mworn, me lads." Noo, that was just what we war thinken oorsels; an' when he saw hoo flate we war, he sed, "What will ye gi' me an' I'll tak t' bleàmm on't? If ye'll nobbut gi' me a shillin', ye may say 'at I dud it." We war fain eneùf o' that; an', wi' a deal to deù, an' borrowin' thrippence o' oor Willie, we gat t' shillin' rais't. We gev't to Bob, an' than he telt us 'at we mud say 'at he dud it; seeah we thowt 'at we war aw reet ageànn.

T' neist mwornin', me fadder hed gitten up, an' was peeklen aboot to see what mischieves hed been deùn o' t' Setterday,—an' chancen' to gang on to t' worchet yat, spy't t' grunstane liggen i' two bits. I've hard fwok say 'at it's a bad thing to hev a bad neàmm, an' I think Jacob an' me mud hev hed a bad neàmm, for as seùn as ivver he saw't, he com reet away to us, an' sed, "Who's brokken t' grunstane?" What, we beàth shootit oot as bold as could be, "Oor Bob dud."

He turn't away an' went reet to Bob, an' sed, "Thoo girt lumpheid, thoo, what hes t'e been deùnn to brek t' grunstane i' yon way?" "I duddent brek't," ses Bob. "Who brak't, than?" ses t' auld chap. "Isaac an' Jacob," ses Bob. We thowt 'at we war in for't than, an' we war, teù. We gat twice as mickle as if we'd oan't wi' 't at furst, beside lossen oor shillin'.

We try't to git oor money back fra Bob, bit he dud nowte bit laugh an' mak ghem on us. He sed 'at it was a fair bargin eneùf. He nobbut gev us leave to say 'at he brak't: an' we dud say seeah—an' a deal better we war on't.

## T'auld Farmer's Midneet Soliloquy

Is't thee 'at's cum heàmm sa leàtt, Zarah?
    I been i' bed three 'oors or mair;
I thowt thoo was langer nor common,
    An' lissen't an' twin't mesel sair.

What! hes t'er been owts iv a deù, than?
    War owts o' them Gursmer fwok theer?
When I use to gang menny year sen,
    Fwok than use to com far an' near.

I think thoo hes somebody wi' the';
    I hard summet talken, I's seùr:
If 't sud be that ill Charlie Tirner,
    Send 'im oot gaily sharp, an' bar t' dooer.

What ses t'e?—O! if it's Tom Sokelt,
    Thoo'll give 'im some pie an' some yal;
Thoo'll finnd t' kay i' my brutches pocket,
    An' tell 'im to mak a good meàll.

His fadder's a gay yabble steàtsman;
    An' hes brass at Wakefield's* an' aw;
An' theer nobbut Tom an' anudder,
    Thoo'll nivver deù better, I know.

If thoo can git Tom Sokelt, Zarah,
 I'll gi' the' five hundred or mair:
Bit if thoo taks that tudder waistrel,
 Thoo's nut hev a plack, I declare.


I've mair nor fower thoosand at Wakefield's;*
 I dream't yesterneet 'at 't bank brack;
If t' dream sud co' trew, I'll be beggar't;
 I may just tak a pwok o' me back.


I keep talken on, bit I hear nowt;
 What, mappen oor Zarah's asleep:
I've a hundred or two i' t' kist corner.
 An' than I've a good stock o' sheep.


Theer three clips o' woo up i' t' woo-loft;
 Them Kendal chaps bad me elebben;
I thowt I sud hev twelve an' sixpence,
 An' noo, dang't, it's come't doon to sebben.


Sec prices ur fair beggaration;
 I'll nivver tak sebben, I's seùr;
But whoar mun we put it neist clippin',
 For t' woo-loft's mew't full up to t' dooer.


I's turn't rayder sleepy, bit mappen
 I'll dream that ill dream ower ageàn;
Bit, what, hang them Wakefield's,[42] they'll brek nin,
 If I nobbut let them aleànn.

---

[42] Wakefield's was a banking business.

## *Lord! Sek a laugh I gat last week*

Lord! sek a laugh I gat last week,
    At that bit lad iv oors;
He's sek a thing as nivver yet
    I saw gang oot o' doors.

I hed a lock o' sheep to clip,
    An' he wad gang an' catch;
Thinks I, laal divvel as thoo is,
    Thoo'll mebby git thee match.

Ye wad ha' been devartit, barn,
    (He's nobbut six year auld,)
To see 'im buckle an auld yowe,
    An' hing on aw roond t' fauld.

He tugg't an' held, an' whing't an' held;
    I laugh't till I was wake;
Cush, barn! I thowt he wad be leàmm't,
    An' sent 'im off to laik.

He went to t' scheùll ya efterneùnn,
    An' it's true as I's here,
He larn't far mair nor some 'ill deù,
    'At gang for hofe a year.

He's flate o' nowte; he'll tak a stick,
    An' gang to fetch t' kye in;
For aw we hev t' bull in t' seàme field,
    He dussent care a pin.

He went to fetch t' auld meer ya day,—
    It was a reet good brek;—
When wi' his helter he gat theer,
    He cudden't reach t' yat sneck.

Says I, "Thoo's a nice gentleman,
    To gang to fetch t' auld meer;
Thoo thinks to catch an' helter hur,
    An' cannot git throo theer."

I'll lay, for twenty mile aroond,
    Ye'll nut finnd sek anudder:
Bit what, ye'll wonder nin – ye ken
    His fadder an' his mudder!


### He sed 'twas for his wife an' barns

If 't wassent for his wife an' barns,
    Auld Griper use to say,
He waddent care to seàve a pund,
    Or leeve anudder day:
'Twas aw for them he screap't an' seav'd,
    He all'as use to tell;
He care't nowt for his money-bags;
    He care't nowt for his-sel.

He keep't them toilen day by day,
    Fra t'dawn till dusk at neet;
An' if yan teùk a helliday,
    He thowt it wassent reet.
He sed it aw was for theirsels,
    'Twas nut for him they wrout;
For them it was he seàv't up aw;
    For him, he wantit nowt.

Bit yan by yan his barns wearr off,

 An' sank doon into t' greàve;

An' still auld Griper harder grew,

 An' still his brass wad seàve.

He sed 'twas for his wife he seàv't;

 He cuddent bear to think,

'At she sud come to poverty,

 When he to t' greàve dud sink.


Bit seùn wi' grief an' constant toil,

 She boo'd her weary heid;

An' Griper than was left aleànn.

 For t' wife an' barns war deid.

An' than it was 'at t' treuth com oot,

 For when they aw war gone,

He harder still an' stingier grew,

 An' still keep't seàvven on.


Some sed he seàvv't it for his-sel;

 Bit that could hardly be,

For nut a cumfort dud he buy,

 'At ivver yan could see.

Some sed he seàvv't for seaven seàke;

 An' that was likely trew;

For mair he gat, an' mair he seàvv't,

 An' poorer still he grew.


An' when auld age com creepen on,

 An' he was deaf an' leàmm,

He still keep't seàven up his brass,

 An' hurden up just t' seàmm.

He hed relations nut far off,

 An' t' poor auld silly ass,

Knew weel eneùf they wish't him deid,

 'At they mud git his brass.

An' than, when aulder still he was,
 An' daft an' dwoten groun,
He'd gedder't aw his money up,
 An' in an auld pwok sow'n.
An' than he steàll away i' t' dark,
 An' bury't it in t' grund;
Bit whoar aboots neah-body knew,
 For it was nivver fund.

An' when they ax't him whoar it was,
 He glower't, an' cuddent tell:
He heddent keep't a penny piece.
 To buy a leàff his-sel.
An' that was t' endin' o' his life;
 He leev't to screàpe an' seàve
An' deit wi'oot a plack at last,
 An' hed a pauper's greàvv.

### Auld Scheull Frinds

Come, Gwordie, sit the' doon,
 Let's hev a frindly crack;
It's menny year sen thoo left heàmm,
 I's fain to see the' back.

Na doot thoo's seen a deal
 O' different fwok an' ways;
It's laal yan sees or knows, 'at bides
 Aboot heàmm aw yan's days.

Sen us two went to t' scheùll,
 Leùks just like t' tudder day;
For aw, I lay, it's forty year
 Sen thoo furst went away.

Bit when I saw the' noo,
 It Browt things back as breet
As if They'd happen't yesterday,
 An' I'd just sleep't aw neet.

Oor lessins an' oor tasks,
 Oor fishin' an' oor fun,
Come Back ageànn when I saw thee,
 As if They'd bit just gone.

Still when yan thinks it ower,
 What ups an' doons theer been;
Aw things ur different noo fra than,
 Wi' forty year atween.

Thy hair, like mine's, grown thin,
 An' what theer is, is gray;
It was jet black, an' curly, teù,
 When furst thoo went away.

Thoo's travert up an' doon,
 Na doot thoo's seen a deal;
An' thoo'll ha' hed thee sunny days,
 An' cloody days as weel.

What, I've hed that at heàmm,—
 Breet times an' dark an' aw;
Bit as I nivver gat much height,
 I heddnt far to faw.

I've all'as try't me best,
 To mak mesel content,
Wi' what I gat for deùn me best;
 An' teùk still what God sent.

If enny frind drops in,
    We're fain, as I can tell;
Bit if a frind gangs swaggeren by,
    We let him suit his-sel.

If an auld mate like thee
    Hods oot his hand to shak,
Na matter if he's rich or poor,
    I bid him welcome back.

Bit if he puffs an' struts,
    An' marches proodly by,
I nivver let it brek me heart,—
    Neah, hang it, what care I!

We aw hev failins, barn.
    An' we've oor fawts, beside;
Bit that's a fawt I nivver hed,
    That nasty stinken pride.

Bit thoo's been lang away,
    Thoo'll hev a deal to tell;
An' I's sa fain to see the' back,
    I's talken't aw mesel.

### *Auld Willie Boonass Fwok an' t' Hare*

Theer was ya spring, nut varra lang efter I furst went to farmin',—I's warrent ye it 'ill be ameàst forty year sen noo,—'at I was wanten a coaven coo, an' somebody telt me 'at auld Willie Boonass hed yan to sell 'at wad be like eneùf suiten me. I'd hard a deal o' funny stwories telt aboot auld Willie an' his wife Betty, bit I'd nivver seen them. I thowt to mesel 'at it wad be an earent for me gaan to see this coo, an' if she suitit me I mud mebby buy her.

They leev't ower Ireby way, nut sa varra far fra whoar auld John Peel, "wi' his cwoat seeah gray," use to leeve, an' keep his famous pack o' hoonds. It wad mebby be aboot nine mile to gang; bit, awivver, ya day efter I'd gitten me dinner, I teùk t' meer an' reàdd ower to see this coo.

When I gat theer I saw nowt astur, an' seah I ty't t' meer to t' foald yat, an' went on to t' hoose dooer 'at was stannen wide oppen. I leùk't in, an' t' furst thing I saw was a girt auld sewe liggen snworen on t' mid fleùrr; an', I's warrent ye, theer wad be eight or nine ducks dabblen away in laal dubs o' durty watter up an' doon on t' flags; an' than theer was mebby hofe a duzzen hens,—some on t' teàble, an' some ya pleàce, an' some anudder. What, I gev a laal bit iv a shoo an' theer was sek a hay-bay as ye nivver hard i' yer life! Some flew ower me shooders, some through atween me legs, an' some reet i' me feàce.

Auld Betty hed been some way nut far, an' when she hard t' uprwoar, she com waddlen away 'cross t' foald wi' t' burk besom in her hands. As seùn as she saw what was up, she fell to yarkin t' auld sewe wi' t' besom, an' sed, "Hang ye! Ye're nivver oot o' t' hoose." I wonder't what meàdd her say ye, when theer was nobbut yan; bit presently, when t' auld sewe began to squeel, theer was hofe a duzzen pigs com scamperen doon t' stairs, an' oot at t' doer, whilk to be t' furst. Efter t' row gat settlet a laal bit, an' I gat me earent telt, Betty axt me to gang in an' sit doon an' she wad mak me some tea, as Willie wad be cummen seùnn, an' than we cud talk aboot t' coo.

What, she hang t' kettle on, an' gat t' bellis, an' blew t' fire up, an' fuss't aboot gitten t' tea ruddy; an' talk't aw t' time, as fast as her tongue could gang, furst aboot ya thing, an' than anudder, while I sat an' leùk't aboot me, an' spak a word noo an' than, when I could git yan in edge way. It was a gay rough untidy swoart iv a hoose, when yan gat a fair leùk at it. Amang udder queer things, theer was an auld hen sitten on her nest amang a lock o' brackens in t' neùk, within two yerds o' t' firepleàce. When auld Betty hed gitten t' fire blown up, an' t' kettle began o' singin', she went an' gev 't a kick off t' nest, an' sed, "Git oot wi' the', an' let me hev thee egg." What, t' auld hen went cocklen oot at t' dooer, an' Betty bucklet hoald o' t' egg, an' boil't it for me tea. It wassent lang till Willie com, an' when we'd deùn oor tea we went an' leùk't at t' coo, an' a rare good coo she was. Theer warse selt noo

for eighteen or nineteen pund; an' I bowt her for sebben-pund-ten. That's t'
difference o' times, ye see.

Bit when I startit I was gaan to tell ye aboot auld Betty an' t' hare. T' man
'at they farm't their bit land on, leev't iv a good hoose aboot two mile off,
an' hed a gay bit o'property aboot theer. He was like a deal o' landlwords,
keen o' shuttin'; an' like't to see a gay lock o' hares an' rabbits on t' grund.
Wy, he'd been oot wi' t' gun ya day, an' happen't to be gaan through auld
Willie foald as he went heàmm, an' leet o' Betty, an' axt her if they hed owts
o' hares aboot their land.

"Aye," says Betty, "theer is a lock, I think. Oor Laddie puts yan off
sometimes, bit it's all'as t' narrest at furst. Willie all'as shoots, 'Hy the',
git away on, Laddie.' I tell him if he wad nobbut shoot, 'Hy, the', git away by,'
as he does when he sends 't for t' sheep, it wad mebby fwoorsett yan an'
bring't back; an' than yan mud git a stew." T' landlword rayder laught, an'
sed 'at if she wad like a stew, he wad give her a hare; an' as he'd shot yan just
afwore, an' hed it in his bag, he teùk 't oot an' gev her 't. What, she was t'
girtest 'at ivver owt was; an' when Willie come in, she sed tull him, "I telt
oor landlword 'at thee an' Laddie wad nivver git us a hare, an' seah he's geen
us yan, an' we'll hev 't stew't for Sunday dinner."

Well, Willie was varra plea't an' aw, an' thowt 'at it wad be t' best way to
hev 't o' Sunday. Seah, theer was nowt mair sed aboot it till Setterday neet.

When Willie com in o' Setterday neet, he sed, "Wy, Betty, hes t'e gitten
thee hare druss't riddy for to-mworn?"

"Aye," says Betty, "I gitten 't deùn, bit I hev hed a terrible job ower 't. It's
teànn me aw this efterneùn; an' I'd a gay deal on 't to swinge off at last. I wad
rayder poo a duzzen geese nor ya hare."

"What, dud t'e poo 't?" says Willie.

"Aye, what mud I deù wi' 't?" says Betty, "I cuddent stew 't wi' t' doon
on, cud I?"

"Neah," says Willie, "bit thoo sud ha' screàp't it, barn."

"Lord bless me weel!" says Betty, "issent it a wonder I nivver thowt o'
that mesel? Bit if ivver oor landlword gi's us anudder, *I'll screap 't, thoo may
depend on't!*"

## *Drucken Bill's Welcome Heamm*

WHOAR hes t'e been, thoo maislen feùll,
　At t' public hoose ageànn?
Thoo promis't me a fortneth sen,
　To let that drink aleànn:
An', noo, thoo's drunk as muck ageànn,
　An' shamful to be seen;
I wish thoo saw thee snuffy nwose,
　An' silly, bleudshot een.


Thee cheeks, at ayder end o' t' mooth,
　Wi' 'bacco slavver's dy't;
Like treacle it's been runnen doon
　Thee chin o' ayder side.
Thoo's rowl't aboot i' t' muck an' mire,
　An' spoil't thee cleàss for mense;
An' oot o' aw thee reavellen' talk,
　Theer nut two words o' sense.


Thoo works for brass just like a horse,
　An' than spends 't like an ass;
Thoo'll bring thee-sel, afwore thoo's deùnn,
　Intul a bonnie pass.
Thoo's guzzlet doon thee greedy throat,
　What t' barns an' me sud hed;
Od rot the'! hod thee silly noise,
　An' tak thee-sel to bed.

Thoo wants thee supper? Thoo may want:
　　Theer nowt i' t' hoose to eat:
Thoo's spent aw ower thee nasty drink
　　We sud ha' hed for meat.
Thooll gang to t' public hoose ageànn!
　　I'd like to see thee try't;
Thool off to bed, an' sharply, teù,
　　Or be to t' teàble tie't.


Tom, run away an' bring me t' cword
　　We use to helter t' pig;
I'll tie him up to t' teàble frame,
　　An' on t' bare flure he's lig.
Oh! what, thoo's gaan to bed, I see;
　　I think it's t' wisest way;
Bit seùr eneùff thoo'll vex me, till
　　I'll brek thee heid some day.


### *Auld Jwohnny' Hoose*

*About two miles above Stonethwaite in Borrowdale, near the track that leads over the Stake between Borrowdale and Langdale, is an old ruin which was formerly a dwelling house, inhabited by an old man and his wife, and called "Jwohnny' hoose," from the circumstance that the old man's name wa' Jwohnny. The tradition embodied in the following verses has long been a current story in Borrowdale. Ed.*


Theer was, some sixty-five year sen,
　　I've hard some auld fwok tell,
A cottage hoose steùd whyte away,
　　Up t' side o' Langstreth fell.

They use to caw't "auld Jwohnny' hoose,"
    An' twea auld fwok leev't theer;
Their lives war lonely, ye may think,
    For they'd na nebbors near.

They use to poo this beesom moss,
    'At grew on t' top o' t' fell;
An' tak their beesoms yance a week,
    To Kessick toon to sell.

O' Setterdays they still war seen,
    Togidder trudgen doon,
To sell their beesoms, an' bring back
    Their few odd things fra t' toon.

Ya Friday neet, some Langdale chaps
    Hed cum't ower t' fell leàtt on;
An' when they gat to Jwohnny' hoose,
    T' auld fwok to bed war gone.

They thowt they just wad hev a jwok,
    An' mew't aw t' hoose aboot
Wi' brackens, fra auld Jwohnny' stack,
    Till t' leet was aw dem't oot.

An' than they went to Kessick toon,
    An' royster't aw t' next day;
An' neet was drawin' on afwore
    They heàmward teùk their way.

An' when they gat to Jwohnny' hoose,
    They teùk aw t' brackens back
To whoar they fand them t' neet afwore,
    On t' top o' Jwohnny' stack.

At last when Jwohnny waken't up,
 He to t' auld deàmm dud say:
"We mun be sturren, dayleet's cum't,
 An' this is t' market day."

Sa up they gat, an' seùnn they war
 Gaan trudgen wi' their leàdd;
Bit when they gat nar to t' Rostwhate,
 They stop't, an' geàpen steàdd.

They met fwok i' their Sunday cleàss,
 Nut as they gang to wark,
An' axt yan whoar they aw war gaan:
 Says Dick, "We're gaan to t' kurk."

"What, gaan to t' kurk o' Setterday?"
 "It's Sunday, min," says Dick:
Says Jwohnny, "We've laid ower a day,
 As seùrr as we're aw whick.

"An' we may e'en ga back ageànn,
 I know na udder way;
We've laid i' bed, theer nowt sa seùrr,
 Ower two neets an' a day!"

## *Auld Jemmy's Advice*

*The same Jemmy Stubbs and his family, as previously mentioned (Jemmy Stubbs'
Grunstane), who lived at the foot of Skiddaw and won notoriety for their foul
language. Ed.*

I'll tell the' what, Gwordie, what I've just been thinken,
    Aboot fwok an' things 'at yan sees noo an' than:
If a chap talks o' honesty, nivver thee trust him;
    It's nut oft he'll turn oot a reet honest man.
A man may be honest, when honesty pays best,
    An' nowt comes across him to lead him astray;
An' turn oot a rascal if enny misforten,
    Or enny temptation, sud come in his way.

If thoo hears a chap brag iv his curridge an' boldness,
    He'll turn oot a cooard as seùr as a gun;
He'll bluster an' bully, when nowts nar to hurt him,
    Bit if theer be danger, he'll seùnn cut an' run.
An' if a lad thinks 'at he's groun varra clever,
    An's gitten to be nar t' best scholar i' t' scheùll,
I's varra weel seùr 'at he'll nut grow much better;
    He may think 'at he's sharp, bit he'll turn oot a feùll.

An', than, theer some fwok 'at show off their religion,
    An' hing as lang feàces as fiddles; bit, than,
They're riddy eneùff to talk ill o' their neighbours,
    An' 'ill nut stick at takkin them in if they can.
They'll lecter poor fwok aboot bein' rag't an' durty,
    An' gi' them a tract when they're wantin' a meàll;
Bit if they war meàdd for a while to change pleàces,
    I guess they wad be in a different teàll.

If a man be reet honest, thoo'll nut hear him speak on't;
    If a man be bold-heartit, he'll nut mak't a sang;
If a man be religious, he'll show't be his actions,
    An' nut be his preùvin' aw udder fwok wrang.
Noo, Gwordie, tak nwotish an' mind what I tell the';
    Be smooth leùks an' fine speeches dunnet be led,
Or else when thoo finnds them aw false an' deceivin',
    Thoo'll wish 'at thoo'd mindit what auld Jemmy sed.

## *This love's a curious thing*

Ya bonny summer neet it was,
 When days war lang, leàtt on i' June,
'At efter I'd me darrick deùn,
 I hed an earen'd into t' toon.

'Twas gitten dusk when I com back,
 For t' sun hed sunk doon into t' sea;
An' burds the'r merry sangs teùn't up,
 Ameàst fra ivvery bush an' tree.

When just a bit fra t' toon I gat,
 I met a young an' gradely pair;
I saw 'at they war gentry fwok,
 For beàth leùk't smush, weel dress't, an' fair.

She held his arm, he held her hand,
 She leuk't up smirken in his feàce:
Thinks I, a witch yan needn't be,
 To know 'at that's a cwortin' keàse.

I thowt hoo happy they mud be,
 Withoot a single want or care;
An' nowt to deù bit bill an' coo,
 An' wander when they wad, an' where.

When meùsen on, nut quite content
 'At things sud seàh unequal be—
'At some sud nowt but plesser know,
 An' udders nowt but hardship see:

Anudder pair com trailen on,

    Bit they war tramps as rag't as sheep;

They'd nowder shoon nor stockin's on,

    An' t'chap leuk't like a chimley sweep.


He hed his arm aroond her waist,

    An' she leuk't smirken in his feàce:

Thinks I, be aw the powers abeùn,

    That's just anudder cwortin' keàse.


They seem't as happy as two burds,

    'At flit frae tree to tree i' spring;

For sceàrse ten yerds I'd gitten by,

    When beàth began to lilt an' sing.


Thinks I, this love's a curious thing:

    Them two gaan wi' the'r barfet feet,

Seem just as happy as yon two;

    Their kiss, na doot, 'ill be as sweet.


### *Dalehead Park Boggle*


Dalehead Park is a low hill, over which the road from Keswick to Ambleside passes, and is about six miles from the former place. It is partly woodland and partly rough pasture, and slopes down to the margin of the beautiful lake Thirlmere. From its higher part, where the road crosses, there is a charming view of the lake, with the fine scenery on its western shore; consisting of precipitous mountains partly clothed with wood, and rocks grey with age, of the most fantastic forms, like some huge, fabled monsters peeping out among the trees, and in several places overhanging the lake. But the road over Dalehead Park, though an exceedingly pleasant walk or drive on a fine summer day, is dismal and lonely enough on a dark winter night; and is precisely such a place as a superstitious or timid person, if compelled to travel over on a dark night, would do so at a pretty brisk pace, without daring to look behind, lest some ghost or hobgoblin should be following. It is upwards of two miles from the King's Head inn, the last house in the vale of Legburthwaite, to Waterhead, the first in the more southerly vale of Wythburn [pronounced Wy-burn]: and, in addition to its loneliness, it has time out of mind had the reputation of being haunted.

Having frequently heard of Dalehead Park Boggle, and being rather curious to know some particulars respecting it, I not long since enquired of an old dalesman—who I knew had traversed it frequently for fifty or sixty years—if he had ever seen anything supernatural there.

I give his answer in his own words.

"Aye, I've seen t' Park Boggle o' neàh different times, an' Armboth Boggle an' aw; bit, what, I mindit nowt aboot them. Theer nowt to be flate on; for they nivver mellt body 'at ivver I hard tell on. I yance spak to t' Park Boggle, bit it ga' me neàh answer; an' I'll tell ye hoo it happen't.

"We'd hed t' hogs off winteren doon below Hawkshead. I'd been fetchen them back, an' as it's a gay lang gete, an' I've a canny lock o' aquentance ower that way, 'at keep't me santeren on a langish time, it was rayder darkish afwore I gat ower t' Park. As I'd just gitten ower t' top, an' was beginnen to come doon o' this side, t' hogs aw stop't i' t' mid rwoad, an' wadden't gang a step farder. What! I shootit t' dog up to help me on wi' them; bit it wad nowder bark nor nowt, an' keep't creepen in ageàn me legs, like as if it was hofe freeten't to deith. I began to leùk than if I could see what it was 'at was freetenen beàth t' dog an' t' hogs; seàh, an' seùr eneùf, I saw reet afwore them what leùk't like a girt lime an' mowd heap, 'at reach't clean across t' rwoad. It went up heigher nor t' wo' o' teàa side o' t' rwoad, an' slowp't doon tull aboot hofe a yard hee o' t'udder. Noo, I was seùr at neabody wad put a midden across t' rwoad i' that way, an' I thowt 'at it mud be t' Park Boggle. I steùd a laal bit consideren what to deù, an' than I shootit an' ax't what was t' reason 'at t' hogs was to gang neàh farder; when just wi' that yan o' them gev a girt lowp ower t' low end o' t' heap, an' than t'udder aw went helter-skelter efter 't doon t' rwoad. When that was ower, I went on tul't, an' thowt I wad set me feùt on't to see what it was; bit when I sud ha' step't on't theer was nowt, nor I could see nowt. It was geàn awtogidder.

"Theer was anudder time, teù 'at I saw t' Park Boggle, in anudder form; bit I wassen't seàh nar't that time, as I was when I'd been fetchen t' hogs. I'd been wo-en a gap 'at hed fawn ower o' t'udder side o' t' Park; an' as t' days war nobbut short, I wrout on till it was gitten to be duskish. I happen'd to nwotish 'at some sheep hed gitten intul an' intack 'at we hed away up t' fell side; seàh I thowt I wad gang up an' put them oot, an' mebby stop a thorn into t' gap whoar they'd gitten in, if I nobbut could finnd t' spot. Wi' that I clam up, an' bodder't on wi' putten t'sheep oot, an' stoppen t'gap up, an' ya thing or anudder, till it was pitch dark. When I gat to cummin doon ageàn, I saw sec a fire on t' top o' t' Park, as I nivver saw befwore i' o' my life. It lowe't up sec a heet, an' sparks fell i' shooers o' aw sides on 't! What! I thowt it was varra queer 'at enny body sud kinnel sec a fire as that up theer, seàh I thowt I wad gang an' see what it meant. Bit when I gat to t' pleàce, theer was nowder a fire nor enny spot whoar theer hed been yan! Theer was nowder a black pleàce, nor a bit o' gurse swing't, nor owt 'at I could see, for aw it wassent a quarter iv an 'oor efter I'd seen t' girt fire blazing away furiously. Noo, ye may mak what ye will on't; ye may believe me or nut, just as ye like; bit nivver neabody 'ill persuade me 'at it was owt bit t' Park Boggle 'at I saw beàth times."

Having noticed that haunted places had almost invariably been the scene of some murder, or suicide, or other tragical occurrence, I enquired if there was any account of any thing of the kind having happened in Dalehead Park, when he related to me the following tradition, which I give as before in his own homely but expressive words.

"I've hard some auld fwok say 'at theer was an ill hang-gallows iv a tailyer leev't at Foneside, 'at they cawt Robin Sim, who went up an' doon to sowe whoarivver enny body wad hev him. At t' seàmm time theer was a middle age't man leev't at Dalehead, 'at they caw't Bob Simpson, an' he use't to gang aboot worken labouren wark, sec as threshin', an' dyken, an' owt o' that mak. Whoarivver he was worken he mainly-what stop't till t' week end, or till he'd deùn his job; bit t' tailyer use' to all'as gang heàm ivvery neet. Noo, it seeah happen't 'at they war beàth worken at Wyburn at t' seàmm time, bit nut beàth at t' seàmm hoose; an' Bob Simpson, hevven finish't his wark ya Thursday neet, set off to ga heàm efter it was dark, wi' two or three weeks' wages in his pocket. Well, as it happen't, poor Bob nivver gat heàm at o', an' he was nivver miss't for two or three days; becos their fwok thowt 'at he was at Wyburn, an' Wyburn fwok thowt 'at he was at heàm. At t' last he was miss't sure eneùf, an' t' hue an' cry was rais't o' t' country ower. As Robin Sim hed come't frae Wyburn t' seàmm neet, they inquire't o' him; bit Robin waddent oan 'at ivver he'd seen him. What, theer war fwok oot laten i' aw directions; an' efter a while he was fund in t' watter, as neàkt as he was bworn; an' theer was a laal wholl in his heid, just sec a yan as mud be meàdd wi' a bodkin, or a pair o' scidders, or owt o' that mak.

"This Robin Sim hed a lad 'at use' to gang wid him sometimes. Well, it com oot efter 'at he wassent wid him at Wyburn on t' Thursday; bit he hed to gang o' t' Friday. Noo, at that time theer was a feùt rwoad went doon t' Park partly by t' watter side, an' that Friday mwornin Robin meàdd t' lad gang wid him through by that feùt rwoad. Nut sa varra far frae t' watter side they fand a bundle o' cleàs, an' heàdd them till they com back at neet, an' than carry't them heàm wi' them. It was strangely suspectit 'at they war this poor Bob Simpson' cleàs, an' 'at Robin hed murder't him an' strip't him t' neet afwore.

"What, theer wassent policemen to leùk efter sec things than as theer is noo; bit fwok war mickle t' seàmm for talkin, an' they gat to talkin aboot this Robin Sim, an' givven him bits o' hints on't at t' public hoose. He was all'as terrible mad aboot it, an' wad hae fowten wi' enny body 'at neàmt it. Bit fwok duddent mind his bein' mad, an' keep't talken on, till Robin gat to be sa flate 'at they wad be cummen to tak him, 'at he dursent sleep in his oan hoose at neets. He use' to gang an' lig in a hollow cragg, away up t' fell abeùn whoar he leev't, an' they caw that pleàce "Sim's cave," yet. What, he dud on i' that way for a bit, an' than he teùk off oot o' t' country, an' was nivver mair hard tell on."

## *Auld Abram's Advice to his Son*

THOO'S gaan away fra heàmm, me lad,
    Thoo'll hev to feight thee way;
I want to gi' the' some advice,
    Sa lissen what I say.

Theer two things I wad ha' the' deù,
    Whoarivver thoo may gang;
An' than whativver else may come,
    Thoo'll nivver be far wrang.

Git hoald o' brass, be heùk or crek,
    It's that 'at maks a man;
An' spend na mair nor thoo can help,
    But still seàvv aw thoo can.

Thoo's larn't to sevv thee hawpennies,
    Sen ivver thoo could walk;
An' that's t' main thing for barns to larn,
    Whativver feùls may talk.

They talk o' honest neàmms, bit what
    That's nowder here nor theer;
If thoo hes brass thoo'll hev a neàmm,
    Thoo nivver need to fear.

Theer some fwok mak a parlish fuss
    Wi' sendin' barns to t' scheùll;
Bit if thoo hessent brass as weel,
    Thoo'd better be a feùll.

I've kent some chaps wi' sense eneùff,
    Bit they war nobbut poor;
An' slender welcome they could git,
    At enny body's dooer.

An' some I've kent, girt blodderen' feùlls,
    'At sceàrce knew reet fra wrang;
Bit if they'd brass they welcome war,
    Whoar they'd a mind to gang.

I've kent some chaps 'at struggle't hard,
    To keep an honest neàmm;
Bit they war poor, an' aw they gat
    Was laal but kicks an' bleàmm.

An' some I've kent 'at's gedder't brass,
    They dudden't care much hoo;
Bit as they hev't, their roguish tricks
    Ur aw forgitten noo.

I've kent some chaps 'at wadden't lee
    Anudder to deceive;
Bit they war poor, an' t' treùth fra them
    Fwok hardly wad believe.

An' some I've kent, 'at hardly mix't
    They're reàvellen' talk wi' treùth;
Bit they hed brass, an' aw was still
    Thowt gospel fra their mooth.

Sa thee git brass, be heùk or creùk,
    It's that 'at maks a man;
It matters laal, barn, hoo thoo gits't,
    Bit git it if thoo can.

## T' Bonnie Deall

Come, climm wi' me up t' moontain side,
    An' see a charmen scene;
Aw t' hills, an' craggs, an' hingen' woods,
    Wi' bonnie deàlls atween.

Come, see hoo naater carpets fine,
    On aw t' fell side does spreed;
We crush some bonnie tiny flower,
    At ivvery step we treed.

Just leùk hoo whiet is that deàll,
    Wi' moontains guardit roond;
An' bit for t' watter splashen doon,
    Yan cannot hear a soond.

Low doon i' t' deàll, theer t' ancient kurk,
    Grown ower wi' ivy green;
A sacred pleàce for ages geànn,
    To deàllsmen it hes been.

A barn browt to its rustic font,
    When groun up, comes to kneel
Doon on its altar steps, and wed
    That lass he loves sa weel.

An' than when years hev glidit by,
    Ageànn he's browt an' laid,
To sleep his lang, lang sleep o' deith,
    Whoar t' kurk his greàvv does shade.

Yon hooses shadit wi' green trees,
    Ilk in its shelter't neùk,
Breet picters o' sweet peaceful heàmms,
    Blest wi' contentment leùk

An' t' smeùk 'at up fra t' chimleys curls,
    Climms lazily an' slow,
As if it fain wad langer stay,
    In t' pleasant deàll below.

An' t' watter, teù, 'at slowly twines,
    Wi' menny a bend an' turn,
Noo slowly gliden' in a pool,
    Noo blashen in a burn.

An' see yon kye how nice they leùk,
    Just dottit here an' theer:
They leùk like bits o' snow yan's seen.
    Left leàt at t' spring o' t' year.

It seems sa strange, an' yet it's trew,
    'At in that whiet deàll,
Theer menny a lee gangs whisper't roond,
    An' menny a sland'rous teàll.

Bit, what! It's seàh aw t' warld ower,
    Yan cannot help bit know;
Whoarivver man is, theer 'ill be
    His selfishness an' aw.

## *What Bob an' Charlie thowt aboot t' war*

BOB

Thoo's gitten t' paper—is t'er owt
   'At's fresh fra t' war to-day?
I hard they'd hed anudder feight,
   An' t' French hed run away.

CHARLIE

They've hed anudder feight for seùr,—
   A dreadful feight it's been;
A murderen job, fra what I read,
   As ivver yet was seen.
An' t' French as good a threshin' gat,
   As ivver they've hed yet;
Bit run away they dudden't deù,
   Because they cudden't git.

BOB

If they war lick't, an' cudden't run,
   They likely mud give in;
Bit as I leùk, theer laal i' t' odds,
   Whilk lwoses an' whilk wins.
Beàth sides hev thoosands kilt an' leàmm't,
   An' varra much I doot,
'At owder side could tell yan what
   Aw t' feightin's been aboot.

## CHARLIE

That's trew eneùff. I'll tell the', Bob,
    If two girt country cloons,
Like thee an' me, sud git on t' spree,
    An' knock teànn tudder doon;
We'd be caw't drukken blackguards, an'
    Afwore oor betters browt,
Bit mair they kill, an' mair they leàmm,
    An' better men they're thowt.

## BOB

I hwop oor guvverment girt men
    'Ill mind what they're aboot,
An' nut be meddlen' theirsels wi' 't,
    Bit keep their nwoses oot.
I think, to keep us oot o' t' mess,
    T' meàst part o' them 'ill try;
For aw thur feighten chaps wad fain
    Their fingers hev in t' pie.

## CHARLIE

I think 'at t' guvverment's aw reet;
    T' meàst danger theer 'ill be
Is frae thur traden taistrels,
    'At send their ships to t' sea
Wi' guns an' pooder, an' sek like,
    'At ower to France they tak;
They'd trade wi' t' auld un seùnn as nut,
    If money they could mak.

## BOB

I'll tell the', Charlie, what I'd deù,
    If I mud hev me way:
For ivvery gun they sent to t' war,
    Twice t' value they sud pay;
An' than I'd ship them off theirsels,
    An' set them doon i' France,
Just whoar they're feighten t' warst iv aw,
    An' let them tak their chance.

## CHARLIE

Bit hofe o' t' news I hevvent telt;
    Theer mair i' t' paper, far—
MacMahon an' fifty thoosand men
    Ur prisoners, o' war.
An' Buonaparte's a prisoner, teù;
    An' who wad think it trew?
Aw t' French 'at thowt he was a god,
    Caw him a cooard noo.

## BOB

Aye, that's just t' way them Frenchmen turn;
    It is divarten, teù,
To read sec mighty deeds they talk
    They're some time gaan to deù:
While t' German chaps keep marchen' on,
    An' aw befwore them drive,
T' French chaps keep shooten' as they run—
    "Ye'll nut git back alive!"

## CHARLIE

I saw two lads in t' garden theer,
    Nut mair nor teàble height,
Aboot their marbles they'd fawn oot,
    An' nowt wad deù bit feight.
Teàa lad—an' it was t' bigger, teù,—
    Hed bully't lang an' sair,
When t' laal un threw his jacket off,
    An' sed he'd tak na mair:

He buckel't in, an' drèave him back,
    Farder, an' farder still;
While t' girt un shootit, "If thoo does,
    I'll gi' the' 't aye, I will."
Bit t' laal un doon't him on his back,
    An' telt him to ax pardin;
Says t' tudder lad, "I nivver will,
    Till thoo gangs oot o' t' garden."
I thowt hoo like that was to t' French:
    They say they'll nivver 'gree,
Till t' Germans aw gang oot o' France,
    An' that they'll let them see.

## BOB

If Buonaparte an' t' Prussian king,
    Like t' two laal lads i' t' garden,
Hed bray't teànn tudder's heids a bit,
    It matter't nut a fardin:
Bit when theer tens o' thoosands kilt,
    An' thoosands cripples meàdd,
I think if they've aw t' bleàmm to bear,
    They'll hev a gay good leàdd.

## *What I'd wish for*

If Providence, wi' bounteous hand,
 Wad aw me wishes kindly grant,
An' just wi' wishen' I could hev
 Eneùf to furnish ivvery want:

I wadden't wish for empty power,
 Theer laal o' happiness i' that;
For girt fwok wad be bigger still,
 An' oft feight for they know nowt what.

I wadden't wish for heaps o' wealth,
 For mickle mainly creàvvs for mair;
An' when fwok to hurd begin,
 It's laal for owt 'at's good they care.

Bit furst I'd wish for peace o' mind,
 Wi' conscience free frae owt 'at's wrang;
An' than, whativver comes amiss,
 I cuddent be unhappy lang.

An' next, I'd hev a cottage snug,
 In some weel-woodit shelter't neuk;
A rustic pworch I'd hev at t' dooer,
 To give me heàmm a heàmly leùk.

A bit o' gardin grund aroond,
 I'd hev for yerbs, an' frutes, an' flooers;
Where I could sow me seeds i' spring,
 An' watch them sproot wi' April shooers.

Inside me cottage, I wad hev
    Some shelves o' beùks, lang neets to cheer,
John Bunyan, Shakespeare, Crabbe, an' Burns,
    Wordsworth, an' Goldsmith, sud be theer.

Eliza Cook, Sir Walter Scott,
    An' menny mair 'at I could neàme;
A hoose withoot a row o' beuks,
    I nivver think leùks like a heàmm.

A newspaper, just twice a week,
    I'd like to hev, to tell me aw
O' markets, politicks, an' wars,
    An' news 'at I wad care to know.

Nut far away, a beck I'd hev,
    'At twistit t' hills an' neuks aboot;
Where I wi' fishin' rod could gang
    An' flog, an' watch for t' risen troot.

An' than I'd wish 'at I mud hev
    Just brass eneùf to pay me way;
An' a laal trifle noo an' than,
    To yan i' need to give away.

I'd hev a wife to love an' trust,
    To whom I aw me thowts could tell;
An' I could like 'at she sud hev
    T' seàmm wants an' wishes as me-sel.

An' if I'd barns, I'd hev them be
    Industrious, sober, free fra pride;
Upreet an' oppen-heartit still,
    Affectionate an' kind beside.

If I a frind or two mud hev
   'At I could trust through clood an' shine;
Frinds 'at I knew as trew wad preùve
   I' darkest times, as when 'twas fine.

I think theer nowt I'd want beside—
   Bit oh! We're hard to satisfy;
Oor real wants ur nobbut few,
   If we to limit them wad try.

### Tommy Dobson's Toor to T' Lakes

It's cum't to be a parlish custom noo-a-days to gang off wi' thur excursions to Liverpool, an' Manchester, an' Lunnen, an' t' Isle o' Man, an' o' up an' doon; bit I nivver see enny o' thur fwok 'at's been off 'at can tell enny mack iv a teàll when they come back ageàn. An' hoo sud they? They're shut up in a clwose carridge aw t' way they hev to gang, an' than when they're let oot at t' far end in a strange pleàce, theer mebby neàh body to tell them aboot owt. They may trail aboot till they're tire't to deith, an' than git into t' carridge an' come heàmm ageànn, just as wise as they war when they went. They can say 'at they've been at Lunnen or Liverpool, an' that's aw.

I happen't to hev a few days helliday nut lang sen me-sel, an' I thowt to me-sel, I'll bodder nin wi' the'r railway excursions; I'll tak my excursion o' me shanks, an' than I'll mebby see summet. I'd leev't doon i' t' low side o' Cummerland aw me life, an' hed nivver been nar a fell, an' seeàh I just meàdd up me mind to hev a rammel amang t' fells for a week or seeàh.

I set off o' Michaelmas day, efter we'd deùn oor harvest, an' aim't reet away for Skiddaw. I could see Skiddaw fra whoar I leev't, an' I thowt 'at it leùk't sec a laal bit to gang 'at I wad be theer in a jiffy; bit, my song! I was weel teàn in. I lay I walk't atween fifteen an' twenty mile afwore I gat to Cawdbeck, an' they telt me 'at it was a good hofe day's-wark gaan on to Skiddaw fra theer. When I larn't that, I began to consider 'at it wad be neet when I gat to t' top, an' as I duddent want to lig on t' fell aw neet, I'd better stop at Cawdbeck,

an' than gang ower t' top o' Skiddaw an' doon to Kessick t' neest mwornin'.
An' seeàh I spak for a bed at t' public hoose whoar I'd caw't at, an' than I
went oot to see what I could aboot Cawdbeck.

Cawdbeck awtogidder, I suppwose, is a gay girt parish, bit whoar I was is
just a canny size't villidge. Theer a gay lock o' hooses, an' they're built in aw
shaps an' directions as they ur i' t' meàst part o' villidges. Theer a girt auld-
fashin't kurk, an' a berryin' pleàce beside it wi' a gay lock o' heidsteàns in't; an'
theer was yan 'at I was uncommonly pleas't wi', 'at's been setten up for auld
John Peel, t' girt hunter—him 'at t' sang was meàdd aboot, beginnin' wi—

> "D'ye ken John Peel with his coat so gray?
> D'ye ken John Peel at the break of the day?
> D'ye ken John Peel when he's far, far away,
> With his hounds and his horn in the morning?"

I think I saw three or fower public hooses, an' a bobbin mill, whoar theer a
lock o' fwok employ't; an' theer some mines nut far off, an' t' miners mainly
leeve in t' villidge; an' than theer yan or two bettermer hooses, an' a lock o'
farm-hooses; seeah 'at awtogidder it's a canny size't villidge. Theer a varra
queer pleàce nut far fra t'bobbin mill, kent be t' neàm o' t' *Howk,* whoar t'
watter runs foamin' an' rattlin' ower t' rocks, an' aw t' time maks a din in a
chap's lugs varra nar like thunner. A laal bit 'aboon this theer anudder spot—a
natteral cur'osity in its way—caw't *Fairy Kettle,* It's med up of a lot o' girt
wholls in t' limestone rock, nicely polish't i' t' inside ameàst as smooth as
marble. I think t' wholls hev been wesh't oot wi' t' watter, bit yan can hardly
tell for sarten hoc they've been deùn.

Efter gitten a good neet's sleep, I was up i' good time t' neest mwornin'
an'set off up t' fell. Theer a gay bit o' inclwost grund efter yan leeves t' villidge,
afwore yan gits fairly onto t' fell. I clamm away till I gat ower t' fell wo, as
they caw't, an' a gay bit up abeùn that, an' than I turn't roond an' sat doon
on a steàn to leùk aboot me, an' a parlish fine seet it was. I could see aw t'
low side o' Cummerland, fra on beyont Workinton to t' tudder side o' Carel,
an' it's a fine country, teù; aw t' way through theer be Wigton, an' t' Holme,
an' away on as far as Marypwort. I could see menny a thoosand fields, iv aw

shaps an' sizes, 'at ivver enny body could contrive; an' I just thowt to mesel 'at theer waddent be a laal neùk in aw 'at I could see, whoar I could gang an' greàve a sod oot, bit theer wad be somebody to claim't an' finnd fawt wi' me.

Efter I'd gitten a rust, I set off ageàn an' clamm away till I gat to t' tippy top o' Skiddaw, an' I hed a finer view nor ivver. Leùken partly to t' west, I could see whyte away on to t' sea, for I dunnet know hoo far. Leùken north, I could see cross a gay bit into Scotland; an' east, I could see away to some fells a lang way at t' tudder side o' Peerath. Bit when I turn't to t' sooth it was t' grandest seet iv aw, for theer was nowt but ya fell aback iv anudder, as far as yan could see. Theer war twea or three bits o' deàlls, sec as Borrowdale, an' St. John's, an' some lakes, an' varra bonnie they leuk't; bit farder off yan could see nowt bit ya fell peepen ower anudder for menny a mile. Theer was a lot o' quality on t' top o' Skiddaw, 'at hed cum't up fra Kessick. They hed a guide wi' them, an' some Galloways to ride on, an' baskets, an' bottles, an' I dunnet know what, like as if they war gaan to bide theer for a fortneth. When I leùk't at them, an' than leùk't roond me, I thowt to mesel, 'at God Almighty heddent dealt things oot seeàh varra unequally efter aw. I duddent know bit t' Prince o' Wales, or t' Archbishop o' Canterbury, mud be amang them fwok. Bit I knew for aw I was theer wi' nowt bit a walkin' stick i' me hand, an' a crust o' bread i' my pocket, browt fra t' public hoose at Cawdbeck, 'at He'd geen me as good eyes, an' spread oot o' that fine scenery I could leùk at an' admire, just as much as they could.

When I'd leùk't aboot me till I was tire't, I set off doon towarts Kessick; an' when I gat a gay bit lower, whoar I cuddent see sa far off for fells, I began to admire t' bonnie pleàce t' toon stood in. It's in a girt hollow 'at may seem to be twenty mile roond, an' fells aw aboot it, owt bit just at t' low end. T' sooth end on't, gaan up towart Borrowdale, is teàn up wi' t' lake, an' a fine lake it is. When I leùk't at it fra Skiddaw breest, I thowt I nivver saw owt sa bonnie i' me life. It was glitteren i' t' sun just like silver, an' than t' woods an' craggs aw roond aboot it, an' nice green islands up an' doon on't, meàdd a fine picter to leùk at. Kessick stands partly at t' low end o' t' lake; an' than below t' toon theer a plat o' fine land aw t' way doon to t' low end, wi' hooses, an' villidges aw up an' doon; an' t' beck twinen away throo t' middle, till it gits into Bassenthwaite watter.

I santer't away, leùken at ya thing an' anudder, till it was leeàte on i' t' efterneùn when I gat to Kessick. It's a nice laal toon, mebby aboot t' size o' Wigton, an' hes some varra good shops in't. T' main street, 'at's use't for t' market pleàce, wad be a varra good street if it wassent for a girt ugly building caw't Meùt-haw, 'at stands reet i' t' middle on't, an' varra nar blocks 't up awtogidder. Theer a gay lock o' public hooses i' Kessick, as theer is in aw toons, an' I suppwose theer 'll be somebody to drink at them aw. When I'd wander't aboot till I was tir't, I went tull a decent leùken public hoose an' gat some supper. Efter I'd deùn I thowt I wad hev a glass o' summet afwore I went to bed an' I axt t' mistress if they hed enny good yal. Sed she, "Aye, I dar say it's good eneùff; it's Bobby's." I dudden't know what she meen't be Bobby's. I thowt it was mappen some new-fashint neàme they'd gitten for some o' their bitter yal or summet, an' seeàh I tell her 'at I dudden't want owt o' that mak. I just wantit a glass o' good Cummerland yal, if I could git it. "Wy," she says, "it is good Cummerland yal; it's 'double X' fra Bobby Faulder' brewery; neàh body drinks owt else bit Bobby' yal at Kessick, if they know't." "Varra weel," says I, "fetch me a glass on't;" an' when it com I thowt it sa good 'at I wad hev anudder, an' than I went to bed. When I gat up t' next mwornin I axt hoo far it was to Borrowdale. They telt me it was nine mile to t' hee end on't; bit theer was a cwoatch went ivvery day up through Borrowdale to Buttermer, an' back be Newlands, 'at wad tak me aw t' way roond for five shillin'. I thowt it was cheap eneùf that, bit I wad rayder walk, an' than I could tak me awn time an' see owt 'at I wantit to see.

Varra weel, I startit off up t' Borrowdale rwoad, an' when I gat hofe a mile or seeah, I thowt if aw t' Borrowdale rwoads war as durty as that they wad hev plenty o' mire i' Borrowdale, if they'd nowt else. Bit efter I gat a bit farder, t' rwoad went on be t' watter side, an' was a varst cleaner. T' furst hoose I com teù was a gentleman's pleàce they caw t' Barrow Hoose, an' I thowt it was t' bonniest spot to leeve at I'd seen aboot Kessick. It frunts reet doon t' lake; an' aw roond aboot it theer nice shrubberies, an' at t' back side t' grund rises up just like a fell, bit it's aw groun ower wi wood, an' girt craggs peepen oot, wi' ivy climmen up them.

Theer was a lad telt me 'at they hed a parlish fine watterfaw up theer, an' I could see't wi' gaan an' axin at t' Lodge: seeah I went an' knock't at t' dooer, an' axt if I could see't. A young lass pot her hat on, an' went to show me t' way; an' I think it was as weel worth gaan to see as owt I saw aw t' time I was away fra heàme. It's a girtish beck wi' a gay sup o' watter in't, 'at comes throo amang a deal o' girt steàns an' craggs, varra nar ebben doon, rworen, an' churnen, an' blashen, ower ya girt steàn, an' by anudder, an' under anudder, till it's aw as white, 'at yan mud think it was menny a hundred gallon o' churn't milk cummen doon. Efter I'd leùk't at it a bit, I com away, an' I gev t' young lass sixpence for gaan wi' me, an' she sed I mud sign me neàme in a beùk she let me see. I thowt to mesel she likely nobbut wantit to know what they caw't me; bit awivver I went an' scribblet "Tommy, fra t' Abbey Holme," an' than I set off ageàn.

I next went by t' Lowdoer Hotel an' t' Borrowdale Hotel, varra nar clwose togidder, an' I cuddent bit wonder what they wantit wi' sa menny hotels i' sec a pleàce as Borrowdale; bit what I dar say theer a deal o' thur quality fwok astur i' summer time. T' next pleàce I saw was a bit villidge ower o' tudder side o' t' beck; bit I was t' meast tean up wi' t' beck iv owt aboot theer. Doon in oor part o' t' country, t' grund's aw sa level yan can hardly tell what way t' watter's gaan in t' beck, an' it all'as leùks meùdy i' t' boddom, teù; bit Borrowdale beck comes runnen away doon ower t' clean steàns an' gravel, as clear as glass; sometimes for a few yerds quite slowly, an' than it sets off ageàn like as if it was in a parlish girt hurry. When I gat a bit farder on, I com at a girt quarry whoar they git sleàte, an' buildin' steàn, an' yat stoops, an' sec like, oot iv a greenish cullert cragg. They tell me it was t' "Whye-feut Quarry," an' t' way it gat that neàme was this. Yance ower, lang sen, a chap steàll a whye fra somebody i' Borrowdale – an' theer's t' feùt-marks o' him an' t' whye, an' auld Harry, ('at was helpen him to drive't,) to be seen till this day on a slape cragg theer-aboots. I teùk t' hee rwoad by t' quarry, an' wasent lang till I gat to "Booder steàn." It's a girt rough steàn, varra nar like t' shap iv oor leàth, if it was stannen wi' t'riggin doon bank, an' I think aboot as big, teu. It's a terrible wild country aboot Booder steàn. Theer nowt to see bit fells, an' craggs, an' gurt steàns iv aw sides, till yan gits a bit farder on; an' than yan may see a lock o' laal fields, an' a few hooses farder up t' deàll. What, I keep't gaan, an' varra seun I com tull a villidge 'at they caw t' Rostwhate. I wassent lang i' cummen tull anudder villidge, 'at a chap telt me was t' Seatore, an' if I wantit to gang to Buttermer, I mud turn to me reet hand up t' fell. I dud seeàh, an' clamm away a gay bit up, an' than I sat doon to hev a rust. I thowt to mesel when I was sitten theer, 'at I'd hard a deal o' queer teàlls aboot Borrowdale an' Borrowdale fwok; sec as ther tryen to wo t' cuckoo in, 'at they mud hev spring aw t' year roond, an' aw sec stuff as that; bit noo when I'd seen them, I dudden't see 'at they war much different fra enny udder country fwok.

Efter I'd rustit a bit I set off ageàn, an' efter a lang climm I gat to t' top; an' when I leuk' in at t' tudder side, I thowt it was a wilder like pleàce ner it was aboot Booder steàn. Up at t' left hand theer was a girt cragg 'at leuk't to ga up as hee as t' cloods; an' whyte away up t' feàce on't, theer war some sleàte quarries, whoar yan mud ha' thowt 'at newt but a fleein' thing could ha' gitten teù; an' theer was a man cummen doon wi' a sledful o' sleàte, whoar it was that brant 'at yan mud ha' thowt a cat cudden't ha' keep't it's legs.

Whoar I hed to gang doon was a hollow atween two fells, an' theer was just room for t' rwoad an' a laal mad beck, 'at went splashen doon be t' side on 't. When I gat a mile or two doon it gat to be rayder wider, an' than I saw a hoose or two. Than I com tull a lake, an' wassent lang till I gat to Buttermer villidge, whoar theer a few farm hooses, an' two or three cottiges, an' a lal chepel, an' two public hooses. I went to t' public hoose 'at hed t'sign o' t' Fish, an' axt t' landleàdy if I could git a bit o' dinner. While it was gitten riddy, she telt me 'at that was t' hoose at t' Buttermer beauty leev't at; an' aw aboot a scamp iv a fellow 'at they caw't Hatfield cummen, an' pertenden to be some girt lword, an' wedden this Mary o' Buttermer, an' 'at it wassent lang till he was hang't for fworgery.

When I'd gitten me dinner I fand I was time eneùf for t' cwoatch back to Kessick. As I was gitten rayder tir't I thowt I cudden't deù better ner gang wi't. It's nut sa brant ower be Newlens as it is be Borrowdale, for aw it's brant eneùf; bit what t' driver was use't teu't, an' we warrent lang i' gaan to Kessick. Theer was a chap on t' cwoatch, a rare talker, an' he telt me t' neàms iv a deal o' pleàces 'at we saw. He shew't me a rwoad ower t' fell lower doon ner that we com ower, 'at they caw Whinlatter; an' he sed as two Borrowdale chaps were yance gaan ower on i' t' spring o' t' year, t' cuckoo began to shoot in a wood on t' rwoad side, an' they thowt it was somebody shooten at them.

Says tean to t' tudder, "Dust'e hear that, Jwohn? Wy, hang it! We're kent whoarivver we gang!"

When I gat back to Kessick I went to t' seàme hoose I stop't at t' neet afwore. I was sair tean up wi' an auld-fashint picter 'at was fassent up on t' wo' in t' room I was in. It was t' picter o' two chaps; tean o' them an' auld miserable leùken fellow as ivver yan saw, reàken up sovereigns wi' a hay-reàk. He'd gitten a canny heap o' them; an' theer was written doon below him—

> The sordid miser takes a world of pains,
> And often frets himself for others' gains;
> But what is't for? to leave a thoughtless boy,
> To reap what he himself wants wit for to enjoy.

T' tudder chap was a young rakish leùken fellow, wi' his hat cock't o' teàa side. He was throwen t' sovereigns aboot iv aw sides wi' a pitchfork, an' theer was doon below him—

> I am clothed in gold lace and feathers,
> With a heart as light as a cork;
> What my old father raketh together,
> I throw it away with a fork.

They telt me 'at it was pentit by a chap caw't Salathiel Court, 'at leev't i' that neighbourhood menny year sen.

When I gat up t' next mwornin, I telt them I wantit to gang to Gursmer, bit I wad like to see t' "Druid steàns." They said I mud gang on t' Peerath rwoad a bit, an' than turn to me reet through St. John's. It was rayder a donky wet mwornin when I left Kessick, an' when I'd gitten aboot a mile oot o' t' toon, I leet iv an' auld man sitten on a steàn, tryen to bwore a wholl in 't wi' a jumper an' a laal hammer. He was tappen away wi' his hammer on t' end o' t' jumper, an' I stop't beside him an' axt him if it was hard. Sed he, "Aye, middlin'. Dud ye ivver hear tell o' auld Jemmy Andrew?" "An' who was auld Jemmy Andrew?" says I. "Wy," says he, "he was a terrible chap for rhymin'. He yance was varra weel off, bit what wi' drinken, an' cock-feighten', an' ya

mak o' idleness or anudder, he spent what he hed, an' gat to be varra poor. I
remember menny year sen noo, I was gaan up that field just abeùn theer, an'
Jemmy was sitten an' bworen a cobble, just as I is noo, an' when I gat tull him
I sed, "Wy, Jemmy, it's rayder coald this mwornin." Jemmy leùk't up an' sed—

> "On this coald steàn poor Jemmy sits,
>
> Reflecten on his drucken fits."

Efter I'd left t' auld chap, I clamm away up t' rwoad till I gat to t' top o' t'
hill, an' than I saw t' Druid steàns in a field clwose by. I gat ower t' steel an'
went to see what they war like. I fand 'at it was a circle mebby twenty or
thirty yerds across, wi' girt rough steàns, some o' them three or fower ton
weight, set up a bit off yan anudder aw roond. I thowt to mesel 'at they
mud ha' studden theer menny a hundred year; I could just fancy I saw them
auld hofe neàk't savages, gimen, an' liften, an' setten them up, an' some auld
grey-beardit Druid stannen ower them wi' a yak-bob in his hand, tellen them
hoo to put them.

When I'd seen what I could I gat ower on to t' rwoad ageàn, an' went
on a bit farder, an' than tum't up St. John's vale. I went on a bit, an' than
through some fields, an' up by a beck; an' just efter I gat to t' beck I saw
fower fellows fishen aw i' ya dub, two iv ayder side. I axt yan o' them what
they war fishen for, an' he sed, "Salmon." I axt him than if theer was some i'
that dub, as they war aw fishen in't. He sed, "Aye, isn't ther'!" "What," says
I, "hes some o' ye seen some?" He sed, "No, nut to-day; bit theer was yan
gitten oot o' theer last week." I went on than. I thowt that was warse ner owt
I hard i' Borrowdale—aw them fower fellows to be floggen theer for t' fish
'at was gitten a week afwore! I went on up t' deàll, clwose by a girt cragg 'at
they telt me was Cassel rock, an' was seùn into t' Ammelsed rwoad. I caw't
at a public hoose an' inquir't which was t' best way on to Helvellyn. They
telt me I cuddent deù better ner start climmen fra theer; bit they thowt it
wad be varra misty at t' top. I sed I wad run t' chance on't, as I thowt it wad
mebby clear up. Seeàh, I set off reet away up t'fell. I fann it a gay bit branter
an' rougher ner Skiddaw, bit I teùk plenty o' time. I oft stop't an' leùk't aboot
me till I gat away up, an' could see partly ower o' t' tudder side, whoar I was

lucky eneùf to leet iv a guide 'at belang't to Gursmer. We hed to cross ower a narrow ledge to t' reet hand, an' just as we war gaan up theer we met a man 'at sed he'd been lost on t' top for an' 'oor or two, an' 'at t' mist was that thick *he could cut it wi' his knife*. Just as we gat to t' top, awivver, it clear't away, an' a terrible fine view we hed. T' guide telt me t' neàms iv a deal o' spots I cudden't ha' fund oot mesel. Barn! yan mud see ya fell peepen ower anudder for miles an' miles. We could see eight or nine lakes, an' I dunnet know hoo menny tarns; an' we could see t' sea an' ships sailen on't, doon aboot Moorcom'. It's varra bare an' steàny on t' top; theer varra nar nowt growes theer; bit I saw some o' thur laal Herdwick sheep picken away amang t' craggs, whoar yan mud think 'at ther wassent gurse kind to git. They're as wild as thunner: if a body happens to git nar yan o' them on a sudden, it gis a laal bit whissel, an's away ower a hill neùk, ameàst afwore yan can say "What's that?"

Efter we'd leùk't aboot us a bit, we set off towarts Gursmer, an' hed a gay lang travel on t' top afwore we gat to gaan doon t' breest into t' valley. It's a varra bonnie deàll is Gursmer, wi' a nice laal lake i' teà end; an' it's a terrible pleàce for gentlemen's hooses. They're sticken iv aw corners. I think t' gentry ur like rooks; a gay lock o' them like to build nut far off yan an udder. T' guide telt me Dick Hudson's was t' likeliest pleàce for me to stop at, an' he shew't me whoar aboots it was, an' then I gev him hofe a croon for aw t' fash he'd hed wi' me. Efter I'd partit wid him, I met two drucken fellows cummen on t' rwoad, 'at hed fawn oot; an' I hard teàn say to t' tudder, "Thou'd better mind what thou's deùn, or else I'll flounder the', thou girt thickheàdd thou." What, I stopt aw neet at Dick's, as t' guide caw't him, an' t' next mwornin they axt me if I'd been to t' Kurkgarth to see Wordsworth's greàvv, bit I telt them I duddent know 'at he was bury't theer. Wy bit, they sed, he was, an' ivvery body went to see it; an' seeah I fand be t' heidsteàns 'at Wordsworth, an' Hartley Coleridge, an' some o' Wordsworth's family war bury't theer. It was aw paddle't aboot till it was just like a turnpike rwoad. I thowt it was a fair sham, an' I mak neàh doot bit theer menny a duzzen gangs an' helps to treed t' gurse off 'at nivver i' their lives read a bit o' owt 'at owder Wordsworth or Coleridge wreàtt.

Efter I'd studden a bit I went on t' rwoad towart Ammelsed, on by t' Prince o' Wales Hotel just at t' low end o' Gursmer watter, an' through Rydal, whoar Wordsworth leev't, an' I was seùnn at Ammelsed. Yan wad hardly know whedder to caw't a toon or a villidge: it's ower laal for teànn, an' ower big for t' tudder. Theer a canny lock o' shops an' public hooses in't, an' a gay lock o' gentlemen's hooses roond aboot t' ootsides on't. I leùk't aboot a bit, an' than I went on t' rwoad to Windermer, an' a varra nice walk it is iv aboot fower mile. I saw t' Low-wood, an' Booness, an' a deal mair varra nice pleàces as I went on. Windermer's quite a new pleàce: it's aw been built sen t' railway was meàdd, an' theer a deal o' varra good buildins, an' sum girt uns an' aw. An' than it's clwose at t' edge o' t' lake, whoar theer two laal steamers, an' scwores o' bwoats to see, sailen aboot. Es I'd nivver hed a sail on enny o' t' lakes, I thowt I wad try to git yan on Windermer; an' seeàh I went an' axt a man if he knew iv enny body 'at wad let me hev a sail, an' he sed, aye, he wad. What, I gat intul his bwoat, an' we sail't away two or three mile on to t' lake, an' I nivver enjoy't owt sa much i' me life I think. It was a fine day; t' watter was as smooth as glass, an' t' fells, an' t' fields, an' t' woods aw roond, dud leùkk sa bonnie! When we'd sail't aboot a bit we com off ageànn, an' I paid him what he charg't, an' than startit back to Ammelsed. T' next mwornin I startit off to gang ower Kurkstan fell to Patterdale. I'd a gay lang climm afwore I gat to t' top, an' when I dud git theer I fand a public hoose 'at hed t' sign o' t' "Traveller's Rest;" seeàh, I thowt I wad hev a rust at it, an' t' landleàdy telt me at that was t' "Hee'st hoose in o' England." I duddent contradict her, bit I'd read some way 'at t' hee'st hoose in England was on Alston moor.

When I'd gitten a rust I set off ageàn doon t' tudder side towart Patterdale, an' I think it's branter o' that side ner it is o' t'Ammelsed side; bit I wassent lang i' gitten doon into Patterdale. It's whyte a wild fell deàll till yan gits a canny bit doon, an' than it gits to be ameàst like Gursmer. Just at t' hee end o' Ullswater theer a canny lock o' good hooses, an' two or three hotels. They caw aw t' public hooses hotels up amang t' fells. I suppwose it's for t' seàke o' gitten thur toorists to ga to them; an' I dar say theer some o' them 'ill stop at a middlin' leùken hoose when it's caw't a hotel, 'at waddent hev't sed 'at they stopt at a public hoose. I fand I could gang doon t' watter i' t' steamer fra Patterdale to Poola Brigg, an' than I waddent be far fra Peerath.

I thowt, as I wassent gan to walk, I mud as weel gang oot an' leuk aboot me, if theer was owt to see. What, I went up a rwoad a bit 'at seem't to ga reet to t' fell. When I' gitten on a bit I fand it went to t' Greenside Mine. They telt me 'at they git leed an' silver oot on't, an' theer three or fower hundred fwok worken at it. Efter I'd santer't aboot a bit, I went doon to t' watter side whoar t' steamer starts fra. I was just i' time, as they war gitten up t' steàm an' makken riddy to start. I teùk me passige, an' we war off doon t' watter directly. It's a gay lang lake is Ullswatter—nut sa lang as Windermer—bit I think 'at it's as bonnie a sheet o' watter as enny I saw i' me travels. Aw doon t' back side, that was at yan's reet hand as yan com doon, it's a wild felly country as can be; bit t' tudder side efter yan gits doon a bit, seems mair cultivatit; an' theer some varra nice hooses here an' theer. We war seùn doon at Poola Brigg, a nice villidge just at t' low end o' t' lake. Theer war two or three busses waiten at t' landin to tak enny passengers 'at wantit to gang to Peerath. I gat into yan o' them an' went streight away to t' Railway Station; an' teùk t' train to Carel. When I gat theer I happent to be i' time for anudder 'at was just gan' to start to Marypwort; seeàh I gat a ticket for as far as I wantit to gang. I gat heàme i' good time, fand them aw i' girt buckle, an' varra pleas't to see me seàfe back ageàn.

Efter I'd gitten me supper, an' was fairly into my oan bed, I gat to meùsin' an' thinken ower what I'd seen while I was away. I'd hard a deal aboot t' fell-heid fwok bein' daft, an' cloonish, an' sec as that; bit noo when I'd seen them, I duddent see 'at they war enny way different fra udder fwok. Enny o' them 'at ivver I saw war just as civil, an' as sharp; an' seem't to know as mickle as cuntry fwok deù doon here. Bit what, theer'ill be odds o' them, neàh doot. Theer'ill be feùls up theer, as theer ur doon here, an' mebby neàh mair o' them nowder.

## *T' Plesser o' Seavin'*

WHAT'S t' use iv aw this screapin', screapin',
   Seàven, seàven, aw yan's days?
T' bit plesser 'at yan hes i' takkin
   Turns to pain when owt yan pays.
What's t' use o' pinchin', pinchin', al'as,
Till yan's feàce grows ping't and thin;
   An' nut a laal bit smile can git oot,
Through yan's dry an' wrinkel't skin?


What's t' use o' aw this toilin', toilin',
   Al'as at it, seùn an' leàte;
To leave awt' brass for udders' spendin',
   When yan's deid an' oot o' geatt.
I sometimes think I'll alter, alter,
Just to sek a time I'll seàvv;
   Bit habit still gits stranger, stranger.
As yan nearer gits to t' greàvv.


When yan's seàv't ameàst a lifetime,
   Aw yan's better thowts ur geànn;
Nowt 'ill deù bit gittin', gittin',—
   T' heart grows hard as enny steànn.
They may spend it; let them spend it,
I'll hod hoàld on't till I dee;
   An' may the'r plesser be as much as
Seavin', seavin's been to me.

## *A laal bit o' Money's a Wonderful Thing*

A laal bit o' money's a wonderful thing;
    Lord bless us! what changes it maks!
Like some famous mixter for cleanen auld cleàs,
    Oot o' fwok seùn aw t' durtspots it taks.

A chap may be cloonish, an' lazy, an' daft,
    Knock't aboot like a Setterday whelp;
Bit let him a legacy git, an' than watch,
    Hoo he'll gang up three steps at a skelp.

His cloonishness seùn aw gits hap't oot o' seet;
    His laziness fwok seùn forgit;
His stains an' his durtspots ur aw cleàn wip't oot;
    His daft speeches turn into wit.

A lass may be thick-leg't, plain leùken, an soor;
    Bad-temper't, a gossip, an' clat;
Bit if she hes money, she'll seùn hev a chap,—
    Aye, if she be warse ner aw that.

Her thick legs an' plain leùk 'ill nivver be seen,
    If money she hods in her hand;
That turns aw her black spots to ornaments breet,
    Like t' touch of a cunjurer's wand.

A chap 'at hes money hes frinds withoot stint,
    Like as wasps a sweet pot swarm aboot;
Bit when t' money's deùn hoo they'll vanish away,
    Like t' wasps when aw t' honey's gone oot.

An' what efter aw is sec shinen stuff worth,

    Withoot ye've a spirit to use't?

Some hurd, hurd it up till they cannot sleep for't,

    An' some nobbut hev't to abuse't.


## *Lang Years sen*


Tho' lang, lang years have pass't away,

    An' trubles nut a few

Hev turn't my hair to silver gray,

    An' wrinkle't thy fair broo:

Still happy memories hing around

    That weel remember't spot,

Whoar furst we voo't to join oor hands,

    An' share teànn tudder's lot.


When leùken through them lang dim years,

    That nivver faden scene

Leùks on life's wilderness, just like

    A paster, fresh an' green.

I' aw oor ups an' doons o' life,

    Na shade o' dark regret

Hes ivver thrown its shadow ower

    That bonny green pleàce yet.


Aw t' toils an' trouble than unseen,

    'At follow't on that voo,

If dark an' threetnen when they com,

    Seem bit like shadows noo:

'At nobbut add anudder charm

    To that still pleasen' view,'

At rises up like waken dreàms,

    Wi' plessers ivver new.

That day abeùn aw udder days,
    When thoo becom me wife,
Hes been a star to guide me through
    Aw t' lang creùk't rwoads o' life:
An' oft when I could see afwore
    Nowt bit a dark rough track,
I still cud gedder heart ageànn,
    Wi' just yance leùken back.

An' noo, when we're gaan hand i' hand,
    Doon t' tudder side o' life,
It's nut sa much I want beside,
    While I've me faithful wife.
We cannot tell what's on befwore;
    Bit, than, when we leùk back,
That bonny breet pleàce rises still
    On life's lang winden track.

### *What Tom Briggs sed aboot Pride*

Tom Briggs an' I war scheùlmates yance;
    Bit Tom's been lang away,
An's just cum't doon to see his frinds,—
    I met him t' tudder day.
He's just t' auld chap for aw the world,
    As when he went fra heàm;
A deal wi' stinken pride git spoil't,
    Bit Tom bides al'as t' seàmm.

Ses I to Tom, "Reet fain I is—
    This minds yan o' lang sen;
Theer some sa stuck up when they come,
    'At auld frinds they dooent ken.
Hoo is't 'at thoo keeps free fra pride?
    Theer some 'at boonce an' strut;
It maks me mad as a poo't swine,
    When they sec capers cut."

Ses Tom, "It's mebby want o' sense,
    Or, mappen, want o' thowt;
Bit dunnet think 'at stinken pride
    Is aw fra Lunnen browt:
I've travvel't England through an' through,
    Fra teàa end on't to t' tudder;
An' pride I fand at ivvery pleàce,
    I' ya shap or anudder.

Fra lwords an' dukes, to tramps on t' rwoad,
    I nivver saw yan yet,
'At care't to bide in t' lower room
    When he could heigher git:
An' if thoo'll leùk aboot the' here,
    Thoo needent leùk sa lang,
To see some fra their brudders turn,
    Wi' finer fwok to gang.

Thoo munnet think 'at pride's confin't
    To him 'at struts an' brags;
Theer pride 'at's whisht as enny moose,
    An' pride 'at's don't i' rags.
Theer some, neàh doot, quite prood to think
    They're humbler far nor t' rest;
An' whoar theer hoaf a duzzen rogues,
    Yan's prood to think he's t' best.

It's want o' thowt 'at maks us prood;
  If we could nobbut see
Oorsels as udders see us, barn,
  Sec things wad nivver be.
Bit while we're watchen udder fwok,
  An' hunten for a fawt,
We hev yan riddy catch't at heàm,
  If we could nobbut know't.

## T' Country for me

They may talk o' the'r wonderful cities,
  An' brag o' the'r toons as they will;
Bit moontans, an' valleys, an' rivers,
  To me ur mair wonderful still.

They may talk o' the'r railways an' stashons,
  An' tell hoo the'r trains swift can glide;
Bit what's aw the'r speed to yon storm-clood,
  'At darts across t' craggy fell side?

They may talk o' the'r buildin's an' steeples,
  An' tell yan they're wondrous to see;
Bit t' ivy green craggs ur far grander,
  Or t' gnarel't auld moss-cuver't tree.

What is t'er in t' toon to compare wi'
  T' green woods when they're brusten i' spring?
What music o' art can be sweeter
  Nor t' burds, when sa blithely they sing?

They may talk o' the'r picters an' statues,
    O' the'r foontans sa fine they may brag;
Bit what ur they aw to sek foontans,
    As spring fra an' dash doon yon crag?

Just gi' me a fishin' rod limber,
    An' leisure to wander away,
Where t' watter winds roond be t' fell boddom,
    An' t' craggs wi' auld age ur turn't grey:

An' neàh mair plesser I'll wish for,
    Nor t' beauties o' nater to see;
The'r toons, an' the'r railways, an' ingins,
    May puff to auld Neddy for me.

### Oor Wants

When burds war singen merrily,
    An' trees wax fresh an' green,
An' daisies peep't fra 'mang t' young gurse,
    Wi' bonnie laughen een;
I sat doon clwose to t' edge o' t' Beur,
    To watch t' breet sparklen stream,
When thowts o' days lang past away,
    Com ower me like a dream.

I thowt aboot that happy time,
    When i' sweet smilen May,
To poo a bunch o' daisies fresh,
    I oft wad steàl away:
I thowt thur daisies near me noo,
    I' colour, form, an' size.
Just like them daisies, lang, lang sen,
    'At dud i' memory rise.

I thowt aboot me scheùl-lad days,

    When caw't sa seùn to rise,

Unwillin' I creàpp oot o' bed,

    An' rub't me sleepy eyes:

Than wi' me setchel an' me beùkk,

    Wi' sledderen steps I went

On t' rwoad to t' scheull; bit nut o' beùkks,

    Bit laken I was bent.

I thowt aboot them ibnins, teù,

    When aw oor tasks war deùnn,

Let lowse fra t' scheùll sa wild we war,

    We meàst cud lowp to t' meùnn:

We than thowt if auld scheùll was gone,

    We wad hev nowt to fear;

Sen than, for idleness at scheùll,

    I've hed to pay reet dear.

I thowt aboot me youthful days,

    When scheùl-lad days war deùn;

'Twas than I thowt 'at nowt bit joy

    Wad be me portion seùnn:

Bit still I fand na happiness,

    I wish't to be a man;

An' than to think o' t' lasses, an'

    To cwort them, I began.

I thowt if I a sweetheart hed,

    Hoo happy I wad be;

An' nowt worth leùken at i' t' warld

    Bit lasses, I cud see.

Bit when I hed a sweetheart fund,

    As dear to me as life,

I thowt I wad be happier still,

    If nobbut I'd a wife.

I thowt if I but hed a wife,
 I wad want nowt mair than;
Bit seùnn I fand it oot 'at noo
 Me wantin' just began.
Me wants afwore hed been bit few,
 An' them few war ideal;
Bit noo they ivvery day grew mair,
 An' ivvery day mair real.

Sen that I've larn't 'at ivvery want
 Hes sisters an' hes brudders;
For when I banish yan away,
 Theer seàfe to be anudder.
Wi' me it ivver hes been seeàh,
 An' mebby ivver will;
For when I git ya want supply't,
 I finnd anudder still.


## The Mother's Appeal


O! dunnet leave us, Willie, dear,
 Bit stay content at heàmm;
What signifies if thoo sud git
 A fortune, or a neàmm?
Thoo'd lwose far mair o' happiness
 Nor owt 'at thoo wad gain;
O! Willie, wad t'e nobbut stay,
 We wad be glad an' fain.

This menny a week I've twin't an' fret.
 Sen furst thoo sed thoo'd gang;
It maks yan good for nowt at aw,
 'At's nivver varra Strang.

Theer menny a neet I gang to bed,
    An' nivver sleep a wink;
I turn an' cough, an' cough an' turn,
    An' than I lig an' think.

What could t'e deù when for fra heàmm,
    If thoo sud ailen be;
An' nut a creeter 'at thoo kent,
    Nor frind 'at thoo could see?
O! Willie, deù consent to bide,
    I's seùr thoo'll nivver reù;
Just stay content, for t' seàke o' us,
    An' Lizzie, teù, sa trew.

What, thoo mud dee, when far away,
    Yan knows nowt when nor where;
Whoar nut a single yan theer is
    To drop a tear, nor care.
Oh! Willie, dear, if gang thoo will,
    I'll nivver dow that day;
I'll twine an' freet fra mworn to neet,
    An' seùnn I'll pine away.

An' Lizzie, teù, peer sairy thing,
    She's just as bad as me;
An' fadder, if it's laal he says,
    He's mebbie t' warst o' t' three.
Just deù give up them wanderen thowts,
    For t' seàk o' them an' me;
Just say them two laal words, "I'll stay,"
    An' happy we will be.

## *Tommy an' Joe:*
## *A Dialogue*

One evening, when wandering along by a wood,

I came to a place where an old pollard stood;

Its trunk was all matted with ivy still green,

But its centre was hollow, where heart had once been;

One side was quite open, and serv'd for a door,

So I stepped inside, where I'd ne'er been before;

Some one had there placed a stone for a seat,

When they'd crept in to shelter, from rain or from heat:

The place seem'd so snug and inviting to me,

That I sat down to rest in this old hollow tree;

Just over the hedge, close to where I sat down,

Was the highway that led to the next market town:

I had scarcely sat down when there driving up came

A neighbouring fanner, Joe Grasper by name,

Who had been to the market his produce to sell;

And the bargains he'd made, they had pleased him well;

You might see by his phisog, oft gloomy and dark,

But now it seem'd cheerful and blythe as the lark.

While to his old dame he did cheerily chat,

As, pleas'd with the change, quite delighted she sat;

Just then Tommy Trueman came sauntering along,

His hands in his pockets, and humming a song;

Though his looks were but poor, and his dress coarse and mean,

In his features blunt honesty plainly was seen:

The two neighbours met when just opposite me,

Where I sat snugly hid in my old hollow tree.

I knew that the news would be fresh from the town.

So my pencil I took, and their dialogue wrote down.

## TOMMY

Wy, Joe, thoo's been to t' market, than;
  What news fra t' toon to-day?
I sud ha' geànn to t' market, teù.
  Bit stay'd to help wi' t' hay.
It shin't oot breet at mwornin,
  An' we brack't aw oot o' cock,
Bit seùnn it com on rain ageànn,—
  We duddent git a lock.

## JOE

I thowt at mwornin' it wad rain,
  I telt oor fwok it wad;
It shin't oot far ower breet be hofe,
  It dry't a bit like mad.
I telt them nut to brek ower much,
  But see hoo t' day turn't oot;
I' brokken wedder sec as this,
  It's best when yan's aboot.

## TOMMY

Aye, wy, it mebby is, but still
  Yan mun gang, noo an' than;
An' t' wife an' barns, when yan's away,
  'Ill deù t' best 'at they can.
Bit, what sec markets hes t'er been
  For butter, eggs, an' cworn?
I think 'at breid 'ill nut faw much,
  Till t' new crop's gitten shworn.

JOE

Wy, meàst o' things aboot sek like;
    I hed some taties theer,
I selt them aw terectly, teù,
    I thowt nut ower dear.
I selt them aw at fow'teen pence,
    An' some fwok grummel't sair;
Bit they war heàmm taties, thoo knows,
    They're worth a gay bit mair.

TOMMY

They mebby ur, but still they're dear,
    For them 'at hes to buy;
Yan cannot wonder if they deù,
    To git them cheaper try.
A steànn o' taties issent much,
    Crack o' them as thoo will;
An' if they be heàmm taties,
    They're nobbut taties still.

JOE

I wassent cracken o' them, Tom,
    Thoo knows I nivver deù;
An' yet me things ur aw as good
    As enny body's, teù.
An' mebby better nor a deal—
    An' who can bleàmm me than,
If oft I deù git rayder mair
    Nor udder farmers can?

## TOMMY

I think it's best to tak what's fair,
    An' nut be ower hard;
A clever chap may be teànn in,
    When rayder off his guard.
An' if yan be teànn in yan's sel,
    Yan dussent like't ower weel;
I think it's t' best to deal yan's sel
    As yan wad hev fwok deal.

## JOE

What does t'e mean be takkin in?
    Thoo dussent mean to say
'At ivver I dud owt 'et mak?
    Nay, nivver i' me days.
For gitten aw yan nicely can,
    I think yan's nut to bleàmm;
An' them 'at cannot bargins mak,
    They'd better stay at heàmm.

## TOMMY

Bit if thoo knows what a thing's worth,
    An' axes a bit mair,
An' cracks it off to git that price,
    I think it's hardly fair.
An' than it mebby hes some fawt;
    O' that thoo'll nut let wi't;
Noo, that, I think, is just as bad
    As leein', ivvery bit.

## JOE

Hoo can yan lee, an' nivver speak?
    Thoo talks just like a feùl;
I nivver larn't sec stuff as that,
    Aw t' time I went to t' scheùll.
To lee's to say what issent trew,
    Me mudder still telt me;
An' if yan nivver speaks at aw,
    Hoo can yan tell a lee?

## TOMMY

A man may act a lee as weel
    As tell yan wi' his mooth;
It's just as bad as leein', if
    He keeps back part o' t' treùth.
If just a bit o' t' treùth he tells,
    An' fwok think he's telt aw,
Is that nut ivvery bit as bad,
    I just wad like to know?

## JOE

Does thoo think 1 wad be sa daft
    As tell fwok aw I knew?
I dunnet think it's t' wisest plan
    To say still just what's trew;
A lee or two i' t' way o' trade
    'Ill nut deù mickle ill,
An' than, yan dussent tie fwok to
    Believ't, withoot they will.

## TOMMY

Thoo all'as aims fwok to believ't,
 Or else what good can't deù?
Thoo's caw't a leear for thee pains,
 An' thoo's reet sarret, teù.
Bit if thoo tells a lee or two,
 An' fwok, thee lees believen',
Gi' mair nor what thee things ur worth,
 It's nar as bad as thieven'.

## JOE

I cannot see a bit o' fawt,
 I' gittin' aw yan can;
Me mudder all'as use to say
 'At they mud laugh 'at wan.
I all'as hed an honest neàmm,
 An' all'as paid me way;
An' him 'at does that needn't care
 What enny man may say.

## TOMMY

It's fine to talk iv honesty,
 Bit nut sa good to know;
If aw war bworn an' try't alike,
 Who'd stand, an' who wad faw?
A chap like thee, 'at nivver knew
 What 'twas to want five pund,
An' ivver sen thoo wantit owt,
 Hed what thoo wantit fund.
It's neah greit preùf o' honesty,
 For thee to pay thee way;

Thoo dussent pay a penny mair
    Nor what thoo's fworc't to pay;
Theer menny a fellow cannot pay,
    'At gladly wad pay, teù;
Bit if he hessent brass eneùff,
    What can a fellow deù?

### JOE

He suddent git things, when he knows
    He hessent brass to pay;
He issent honest if he does,
    That's aw 'at yan can say.
I think 'at fwok sud ha' their awn,
    It's nobbut just an' reet;
An' poor fwok gitten into debt,
    I cannot bide to see 't.

### TOMMY

I'll awn it's t' warst iv owt 'at comes
    To any labouren' man;
Bit sometimes it may happen, teù,
    When he does t' best he can;
For want o' health or wark 'ill mak
    Want in his feàce to glower,
When ivvery penny he could mak
    Was laal eneùf befwore.
It's hard for wife an' barns to starve,
    When bread an' money's deùn;
He knows 'at he can credit hev,
    An' thinks he'll git wark seùn.
Bit pay-day comes afwore he thinks,
    An' mebby part he'll pay;

Bit when he's gitten into debt,
    He's hamper't menny a day:
It's than it tries his honesty,
    When dun't an' cannot pay;
An' threeten't oft, an' blackguardit,
    An' bully't ivvery way.
If he can stick to t' thing 'at's reet,
    An' tell t' treuth all'as than,
Yan may wi' reason set it doon,
    'At he's an honest man.
It's nut for sek as thee to brag,
    'At thoo can pay thee way, ·
An' 'at thoo's honest, an' sek stuff,
    As I've just hard the' say.
If thoo was drovven tull a strait,
    I waddent think 'at thoo
Wad stick at trifles, when thoo awns
    Thoo'll lee for profit noo.

## JOE

Come 'op! Sally, we mun gang,
    We're gaan to talk aw neet;
We sud ha' been at heàmm to milk
    At six o'clock, wi' reet.
Bit ivvery body 'at yan met
    Persuadit yan to stop;
Bit noo we mun gang, seàh, "Good neet:"
    Auld meer, I say, come 'op!

# Miscellaneous Pieces in Verse

## *The Medical Students*

Two medical students, on science intent,
One night to a churchyard clandestinely went;
To steal a dead body to anatomize,
And quickly had dug up and seized their prize.
But the great difficulty was still in the way,
How the corpse unobserv'd to the town to convey;
But, both being clever, this plan they contriv'd,
To dress up the body just as if alive:
Which, having performed quite well, as they thought,
To the church gates their covered vehicle brought;
And hoisted it in, and then whispering "All right,"
They jump'd up and drove at full speed through the night.
Thus they travell'd ten miles, till they came to an inn,
Where the people sold grog, whiskey-toddy, and gin;
And thinking the worst of their journey was o'er,
They drew up their now jaded horse at the door.
And, leaving their subject all snugly propped up,
They enter'd the tavern to smoke and to sup;
The ostler was order'd the horse to attend,
And, thinking the man in the car was their friend,
He thought he might venture to be just so bold,
As civilly ask him if he were not cold:
But the mysterious personage silence did keep,
So the ostler thought he was drunk or asleep.
But wishing to get at the truth if he could,
He climb'd up, and soon found out how matters stood.
Now, being a wag, for a moment he thought,
And then the dead body he quietly brought,
And cover'd it up in the stable unseen,
Then went and sat down where the body had been.

He had not thus long in the car to remain,

Till the young doctors mounted and drove off again;

Refresh'd by the rest, and the whiskey they'd quaff'd,

Their hearts were now light, and they joked and laugh'd.

At length, just to feel if the corpse was all right,

One stretched out his hand, but drew back with affright:

"It is warm!" he exclaimed, not suspecting the trick;

"So would you," said the wag, "if you'd come from old Nick!"

Confounded with terror, they jumped down apace,

And ran 'cross the fields as if running a race;

And they never came back; so the ostler, of course,

Had gain'd by his trick, both a car and a horse!


### *Lines written at "Druid Stones," near Keswick*


Sometimes when the mind wanders back in its musings,

And looks through time's vista to ages gone by;

When left in the gloom of uncertain tradition,

From the pages of fancy the blank we supply:

We in fancy can picture the rude ancient Britons,

On their small sea-girt island, unknowing, unknown;

Undiscover'd by Romans or hardy sea-rovers,

Their world was contained in Britain alone.

How simple their wants we may learn from the climate,

The fruits of the island insipid and few;

The land with black morasses cover'd, an' forests

Where the birch, and the oak, and the alder tree grew.

There the fierce wolf would prowl, and contend for the mastery
With man, who, half-naked, and arm'd with his spear,
Would stealthily steal down among the rank brushwood,
To watch for the wild boar, the hare, or the deer.
How rude were their dwellings: the hut, or the cavern
Would serve them for shelter when tempests howl'd round;
Their seats would be stones, with the green moss for cushions,
Their beds a few branches spread over the ground.
We can fancy the Druids with dark superstition,
And mystery awful enchaining the mind;
For ages no ray of enlightened knowledge,
Its way to this dark gloomy region could find.
Yet o'er all this dark prospect the fair face of nature
Was smiling as lovely, and blooming as fair
As now, when 'tis Britain the seat of refinement,
With cities and palaces everywhere.


Even then the grey skylark would soar towards heaven,
And sing the same song it is singing to-day;
Not a trill has been lost, not a note has been added,
Since it sang to the Druids its sweet morning lay.
Then, as now, would the swallow migrate in the autumn,
And return with the cuckoo when winter was o'er;
In summer the plover would dwell in the mountains,
And in winter return with its brood to the shore.
We can see some old priest in this temple of boulders,
Its floor the green turf, and its roof the blue sky,
Performing some strange act of mystical mummery,
While his rude congregation stands silently by;
The skylark is carolling sweetly above them,
And soaring up higher till lost to the sight;
The thrush on the hawthorn so sweetly is singing,
While the hawthorn itself is all blossom'd with white.
How constant is nature! for successive ages

The beautiful process is ever the same;

Self-renewing, self-acting, and self-recreating,

It was perfect when first from its Maker it came.

That Almighty being, the Father of nature,

Left nothing to alter, and nothing to mend;

With wisdom omniscient, He from the beginning

Could see through all time, even unto the end.

### *Blencathra*

*Blencathra is the ancient name for the mountain also known by the name of Saddleback. Ed.*

I stood on the summit of lofty Blencathra,

And gazed with rapture on mountain and vale;

As far as the eye could reach endless variety

Of hills intermixed with streamlet and dale?

From the brink where I stood on the south of the mountain,

The grey rocks fall sheer down and steep as a wall;

While far down below in the dark humid caverns

The mountain born waters o'er rocky beds roll.

At the foot of the mountain, the hamlet of Threlkeld

Is nestling beneath it, its shelter to crave;

With its houses all white, as the snows of December,

Which its bold hardy shepherds oft fearlessly brave.

Beyond is the verdant Saint John's in the valley,

Spread out like a picture of beautiful sheen,

With its clear winding Beùr, like a long thread of silver,

And its meadows and pastures all brightest of green.

Still more to the south, lies the clear lake of Thirlmere,

Like a sheet of pure crystal with emerald fram'd round;

And beyond, in the distance, the valley of Wythburn,

Where the fabled Dunmail-raise the vision does bound;

From the margin of Thirlmere, the mighty Helvellyn

Towers up steep and rugged, till capped with cloud;

It frowns high above all the neighbouring mountains,

Like a giant who stands in the midst of a crowd.

To the east, where the prospect more uninterrupted

Over fields cultivated, the eye stretches far

Till it rests on the distant and dark line of Crossfell,

Where helm winds and tempests incessantly war.

To the North, I could see through a gorge in the mountain

A rich fertile country slope gently away,

To the flat of Burgh-marsh, on the shore of the Solway,

Where the first Edward died, when his army there lay.

'Cross the Solway, distinctly I saw the white home-steads

Of Scotland, the land of the free and the brave;

Where the dear names of Wallace and Bruce are held sacred,

Who bled their lov'd country from thraldom to save.

Turning more to the left, there the prospect is bounded

By Skiddaw, whose summit seems rocky and bare;

Between is a long reach of heath-cover'd mountain,

The home of the plover, the grouse, and the hare.

Still more to the west is the sweet vale of Derwent,

The loveliest far of those beautiful scenes;

With its lake like a mirror reflecting the sunbeams.

And border'd with woods, meads, and pastures all green.

Beyond is the picturesque valley of Borrowdale,

Hemm'd in by steep mountains, which, starting from Grange,

Stretch for miles 'cross the country, still mountain o'er mountain,

The stupendous Scawfell o'ertopping the range.

Having view'd all the scenes in the vast panorama,

Reluctant and slow I began my descent

To the east, and then turn'd to the right down a hollow;

Where the damp rocks were shatter'd, and broken, and rent.

From the fissures and cracks, in the dark colour'd clay-slate,

The pure waters issue in bubbling springs;

Which, collecting their forces, then form a small streamlet

That falls down the rocks as it murmuring sings;

Its course is but short till it reaches a basin,

Surrounded by rocks, sloping, rugged, and steep,

Where its waters dam'd up form the small tarn of Bowscale,

Whose transparent waters are placid and deep.

Tradition asserts that two immortal fishes

Have dwelt in this tarn since that far distant day,

When its waters were first in this bason collected,

And the mists on the top of Blencathra first lay.

Oh! 'tis healthful to climb to the mountain's high summit,

And gaze on the grandeur of objects around,

Or to range through its lonely and curious recesses,

Where nature unaltered by art is still found.


## *The Changes of Life*


Two young and guileless happy hearts,

   Go on their separate ways;

As buoyant as the feathery foam,

   Which on the ocean plays.


To them all nature wears a smile,

   Their thoughts are pure and bright:

By day their load is light as air,

   And sound their sleep at night.

While gliding on their lightsome ways,
    These two together meet;
A new sensation springs to life,
    A feeling, O! how sweet.

This feeling though unfelt before,
    Is now the polar star;
The magnet that will draw these hearts
    Together from afar.

The dreamy days of courtship now,
    Their every thought engage;
Of all the ups and downs of life,
    This is the brightest stage.

The joys of life, without its cares,
    The lovers now enjoy;
Without a thought, without a fear,
    Its pleasure to destroy.

But soon this life of dreams is o'er,
    And they are man and wife;
They've sworn to cherish and to love
    Each other, through this life.

This pledge to comfort and to help,
    For better and for worse;
If kept, is life's most precious boon;
    If broke, its bitterest curse.

But life in earnest now begins,
    The past has been a dream;
While future days, perhaps to them,
    As bright and lovely seem.

They enter on their new abode,
    No thoughts of sorrow near;
They dream not of the many cares,
    Which soon will gather here.

Alas! how little do they see
    The rough and stony road;
How little burdens one by one,
    Will add unto their load.

A few short years, the changing wheel,
    Again is turned round;
Where then two, only two, were left,
    Is now a family found.

The little blessings, one by one,
    Have gathered round the hearth;
And now the cheerful home resounds
    With childhood's joyous mirth.

Perhaps some friend or parent dear
    Is added to the ring,
And though they're ever welcome, yet
    Some added care they bring.

Home is the blest abode of peace,
    And if conducted right,
The pleasures will out-weigh the cares,
    And make the burden light.

No happier scene on earth is found,
    If through the world we roam,
Than sweet domestic happiness,
    In home, sweet, happy home.

But years again have roll'd around,
    Again we view the scene;
But oh! how altered is the place,
    What changes here have been.

The sons and daughters, one by one,
    Have left the parent hearth;
Some laid within the silent tomb,
    Some scattered o'er the earth.

Two, only two, are at the board;
    Oh! can it be the same—
The same two light and merry hearts,
    Which first together came?

The fading autumn of their lives,
    How different from the spring;
What different thoughts, and joys, and hopes
    And feelings it does bring!

They then look'd forward high with hope,
    Nor thought that they could mourn;
They now look back to joys long past,
    And never to return.

The quiet evening of their lives,
    Is now before them spread;
Their chastened spirits now are calm,
    Their thoughts are upwards led.

They've tasted all the joys of life,
    And many of its pains;
They now look forward to the place
    Where joy unmixed reigns.

A few short years, once more we come,
    To view the changing scene;
The place is there, but they are now
    As if they had not been.

## *Childhood and Age*

When lightsome childhood bounds along,
    With loud and merry laugh;
How different 'tis from age bent down,
    And leaning on a staff.

How different are the scatter'd locks,
    When silvery white with years;
From the luxuriant glossy curls,
    Which happy childhood wears.

How different too the dimpled cheeks,
    And brow so smooth and fair;
From age's sunken cheeks and brow,
    Furrow'd by years and care.

And yet that feeble tottering frame,
    And deeply wrinkled brow;
Were once as lithesome and as fair,
    As this sweet child's are now.

A few short years have made the change,
    A change that comes to all;
The child is raised from the dust,
    Age into dust shall fall.

The child grows up with beauteous bloom,
    Like a sweet flower in spring;
And age sinks down, like that same flower,
    A dry and shrivelled thing.

# SERIES 2 (1876)

## Preface

IN publishing this Second Series of Dialect Pieces, the author begs respectfully to inform his readers that the present volume, like the former one, consists of sketches in prose and verse, illustrative of the dialect, as well as of some of the habits and modes of thought which still prevail in all the rural parts of Cumberland. The stories and rhymes introduced are, with one or two exceptions, strictly Cumbrian in character and idiom, the author having taken pains to ascertain that the real incidents related actually happened in that county; while in the few pieces which are purely imaginary, he has been careful to preserve the same characteristics.

It may perhaps be objected by some critics that the dialect as here written is exaggerated, or, in other words, made broader and more bucolic than it is anywhere spoken at this time of day. That, however, is not so; but, on the contrary, in the more purely pastoral and agricultural parts of the county the vernacular used is very much ruder than anything to be found in this volume. In fact, any one who attempts to write in the dialect will find that if he intends to make his composition in any degree understandable, he will be under the necessity of modifying to some extent the folk-speech which he has heard. One of the greatest impediments in the way of writing the dialect exactly as it is spoken, is the tendency which many of those who speak it have to disregard all the rules of grammar. A single specimen, taken at random, may serve to illustrate this habit. A country man, speaking of his wife and himself going to market, will say, "Hur an' me's gaan." Here we have two pronouns in the objective case in place of two nominatives, and a singular verb instead of a plural one—three palpable errors in a sentence of five words. Considering, however, such anomalies as nothing more than corruptions and abuses, the omission of which would not in any way affect the expressiveness of what Dr. Gibson lovingly styled "our grand old dialect," the writer of these pieces has thought himself justified in discarding many of at least the more glaring of such solecisms.

There being no arbitrary rule for spelling dialect words, as might be expected, almost everyone who tries it has a method of his own; and some writers seem to think that if they can only manage to spell every word, dialect and non-dialect, in some outlandish way, that is all that is required. Failing to see the utility of making what is difficult enough at any time, to outsiders, more unreadable still by such a system, the author has in this volume adopted the opposite plan of spelling all ordinary English words in the usual way, while in spelling dialect words he has followed to a large extent, though not altogether, the phonetic system, as used by the late Dr. Gibson and Mr. Dickinson. With these few remarks, he offers to the public this second volume of trifles, hoping that it may meet with as cordial a reception as greeted the first, and trusting also that it may afford entertainment and amusement during an idle hour to at least all Cumbrians into whose hands it may chance to fall.

J. R.
SAINT JOHN'S.

# "Cummerland Mak O' Talk"

### Coming Home Sober

*Geordie Tarlton, the tailor, used to sew for a week at a time at Waterend, Lord William Gordon's house on Derwentwater. On one occasion, he joined the footman and the butler to patronizz a merry neet at Rosthwaite: the guinea Lord William had given them was more than enough to get them drunk twice over ... of course they promised to come home cold sober. A final glass of whisky for the road after a riotous night of merry-making proved too much. They struggled back to Waterend ("oft eneùf two on us war liggin in' gutter togidder"), only to find his lordship was not abed. A series of accidents revealed their condition to Lord William: they expected "'at ivvery man-jack on us wad git t'seck next mwornin'" but fortunately they never heard another word. Ed.*

SAYS laal Gwordie Tarlton, t' tailyor, to me tudder neet—as he was sittin' cross-legg't on oor teàble at heàm, wid his lapbwoard an' geùss, his needles an' threed, an' aw t' rest iv his knickknackeries scatter't aboot him—says he to me:

When I was a young buck iv a chap, a gay deal different to what I is noo, I oft went to sewe for a week togidder at Lord William Gordon's, at t' Watterend—it was a grand shop that i' Lord William's time—an' as he keep't a gay lock o' sarvents an' fwok a boot him, we hed some rare fun at times.

It happen't yance ower 'at I was theer when auld Mary Cwoats o' Rostwhate was gantè hod hur merry neet; an' t' footman, an' t' butler, an' me meàd it up, (if we could nobbut git leave fra my lword,) we wad gang; an' t' butler promis't to ax him t' furst chance he hed. Noo, as good luck wad hev't, it wassent varra lang till t' bell rang aboot summat or anudder; an' seeàh, what, t' butler meàd free to ax his lwordship.

"Well," sed he, "I'll consider about it, and let you know before night."

Some time on i' t' efteneùn he com oot o' t' drawin' room into t' kitchen, an' telt us we mud gang to t' merry neet if we like't; an', handin' a laal parcel to t' butler, says he, "You must give this, with my respects, to old Mary

Coats, and tell her it is something to pay your reckoning with. I hope," says he, "you'll enjoy yourselves; and you must all be sure to come home sober."

What! we aw meàd oor best boos, an' thank't him varra muckle for his kindness, an' sed we wad tak good care to come back ageàn aw reet an' square. He rayder smil't at that, an' than left us to mak oor oan arrangements amang oorsels as best we could.

Just aboot dusk we set off to t' merry neet, an' gat to Rostwhate famishly. T' butler handit t' laal parcel to auld Mary; an' when she oppen't it oot it was nowder mair nor less than an auld speàd yas guinea, lapt up in a bit o' brown paper. T' auld body was quite stunn'd when she saw't glitterin' befwore her, an' sed, "Lord, bless me weel! Dud ivver enny body see! Ye'll nivver can drink t' worth o' aw this! It 'ill pay your shots twice ower, barne!"

Bit we telt her she was to hev't an' neahbody else, as it was sent for her specially by lword William hissel'.

"Wy, wy, good lads!" sed she, "Ye mun just drink what ye will, an' as mickle on't as ye can, that's aw." Wid that she went an' browt ivvery yan on us a glass o' rum to be gaan on wi', an' gay stiffeners they war, ye may depend on't.

Efter we'd sitten a laal bit an' drucken oor glasses off, we went up into t' dancin' room; an' I's nut far wrang when I say, we meàd a bit iv a sensation theer. I was a bit iv a buck mysel' i' them days; bit t' butler an' t' footman war a parlish deal finer nor owt I was, wid their white powder't wigs, their reed plush waistcwoats, white neckleths, short-knee't buckskin brutches, an' white stockin's. An' when it gat whisper't aboot 'at we'd browt a heàl guinea wid us to spend, we war leuk't on an' thowt summat wonderful i' sec a pleàce as Borrowdale.

Loavins me! hoo we danc't, an' drank, an' sang, an' squeez't t' lasses, an' enjoy't oorsels to oor heart's content! An what wi' t' drink auld Mary an' udder fwok wad ha' geen us, we could aw ha' gitten drunk twice ower! We sartenly dud git middlin' fresh; bit as lword William hed telt us to keep swober, we thowt 'at if we could we mud. We agree't amang oorsels to stop an' see t' end o' t' hake, an' than he mappen wad ha' gone to bed when we gat heàm, an' wadden't see if we chanc't to be rayder blash't like.

Well, t' dance brak up at last; an' just as we war gaan to start, auld Mary shootit oot: "Stop, lads, ye mun ivvery yan hev anuddcr glass afwore ye gang!

Ye hevvent gitten hefe t' worth o' your guinea yet!" An' wi' that she set off an' browt us a girt yarken glass o' whiskey a piece, eneùf to knock a fellow doon if he'd gitten nowt afwore.

I was allus a varra bad sayer nay, when I hed t' loff iv owt to drink, an' I think my mates war aboot mickle sec like; seeàh, we swipe't them up, bade "Good neet" to auld Mary, an' off we set doon t' rwoad.

Dar bon! bit them last glasses dud top us off to some teùn. Befwore we gat to Grange t' rwoad was pinch't to be wide eneùf for us. We mannish't some way to keep up on end a kind o' decently as lang as t' rwoad was owts decent. Bit when it grew rougher, doon below Branley, we fand oorsels liggin' fairly maizelt, ivvery noo an' ageàn; an' t' best on't was, we cuddent yan laugh at anudder, for furst t' butler went doon, an' than t' footman follow't suit, an' than I was doon mysel'! Oft eneùf two on us war liggin' in t' gutter togidder; an', as bad luck wad hev't, when we war gaan through t' moss, varra nar at heàm, t' butler lost teà leg intul an auld peet-pot! An' when he poot it oot ageàn, ods wunters! it was as black as tudder was white!

We yan sed till anudder, ivvery noo an' than, "I whop my lword 'ill be geàn to bed when we git heàm!"

Bit we war fairly dumfoonder't, as we gat gaily nar t' hoose, to see a leet i' t' drawin'-room window.

We knew than his lwordship was up, an' wad be lissenin' for us.

Seeàh, we tried to sneak in, yan efter anudder, as deftly as we could, bit it was aw neàh use. We'd hardly gitten weel into t' kitchen till t' bell rang, an' t' footman was wantit. He was fworc't to gang; nowt else wad deù; an' for aw he stiddy't hissel' as weel as he could, he stacker't an' meàd some gye steps, 'at his lwordship saw, bit nivver seem't to nwotish.

"Well, footman," sed he, "you've got back, then? What such a merry-night have you had?"

"A capital merry-night, my lord," sed t' footman. "We've enjoyed ourselves very much indeed."

"Yes," says his lwordship, "I think you've been enjoying yourselves; and you've come home sober, I see?"

"Oh yes, my lord, qui-quite sober."

"Yes," says lword William ageàn. "I see you have! You can go now; and send the butler here."

Fain eneùf to git away, I's warrent ye, oot com t' footman, an' in went t' butler. He was warse iv owt nor t' footman; an' just as he was gaan in at t' drawin' room dooar, his shoe neb catch't t' edge o' t' carpet, an' doon he went heid furst on to t' midfleùr! He gedder't hissel' up as fast as he could; an' as seùn as he'd gitten a kind o' stiddy't, without ivver seemin' to nwotish t' accident at aw, my lword sed, "Well, butler, you've got back? What such a merry-night have you had?"

"Oh!" says he, "a famous merry-night, my lord. We've enjoyed ourselves amazingly."

"Yes," says his lwordship, "I have no doubt of it; and you've come home sober?"

"Oh! yes, quite sober, my lord." "But what is the matter with your legs, butler? Is it usual to go to merry-nights with a black stocking and a white one?" sed his lwordship.

"No, my lord," says t' butler, "it's not that. As we were crossing the meadows, a gust of wind blew my hat off, and in following it I slipped into a ditch."

"Oh!" sed he, "that is what it is, is it? Well, you may go now; and send the tailor here. I want to see the tailor." Cockswunters! when he com oot an' telt me that, I fairly trimmel't ageàn, fra heid to feùt, I was seeàh flate. I thowt to mysel' I wad keep hoald o' t' dooar, an' it wad rayder stiddy me; bit that waddent fit. My lword kent a trick worth two o' that.

"Come on into the room, tailor," sed he. "I want to see you."

I saw a laal bit iv a teàble stannin' on t' mid-fleùr, wi' some writin' things on 't, an' I thowt if I could nobbut mannish to reach that I wad git hoald on't; bit, hang't! it hed neàh mair stiddyness in't nor I hed mysel'. I neàh seùner pot my hand on't nor ower it went, an' t' papers an' t' things flew aw t' room ower.

He leùk't at me a minute, an' than sed, "Well, tailor, you've got back; and sober, too, I see?"

"Oh, yes!" says I, "quite sober, my lord."

"But what have you thrown my table over for?" says he.

"Beggin' your pardon, my lord," says I, "it was an accident."

"Yes," sed he, "there seems to have been a chapter of queer accidents tonight. It was an accident when the butler got into the bog! It was an accident when he caught the carpet with his foot! It was an accident when you upset my table! And, I suppose, it was an accident when you all got drunk together! Go away, tailor!" says he, "go away! I don't want you any longer. You have all three disgraced yourselves in a most shameful manner!"

I was fain eneùf to gang away, I can tell ye; bit when I gat back to t' deùr it was shut. Lord William hed aw his deùrs meàd 'at they wad shut o' the'rsels; an' I cuddent ha' gitten't oppen if I mud ha' hed aw t' Watterend for't. I greàpp't an' fummel't theer I dar say for ten minutes, an' t' auld kneave nivver as much as let wi't he saw me. At t' last he leùkt up, an' sed, says he, "What! there yet, tailor! What's the matter you've not gone?" "Well, my lord," says I, "beggin' your pardon, I can't finnd t' sneck." "No," says he, "mine are all doors, and no snecks." An' just wi' that I gev a bit stacker ageàn t' deùr, An' oppen it flew, an' I went lang streight into t' lobby!

"There! there! tailor," says he, "there's another accident, I suppose!"

I stop't to hear neàh mair; an' we aw three slunk off to bed as fast as we could, leùkin' gay hang't leùks, I dar say; expectin' 'at ivvery man-jack on us wad git t' seck next mwornin.' Bit, lucky eneùf for us aw, we nivver hard anudder word aboot it.

### The Fell King

Breet summer days war aw gone by,
   An' autumn leaves sa' broon,
Hed fawn fra t' trees, an' here an' theer,
   War whurlin' up an' doon;
An' t' trees steùd whidderin' neàk't an' bare,
   Shakken wi' coald an' wind,
While t' burds war wonderin' hoo it was
   Neàh shelter they could finnd.

Helvellyn, toorin' t' fells abeùn,
    Saw winter creepin' on,
An' grummelin' sed, "Hoo coald it's grown;
    My winter cap I'll don."
Clean wesh't an' bleach't, as white as drip,
    He poo't it ower his broo;
An' than to t' fells aw roond he sed,
    "Put on ye'r neetcaps noo."

Auld Skiddaw, lap't i' heddery duds,
    Laal nwotish seem't to tak:
An' seùn wi' lood an' thunnerin' voice,
    Ageàn Helvellyn spak:
"I say, put on that winter cap,
    Broon hill ower-groun wi' ling;
Rebellious upstart! put it on;
    Obey thy lawful king!"

Auld Skiddaw lang hed hanker't sair
    Itsel to be t' fell king;
An' Saddleback hed egg't it on,
    Thinkin' 't wad honour bring;
An' bits o' profit it mud be,
    Fwok see eneùf o' that;
When kings an' girt fwok thriven ur
    Their flunkies oft git fat.

Seàh, Skiddaw stack it' hedder up,
    An' pertly sed, "Is yon
Rough heap o' crags an' shilly beds,
    To tell us what to don?
I'll freely oan it's wise eneùf
    To hap itsel wi' snow;
If I was neak't an' bare like it
    I'd hide mysel an' aw.

"I's nut asham't my heid to show,
 Withoot a neetcap on;
An' claim mair reet to be t' fell king
 Nor a bare hill like yon.
Fra t' farthest neùks o' t' warld fwok come
 Fam't Skiddaw bit to see;
Whoar ten climm up Helvellyn breest,
 Ten twenties climm up me!"


With threetnin' storm, Helvellyn laps
 Dark cloods aroond it' heid;
An' noo a voice fra t' clood com oot,
 "A bonny king, indeed!
A hill thrown up by mowdiwarps,
 An' cuvver't ower wi' ling,
Withoot a crag, withoot a tarn,
 Wad mak a nice fell king!


"Laal brag it is for enny man
 To climm up Skiddaw side;
Auld wives an' barnes on jackasses,
 To t' tippy top may ride:
When theer, it's nut sa' much they see,
 Bit level country roond;
They're better pleas't when gangin' up,
 Nor when they're comin' doon.


"Bit let them climm Helvellyn side,
 If climm't they nobbut can;
They munnet be auld wives or barnes;
 It taks a strang hale man,
To stand on t' dizzy edge, an' leùk
 Doon t' screes, whoar Gough was lost;
An' he's neah snafflin' 'at can say,
 Ower Striden Edge I cross't.

"Than what a glorious scene it is
    'At 's spread befwore his eyes,
O' lakes an' tarns an' woody deàls,
    An' fells ower fells 'at rise.
A dozen lakes, an' twenty tarns,
    Ur spread befwore his een;
An' Skiddaw, like a low black hill,
    Far doon to t' north is seen!"


What mair palaver theer hed been,
    It's hard for yan to tell;
For grummelin' soonds, an' snarlin' words,
    Noo spread fra fell to fell;
An' some their caps o' white don't on,
    While udders went withoot;
An' some proclaim't Helvellyn king,
    While some wad Skiddaw shoot,


Bit noo roond Scawfell Man theer hung,
    As midneet black, a clood;
An' oot fra't brast a thunner clap,
    'At rwoar't beàth lang an' lood:
Than hail an' snow com whurlin' doon,
    An' hap't beàth crags an' ling;
While t' fells aw roond, as whisht as mice,
    Oan't Scawfell as their king!

### "For sham o' the', Mary!" ses I

This clattin' an' tattlin' 's aboot nowt;
    I nivver give ear to sec stuff;
When Mary comes whisperin' an' preachin',
    I oft send her off in a huff.
She comes wi' her mischief an' clish-clash,
    To git me to lissen she'll try;
Bit I'll give neàh ear to her tattle;
    "For sham o' the', Mary!" ses I.


She sed 'at lang Sally was stannin',
    Till midneet wi' laal Gwordie Bell;
'At Scott hed been drinkin' a fortneth,
    An' Jinkison hoondin' on t' fell.
'At Broon sed he'd send him a summons,
    As seùr as t' stars glittcr't i' t' sky;
Bit I give neàh ear to her tattle,
    "For sham o' the', Mary!" ses I.


She telt a lang teàl t' tudder mwornin',
    Aboot Sammy Thompson an' t' wife;
She sed they war scoaldin' an' fratchen,
    An' leadin' a dog an' cat life.
'At Sammy hed gitten on t' batter,
    An' gien t' wife a thumpin', forby;
Bit I lissen nin to her tattle;
    "For sham o' the', Mary!" ses I.

It maks yan as mad as a piper,
    To lissen to this, that, an' t' tudder;
An' that 'at will git in at teà lug,
    I send gayly sharp oot at tudder!
An' when Mary comes wi' her preachment,
    I's vext eneùf sometimes to cry;
Bit I lissen nin to her tattle;
    "For sham o' the', Mary!" ses I.


### *John Crozier's Tally Ho!*

The hunt is up, the hunt is up;
    Auld Tolly's on the drag;
Hark to him, beauties, git away,
    He's gone for Skiddaw crag.

Rise fra ye'r beds, ye sleepy-heads,
    If ye wad plesser know;
Ye'r hearts 't will cheer, if ye bit hear,
    John Crozier's Tally ho!

Hurrah! Hurrah! He's stown away;
    Through t' Forest wild he's geàn:
Sweet music tells 'mang t' heather bells,
    What track sly reynard's teàn.

Rise fra ye'r beds, &c.

To Carrick fell, to Carrick fell,
    His covert theer 'ill fail;
Unlucky day, he cannot stay,
    Blencathra's heights to scale.

Rise fra ye'r beds, &c.

Ower Louscale fell, by Skiddaw Man,
    An' doon by Millbeck ghyll;
To t' Dod he's gone, his reàce is run,
    Hark! Tally Ho! a kill!

Rise fra ye'r beds, ye sleepy-heads,
    If ye wad plesser know;
Ye'r hearts 't will cheer, if ye bit hear,
    John Crozier's Tally ho!

## Thowts by Thirlmere

A bonny summer day it was,
    As mortal ivver wish't for;
When Thirlmer's shore I steùd upon,
    An' prickly bass I fish't for.
Wi' mennums furst, an' next wi' worms,
    And than wi' grubs I baitit;
My cork, wi' anxious eye I watch't,
    An' for a nibble waitit.

Till tire't, my rod in t' grund I stack,
    An' sat me doon to watch it;
Thinkin' if owt sud mak it bend,
    Reet up I'd boonce an' catch it.
Bit lang afwore t' laal cork hed dive't,
    Or ivver fish hed bitten;
Bass bitin', cork, an' fishin' rod,
    By me war aw forgitten.

A skylark, heigh abeùn my heid,
    Was soarin' up an' singin';
While clwose behint was Reàven crag,
    Wood croon't an' ower-hingin'.
Aw roon' aboot war rocks an' woods,
    O' nater's awn creation;
Wi' human habitations nin,
    Nor patch o' cultivation.

A leùkin' glass on t' boddom laid,
    That shore wi' this connectit;
Whoar fells, an' woods, an' shilly beds,
    War upside doon reflectit.
A lang neck't heron, still as deith,
    To strike a fish was waitin';
An' up to t' knees, in t' watter, steùd
    Three crummies ruminatin'.

Musin', thinks I, i' this sweet pleàce,
    So whyet an' delightful;
Neah jarrin' soond 'ill ivver come,
    Or owt 'at's cross an' spiteful.
When just wi' that a kestrel hawk,
    Like flash o' leetnin' gleamin';
A dart at t' Jenny-lang-neck meàd,
    An' sent it off lood screamin'!

In' t' watter clear, a shoal o' bass,
    Clwose on by t' shore com sailin';
Amang them rush't a hungry pike,
    Aw t' swarm like deid leaves scalin'!
Next t' coos began to switch their tails,
    Wi' clegs an' midges hamper't;
An' when t' horse-bees com buzzin' roond,
    Like mad up t' woods they scamper't!

Thinks I, laal peace can be in t' warld,
 Fra teà end on 't to t' tudder;
As lang as brutes, an' fwok ur aw,
 Yan paiken at anudder.
Fra spite an' envy nin 'ill sceàpe,
 Whativver their condition;
Hooivver humble they may be
 Or free fra aw ambition.

Some whyet, honest, bashful soul,
 To git a leevin' strivin';
'Mang croods an' thrangs 'ill venter nin,
 Whoar yan ower udder's rivin'.
An' when it's meàst within his grasp,
 Wi' toilin', waitin', watchin';
Some human kestral doon 'll swoop,
 T' prize fra his clutches snatchin'!

A family blest wi' competence,
 Wi' prospect weel contentit;
Nor dream 'at owt 'ill come atween,
 To hinder or prevent it.
When deith, like hungry pike 'll come,
 As unconsarn't they wander;
T' main prop an' stay just whisk away,
 An' t' rest ower t' warld squander!

Theer few i' life bit summat hev,
 To bodder an' perplex them;
An' if fra bigger plagues exempt,
 They lesser hev to vex them.
Theer human midges, clegs, an' fleas,
 To kittle, plague, an' bite fwok;
Their teeth ur nobbet short; what than?
 They deù their best to spite fwok!

At last my fishin' rod I spy't,
  An' aw my dreams war endit;
Clean oot o' seet my cork was gone,
  Hofe double t' top was bendit.
While I'd been tryin' this an' that,
  To mak oot, an' consider,
An' eel my heùk an' bait hed teàn,
  An' swallow't aw togidder!


### The Cockney in Mosedale


YA mwornin' seùn on i' spring, I think it was t' fwore end o' March mebby – hooiver, it was befwore we'd gien ower fodderin' t' sheep—'at I set off wi' my hay-sheet on my back up into Mwosedale, whoar I'd carry't menny a hundred steàn o' hay befwore. It was a gay fine mwornin' for t' time o' year; an' Wily went trottin' away on aboot fifty yards befwore me, for he kent t' rwoad as weel as I dud mysel.

I clam away up wi' my lyàd, till I gat whyte away up t' hollow, varra nar at t' hee end o' Mwosedale beck, an' clean oot o' seet iv aw t' hooses an' ivvery thing else bit fells; an' than I began howin' an' shootin' at t' sheep to come to their hay; when aw at yance summat jump't up fra back iv a girt steàn aboot a hundred yards off, an' steùd stock still. Fra whoar I was, it leùk't likest a flay-crow iv owt 'at I could compare't teù, bit I thowt to mysel', what the hangment! neàh body wad be sa silly as put a flaycrow up theer! T' crows mud be some pleàce, an' they cuddent be varra weel whoar they wad deù less hurt ner they cud up i' Mwosedale.

Hooiver, I thowt I wad gang an' see what it was, An' sooa I went towarts it, when Wily spy't it an' aw, an' gev a girt bow-wow, as it allus does when it sees owt fresh.

What wi' t' dog barkin', an' me gaan towart it wi' my hay-sheet on my back, it set off across t' hollow, an' ran like a new clip't sheep; bit it duddent git varra far till it went soss intul a peetpot, up tull t' middle, an' stack theer as fast as a fiddlepin! I threw doon my hay-sheet than an' went to see what it was; an' when I gat to beside it, I saw 'at it was a fellow o' some mak, bit he was sartenly sec an object as I'd nivver seen befwore!

T' feàce on him, aw bit a laal bit aboot t' nwose an' eyes, was grown ower wi' reed hair, an' his chin was t' likest a moss beesom iv owt 'at I could compare't teù, an' he was trimmelin' theer in that peetpot, an' sayin', "Oh dear! dunnet kill me! dunnet kill me!"

"What does t'è think I mun kill the' for, thoo maislin, thoo," says I. "I think thoo wad be o' laal use if thoo was kilt, withoot I gat the' stufft an' carry't the' aboot in a show. What! whoar does t'è come fra? an' what is t'è deùn here?"

I could mak laal iv his talk; nobbut he sed summat aboot Lunnon an' Pellmell.

"Aye aye!" says I, "thoo hes pell mell't it tull a bonny pass. Thoo's run pell mell intul a peetpot!"

Wily stop't aboot twenty yards off, an' as he was like me an' hed nivver seen sec a thing befwore, he was girnen neah laal, an' t' fellow keep't sayin', "Oh keep 't off me! Will 't bite me?"

"No!" says I, "it 'ill bite nin. It 'ill nut mell o' the', thoo neudlin, thoo."

An' than he spy't some sheep cummin' blairen ower t' hill, an' was flaiter nor ivver, an' sed, "Oh dear me! What's yon 'at's cummin'?"

"Nowt bit t' sheep," says I. "They're wantin' their hay; they'll nut mell o' the', nowder." "An' what ur aw them girt hee pleàces roond aboot, an' whoar hev I gitten teù?" says he. "Oh dear me!"

"Wy, aw them hee pleàces ur fells," says I; "an' thoo's gitten intul a peetpot, that's whoar thoo's gitten, teù."

What, I thowt it was o' neah use axin' him enny mair questions, for he knew nowt; bit I mud be fworc't to tak him some way whoar he wad be leùk't efter. An' than I thowt ageàn 'at if I set him ageàt he wad mebby tummel doon some crag an' breck t' neck on him, an' I mud be bleàm't; an' seah, I wad just let him bide whoar he was till I gat my sheep fodder't. I knew he was fast eneùf in t' peetpot, an' seah I sed to mysel, "Thoo'll just stay whoar thoo is, my lad, till I git t' hay-sheet empty't, an' than we'll see what's t' best to be deùn."

I kind o' consider't it ower i' my awn mind while I was fodderin' t' sheep, an' it com into my heid 'at I could easily carry him doon on my back, if I hed him ty't decently up i' t' hay-sheet; an' that wad be t' seàfest way for me to deù. Seah, as seùn as I'd deùn, I went away back an' spread t' hay-sheet on t' grund, an' than I teùk him by t' cwoat neck an' poot him oot. I held him a laal bit to let t' durty watter a kind o' sipe off; an' than I clapp't him into t' hay-sheet, an' hed him ty't up in a jiffy. T' thing scraffle't an' fidg't a bit, an' chatter't neàh laal; bit I care't nowt aboot that. I let him hev his heid oot, or else I thowt he wad mappen smudder. When I'd gitten him fettle't up, I swang him onto my back an' set off doon't fell.

Wily wad ha' divartit owt to see hoo he furst ran on a bit afwore, an' than com back to beside me, an' jump't aboot an' bark't ivvery step. I dar say he thowt we hed gitten a fine prize, an' he cuddent ha' been pleaster if we'd catch't a fox, or a foomart, or owt o' that mak. I thowt it wad be t' best way to tak him doon to Trootbeck Station, as it was just possible they mud know summat aboot him theer; an' if they duddent I could leave him till somebody com to lait him or summat, as he wad varra likely belong to somebody someway or anudder.

What, I fagg't away doon till I gat aboot hofe a mile fra t' station, when I met auld Joe Mitchison, an' as seùn as Joe saw me he meàd a full stop, an' sed,

"What, the divvel, hes t'è gitten i' t' hay-sheet!"

"Well," says I, "I've gitten some mak iv a fellow I fand up i' Mwosedale. He says 'at he comes fra a pleàce caw't Pellmell; bit hoo he's gitten up yonder's a capper. I dunnet know wheddcr I could ha' catch't him or nut if he heddent run intul a peetpot, an' mire't sel' on him up!"

"Fellow!" says auld Joe, "fellow! thoo dissent caw that hairy feàc't creeter a fellow, does t'è? What it's some mak iv a monkey, I'll uphod 't."

"Nay," says I, "what he hes cleàs on, an' gay fine uns teù, they hev been; bit they're a gay pickel noo wi' peetmoss watter."

"Aye aye!" says auld Joe, "it's a monkey, I's warrent it; they deù don them up I' that way. It's gitten oot o' some caravan likely."

"Nay, bit than, it talk't to me," says I; "an' I nivver hard tell at monkeys could talk."

"Neàh, nor I nowder," ses Joe. "What dud it say?"

"Wy, nowt varra sensible," says I; "he shootit 'dunnet kill me! dunnet kill me!' an' when I axt him whoar he com fra, he sed, 'Pellmell' an' 'Lunnon.' He was varra nar freetent to deith o' t' dog, an' t' sheep; an' for t' fells he duddent know what they war."

"Wy, it caps me," says Joe, "What is t'è gaan to deù wi' t' creeter when thoo's gitten't?"

"I dunnet know," says I, "I think I'd best tak him doon to t' station; they may know summat aboot him theer; an', what, I cuddent leave him up yonder stickin' in a peetpot."

"Wy, it caps me," says Joe ageàn. "I'll ga wi' the'."

An' seàh, what, we set off to t' Station, an' as seùn as we gat him intul t' waitin' room, an' t' dooar shut, I lows't my hay-sheet an' let him oot.

What, he duddent seem sa' wild at aw when he'd gitten to 'mang fwok: an' seàh, I left him theer, an' thowt 'at I'd gitten varra nicely shot on him.

I enquire't at t' station a day or two efter, an' they telt me he was a chap 'at hed nivver been ootside o' Lunnon befwore, 'at he'd cum't doon iv a neet train, an' whedder he'd been asleep or what he cuddent tell. Bit, neàh doot, he'd gitten oot when t' train stop't at Trootbeck, an' wander't i' t' dark aw t' way to whoar I fand him, an' than laid doon i' back o' that steàn.

It was neàh wonder 'at he was lost when day-leet com, an' he could see nowt bit fells aw roond, an' me gaan wi' my hay-sheet on my back; an' God knows what wad ha' come't on him if I heddent catch't him in that peetpot.

## *Laal Isaac*

*Isaac Todhunter, who during a great number of years hunted the Blencathra hounds with Mr. John Crozier, of the Riddings, was well known in most of the vales in the Lake District as "Laal Isaac." When Crozier retired, he entrusted Isaac with being Master of the Hounds. Ed.*

When cworn wi' thack an' reàpp was hap't,
 An' stubbles aw war bare,
Laal Isaac, in his cwoat o' green,
 For twenty year an' mair,
As constant as October broon,
 An' winter com their roonds,
Was at his post, wi' whip an' horn,
 An' tarriers an' hoonds.

"Howp! come away! my bonny pets!"
 'Cross fell an' deàl wad ring;
An' a clear blast fra Isaac's horn,
 Wad hoonds an' hunters bring.
For miles aroond, 'cross moor an' field,
 They'd come at brek o' day;
To that familiar weel ken't voice,
 That cheery, "Come away!"

Theer sceàrce a crag i' Skiddaw range,
 Fra t' Dod to Carrick fell,
Bit whoar some huntin' feat hed been,
 'At Isaac ower could tell.
Through Borrowdale an' Wyburn heids,
 He ivvery burrent kent;

An' ivvery smoot in t' deàls aroond,
 Which ivver way he went.

Bit noo he's gone, an' nivver mair,
 His cheerful voice we'll hear;
Reet sair Laal Isaac 'ill be miss't,
 By hunters far an' near,
His drag an' chase ur finish't, noo,
 His Tally ho's! ur past;
His huntin's endit; an' poor Ike
 Is run to earth at last!

## *Hoo Gwordie gat a Dinner*

Gwordie was a funny fellow;
 His delight was pints o' yal;
Always spendin' aw his aidlins,
 Oft eneùf withoot a meàl;
Schemes an' tricks he'd withoot number,
 Aw contriv't a pint to git:
Some fwok cawt them barefeàc't swinlin';
 Some fwok laugh't an' cawt them wit.

Yance he'd been a week on t' batter;
 Drinkin', shoolin', aidlin' nowt;
Ivvery trick he hed he'd try't it;
 Monday mwornin' black leùks browt.
Nowder brass nor credit hed he,
 Nor a bite iv owt to eat;
Wark he hed eneùf to gang teù;
 Wage for t' day he'd git at t' neet.

Fastin', off he went to drainin',
 Nar auld Betty Vickers' farm;
Sunshine meàd him throw his cwoat off,
 When wi' hackin' he grew warm.

"Brekfastless I com i' t' mwornin';
    Dinnerless I'll hev to gang:"
Thowts like thur went back an' forrat,
    Gwordie' schemin' brains amang.


Reùten, reùten, Betty's grunters,
    Snuffin' com whoar t' cwoat was left:
"Wons! says Gwordie, "I'll hev dinner;
Lang I've study't,—noo I hev't!"
    Oot o' t' drain, wi' speàd upliftit,
Squeelin' heàm t' two pigs he dreàv;
    Weel he knew 'at Betty Vickers,
Oot wad come her pigs to seàv.


Gwordie sweerin', t' grunters squeelin'
    Kick't up some gay bonnie shines;
Betty shootit, "Lord! ha' marcy!
    Ur ye gantè kill them swines!"
"Kill them! d--m them! aye, I'll kill them!
    Ivvery bite o' dinner geàn!"
"Dinner ye sall hev," says Betty;
    "Pray ye let t' poor swines aleàn!


"Come away, an' git some dinner;
    Come away, an' let them leeve!"
Gwordie leùk't as mad as need be;
    Bit was laughin' in his sleeve.
Nut sa menny could ha' scheme't it;
    Dinner sec a way to git:
Some fwok caw't it mean an' kneàvish;
    Some fwok laugh't an' caw't it wit.

## *Cheap Advice*

It's passin' strange, an' yet its trew,
'At in this warld theer varra few,
Fra t' heighest up to t' lowest doon,
Fra t' wisest man to t' daftest cloon,
  Bit thinks he's qualify't,
Wi' solemn feàce an' leùks sa wise,
To snub, an' lecture, an' advise,
  An' udder fwok to guide.


It 'meàst wad mak a parson sweer,
A ning-nang snafflen thing to hear,
'At 's been a waistrel aw his life,
Beàth starvin' t' barnes and threshin' t' wife,
  Hev impidence to tell,
Some decent youngster t' best way hoo,
To keep his feùt streight in his shoe,
  As if he'd deùn't hissel.


It maks yan mad some snob to hear,
Wi' his five thoosand pund a year,
'At gallops, gammels, drinks an' bets,
Till he's ower heid an' ears i' debt,
  Advise wi' coonsel sage,
Some boor wi' hofe a croon a day,
To keep aw streight an' pay his way,
  An' seàve up for auld age.

It maks yan laugh to see some deàm,
'At likes "My lady" to her neàm,
'At cuddent mak a meàl o' meat,
Fit for a Christian to eat,
    If he was starvin' quite,
Pretend to larn some thrifty wife,
'At 's been contrivin' aw her life,
    Hoo best to keùk a bite.

Some lady fine 'ill scoald an' preach,
Poor fwok economy to teach,
An' tell them hoo to leeve an' dress,
To seàve far mair an' spend far less;
    An' than streight off she'll gang,
To buy a dress an' think it cheap,
At what a family wad keep,
    Through t' winter coald an' lang.

If sec advice was good for owt,
Fwok waddent git it aw for nowt,
For that 'at useful is or nice,
Ye'll hev to pay a market price,
    O' that be seùr eneùf;
What ivvery body gives away,
Unass't an' nut expectin' pay,
    Is nobbut silly stuff!

## *Nancy's Cure*

Wild Lantie was a canker't carl,
    A canker't carl was he;
Mad Nancy was a rattlin' jade,
    A rattlin' jade was she.

Wild Lantie was a jealous tike,
    A jealous tike was he;
Bit nut a peg dud Nancy care,
    Neah! nut a peg care't she!

When ugly things wild Lantie sed,
    An' ugly things sed he;
Far uglier things could Nancy say,
    An' uglier things sed she.

When Lantie sulky was a' soor,
    An' soor eneùf was he;
Far soorer still could Nancy leùk,
    An' soorer still leùk't she.

To t' public hoose wild Lantie went,
    To t' public hoose went he;
To lait him heàm mad Nancy went,
    To lait him heàm went she.

"What's browt thee here?" wild Lantie sed,
    "What's browt thee here?" sed he.
"My awn good shanks," mad Nancy sed,
    "My awn good shanks," sed she.

"Than back ageàn thoo'd better gang,
    Reet back ageàn," sed he.
"I's gaan reet back," mad Nancy sed,
    "Bit thoo'll gang furst," sed she.

Wild Lantie knew 'at gang he mud,
    Seàh, reet away went he;
Mad Nancy follow'd at his heels,
    Hard at his heels went she.

To bed in t' pet wild Lantie went,
    To bed in t' pet went he;
Ses Nancy, "stop till thoo's asleep,
    Till thoo's asleep," sed she.

An' when wild Lantie snworen was,
    An' snworen seùn was he;
Mad Nancy sew't him up in t' sheets,
    Him up in t' sheets sew't she!

"Oh, Lord! ha' marcy!" Lantie rwoar't,
    "Oh, Lord! Oh, Lord!" rwoar't he.
Mad Nancy bray't wi' t' beesom stick,
    Wi' t' beesom stick bray't she!

"Thoo'll gang to t' public hoose ageàn,
    Thoo'll gang ageàn!" sed she.
Wild Lantie greàn't, "Nay, nivver mair!"
    An' nivver mair went he!

## A Crack aboot Auld Times

Come Joe an' hev a friendly crack,
    Draw up thy chair to t' chimley neùk;
Here t' 'bacco piggin, full thy pipe,
    An' while we crack we'll hev a smeùk.
Let's talk o' times i' auld lang syne,
    When country fwok could card an' spin;
To weer a cwoàt o' hodden grey,
    I' them auld times was thowt neah sin.

I've hard me ganny, (rust her soul!)
    Tell hoo fwok don'd i' her young days;
An' hoo they leev't, an' what they eat,
    An' aw their queer auld fashin't ways,
To hear her tell aboot auld times,
    For 'oors I patiently wad sit;
An' pleas't to hev a lissener, she
    For 'oors an' 'oors wad talk an' knit.

She telt hoo t' men, their woo wad card,
    I' winter time when t' neets war lang;
Hoo ivvery neet a pund they dud,
    Hoo while they wrowt they crack't or sang.
Hoo t' lasses, wi' their spinnin' wheels,
    Aw t' cardin's into garn wad mak;
An' hoo t' auld fwok their hanks o' garn,
    To t' market ivvery week wad tak.

Hoo some their garn at heàm wad weave,
    An' than their webs wad tak to sell;
An' when some plague was bad i' t' toons,
    Hoo fwok wad meet on Armboth fell,
To buy an' sell, nar a girt steàn;
    Web-steàn it's caw't still to this day;
Auld shipperds sometimes point it oot,
    To toorists when they gang that way.

An' next she'd talk o' what they eat,
    Laal tea or coffee than they hed;
Bit beef, an' legs o' mutton dry't,
    Wi' butter, cheese, an' havver bread.
Good heàm brew't yal, three times a day;
    "Nowt in 't bit hop an' mawt," ses she;
"'T was wholsomer an' better far
    Nor coffee an' thin swashy tea!"

For plates, wood trenchers aw fwok hed,
    Hom speùns to sup their poddish wi',
Oot o' wood piggins 'at war meàd,
    Just like t' cofe geggins 'at we see.
They'd pewder plates an' dishes, teù;
    Bit they war less for use ner show;
As breet as silver they war meàd,
    An' set on t' drusser in a row.

She sed, for eldin, peats they hed,
    Drowt meàstly doon fra t' hee fell tops;
An' when they sat by t' grateless fire,
    They hed to watch for t' hallen drops.
A rannel boak t'wide chimley cross't;
    An' fra 't a chain some three yards lang;
'At held a creùk at t' smiddy meàd,
    Whoar t' kettle belly't keàlpot hang.

An' next she'd tell aboot their wark;
    Neah cars or carridges hed they;
Ses she, "We carry't t' muck i' hots;
    We sleddit t' peats an' truss't oor hay.
Pack horses dud for carriers than;
    Lang strings, fra toon to toon, wad gang,
A bell to t' fwormost nag was ty'd,
    To keep aw t' rest fra wanderin' wrang.

"T' men fwok hed cwoats o' hodden grey,
    An' buck-skin brutches ty'd at t' knees;
Wi' silver buckles to their shoon;
    It's nut oft noo sec legs yan sees,
As t' men hed than; an' oft their hair
    Was pooder't white as enny snow:
Red waistcwoats, they'd for Sunday weer,
    An' some hed ruffle't sarks an' aw.

"Aw t' women fwok hed bedgoons lang,
    Wi' tails 'at to their knees hung doon;
An' linsey woolsey petticwoats,
    An' clean greas't clogs i' steed o' shoon.
Blue approns they'd for war-day weer,
    Turn'd sides when durty wark was deùn;
A check't un clean, an' bedgoon blue,
    To don o' t' Sunday efternèun."

Ses she, "At Cursmas time we went,
    Fra hoose to hoose sweet pies to meàk;
We use' to yan anudder help,
    Oor Cursmas pies an' things to beàk.
An' theer war feasts at ivvery hoose,
    Beàth rich an' poor war ax't to gang;
Whoar some at three card lant wad laak,
    An' some at whisk, while udders sang."

An' than she'd sigh an' say, "Oh dear!
    What chops an' changes yan hes seen;
This warld's nut like t' seàm warld at aw,
    It was when I was i' me teens!"
Bit what thoo's gaan; aye, varra weel;
    We've hed a good auld fashin't crack;
Thoo'll mappen caw an' tell us t' news,
    An' smèuk thy pipe as thoo comes back.

## *Tom an' Jerry*

Says Ben to t' wife, "Auld wife," says he,
    "We'll hev a Tom an' Jerry;
An' thoo can wait, an' I can drum,
    By jing! but we'll be merry!
We'll hev a cask o' yal for t' start,
    An' than when we want mair,
We'll pay wi' t' brass we've selt it for,
    An' summat hev to spare."

What, t' cask was browt, an' it was broach't;
    Says Ben, "Auld wife, I say,
We'll nivver trust a single pint,
    Seah, them 'at drink mun pay.
I've just three penny pieces here;
    I think a pint I'll hev."
Seah, than a pint t' auld woman browt,
    An' he her t' threepence gev.

Says she, "If fwok sud ax if 't 's good,
    I'll nut know what to say;
I'd better hev a pint an' aw."
    Says Ben, "Bit thoo mun pay."
Seah, she'd a pint, an' he'd a pint,
    An' ivvery time they paid;
An' back an' forret t' threepence went,
    Till beàth on t' flags war laid!

An' when they'd sleep't it off, they up
    An' at it still they went;
Till t' cask was empty, seùr eneùf,
    An' nobbut threepence spent.
Says Ben, "Auld wife, we've meàd a mess,
    An' what 'ill t' brewer think?"
Says she, "He'll git his cask ageàn,
    Just wantin' t' sup o' drink!"

### Sneck Posset

*The old-fashioned mode of courting in the northern counties, which is still common in many places, is for the young man to go to the house where his sweetheart lives, late at night, after all the other members of the family have retired to rest, when gently tapping at the window, the waiting damsel as soon as she has ascertained, by sundry whisperings, that he is the expected swain, admits him. If for any cause she refuses to let him into the house, he is said to have got a "Sneck Posset". Ed.*

Hoo lang it's sen, I willent say;
    For if I that sud tell,
Some busy fwok mud reckon up,
    Hoo auld I is mysel'.

Neah matter 't is hoo lang it's sen,
    I than was young an' daft;
Nin flate o' wark, an' nivver tire't;
    At fash an' care I laugh't.

A strappin', good like chap I was,
    For aw I say't mysel;
An' when to t' merry neets I went,
    I still could gang wi' t' belle.

Bit yance theer was, I'll tell ye where,
    A sneck posset I gat;
Reet sarret, teù, ye'll think I was;
    Ye'll likely aw say that.

Ya Thursday neet, 'twas winter time,
    An' t' grund was hap't wi' snow;
T' wind strang fra t' north, ower Hutton-moor,
    Wi' whisslin' blast dud blow.

'T was t' merry neet at Moorend Hoose;
    For many a lang, lang year,
Auld Isaac' fwok hed keep't it up,
    An' lots o' fwok war theer.

They com fra Threlket, an' fra t' Sceàls,
    An' doon fra t' Paster side;
Fra Sooter fell an' Grizel Mill,
    They com fra far an' wide.

Some drank, some danc't, some laik't at cards,
    An' aw went merrily on;
Yan hardly knew 'at yan was theer,
    Till two or three 'oors war gone.

I danc't oft wi' a canny lass,
    I needent tell her neàm;
We grew quite thick, an' beath agreèt
    At I sud set her heàm.

I thowt I'd see her seàf to t' dooar,
    An' than reet back I'd run;
To t' merry neet at Moorend Hoose,
    An' see some mair o' t' fun.

A single kiss at t' dooar I steàl;
    An' than says I, "My pet,
I'll come ageàn anudder neet,
    My feet ur possen wet."

Thinks I, as back ageàn I ran,
    That wassent badly deùn;
T' wet feet war just a bit excuse,
    For leavin' her sa seùn.

A lot o' jolly dogs war left,
    Gay rivin' yarks we hed;
An' t' cock hed crown it' second roond,
    Befwore I went to bed.

A fortneth efter, off I set,
    My bonny lass to see;
An' nivver yance a doot I hed,
    Bit welcome I wad be.

I gently tap't at t' window pane,
    An' when she saw me theer;
Says she, "Thoo meàd me start, thoo dud!
    What is t'è wantin' here?"

Says I, "I telt the' I wad come;
    An' noo thoo sees I hev."
"Oh! aye, I see who 'tis!" says she;
    An' a laal snirt she gev.

"Thoo's manish't varra weel," says she,
    "To come aw t' way to neet:
I's flate thoo'll git thy deith o' cauld;
    Gang heàm an' dry thy feet!"

## *At the grave of Robert Burns*

Brave Robin! merry, tender, rantin',
Independent, reverent, wanton,
    Peace to thy dust!
Queer checquer't life was thine when leevin'
Plewin', rhymin', singin', grievin',
    Here thoo's at rust.

While hoddin' t' plew, as noo I see thee,
Kind Providence wad dootless gi' thee
    Thy happiest days.
As weel I know, when t' plew stilts hoddin'
Thoo sang, while up an' doon t' furs ploddin',
    Thy sweetest lays.

Wi' bonnie daisies roond thee springin';
Wi' t' skylark up abeùn thee singin',
    At peace thysel:
What meàd thee leave a life sa' bleàmless?
Was it for fear o' deein' neàmless?
    Who can tell?

'Twas worth a sacrifice, hooivver,
To gain a neàm to last forivver,
 Still breet to shine.
But hed t'è still stuck to thy tillin',
That neàm, I'll bet a silver shillin',
 Wad still been thine.

Thy native wit an' inbworn genius,
Hed left a neàm, to bide as green as
 A field i' May.
Fwok still wad been thy sweet sangs singin',
When this pleàce was i' ruins hingin',
 Or pass'd away.

But thirty-eight! when life's delightful,
T' grim tyrant com relentless, spiteful,
 An' snap't life's threed.
Just when t' lamp sud been t' breetest burnin',
A knell was heard left Scotland mournin',
 Her poet deid!

Hed thoo been spar'd to life's October,
When thowts an' passions aw growe sober;
 An' we can see
"Oorsels as udder fwok hev seen us,"
What treasures mair thoo mud hev geen us:
 'Twas nut to be!

## *Auld Gwordie Thompson*

*The author begs to state that in writing this and the piece which immediately follows it, his intention was not by any means to attempt to throw ridicule upon religion, but merely to shew off, from a ludicrous point of view, the absurd notions which some people have regarding sacred things. Ed.*

THEER leev't up on t' edge o' Huttonmoor, for menny a year, an auld chap they caw't Gwordie Thompson, 'at was quite a character in his day. He allus weàr short-knee't, ribb't brutches, an' a Skiddaw grey cwoat, varra nar as rough as an unclip't sheep; an' auld Gwordie his-sel was ameàst as rough as his cwoat.

T' auld chap use' to say 'at t' two things he liket best, iv owt i' this warld, war a pint o' yal an' a pipe o' 'bacca; an' t' two things at he liket warst war priests an' doctors. He oft brag't an' telt fwok he'd nivver nobbut been twice in t' inside iv a church sen he was bworn: 'at t' furst time his mudder carry't him theer to git kursen't, an' t' tudder time t' wife trailt him off to git weddit.

Till a lock o' weeks afwore Gwordie dee't he was nivver off hilth a day in his life; an' as he'd nivver wantit a doctor his-sel, he varra likely thowt they war o' neah use. He reckon'd he duddent wonder at fwok bein' badly when they'd doctors cummin' an' givin' them eneùf o' nasty physic to puzzen a swine, let aleàn a Christian. When he gat to t' public hoose, an' intul his reàvellin' way, he oft sed, if aw t' doctors an' priests war oot o' t' country, it wad be a gay deal better for t' fwok 'at war left. Bit ye'll see theer come a time: he wantit beàth.

When he'd gitten up towards sebbenty year auld, nater began to tak t' tetch wid him, an' wadden't be meàd ghem on enny langer. If he gat drunk he was badly t' next day; an' if he chanc't to git wet, an' dudden't change his cleàs, he wassen't reet for a week or mair. At last he gat a warse coàld nor common, 'at fairly laid him up; an' efter a lang while, an' a gay deal o' persuadin', he consentit to hev a doctor. When t' doctor com an' examin't him ower, an' enquir't hoo he was hodden, he seùn saw 'at t' auld man was aboot deùn, an' hedden't varra lang to leeve; an' as he thowt it was o'laal use fashin' him wi' takken physic, he order't them to give him a laal sup o' rum het, twice a day, to nourish and cheer him up a bit, as lang as he could tak it.

When they telt t' auld chap what he was to hev, he was t' girtest at ivver owt was, an' sed,

"Ods wons! if I'd thowt he wad ha' order't me sec physic as that, ye mud ha' fetch't him lang sen."

As it was than on i' February, he reckon't if he'd anudder month ower, t' wedder wad git warmer, an' wi' his two glasses o' rum a day, he wad seùn be as reet as a fiddle ageàn.

As t' spring went on, hooivver, auld Gwordie, isteed o' growin' stranger, gat waker an' waker, till afwore March was oot he cudden't manage to tak hofe a glass i' t' day; an' than he was fworc't to give 't up aw togidder. He fairly lost heart than; an' if enny iv his neighbours try't to cheer him up a bit, wi' tellin' him 'at he wad growe better efter a while, he sed,

"Nay, nay, theer neah way bit yan for me. Ye may depend on 't if auld Gwordie 's past takken a glass o' rum, he's gaily far on in his journey, an' hessent lang to be here."

When it gat on to t' middle o' April, he'd gitten sa' wake 'at he cudden't git oot o' bed, an' he sed to t' dowter ya day,

"I finnd 'at my time willen't be lang noo. I've meàd my will an' settl't aw my consarns, bit theer' ya thing at rayder bodders me at times: I think I sud hev somebody to pray wi' me. What does thoo think? Does t'è think thoo can git enny body to come?"

"Aye!" ses she, "I'll send for t' priest. He'll come, I'll warrant him, if he be ax't."

"Wy, send for him than," ses Gwordie, "as seùn as thoo can. Theer 'ill mebby nut be ower mickle time to scowp on."

When t' priest hed cum't an' gone ageàn, t' dowter went in to see t' auld man, an' sed tull him:

"What, ye'll be satisfy't noo, likely, when he's been here, an' pray't wi' ye?"

"Satisfy't!" ses Gwordie, "aye, I's satisfy't eneùf wi' him. I'll nut want him ageàn, thoo may depend on 't."

"What hes he sed to ye, fadder, to vex ye seah?" ses Betty.

"Sed!" ses Gwordie, "he sed plenty, an' a gay deal mair nor he durst ha'
sed if I'd been as I was yance. He telt me he'd kent me for menny a year to be
an auld harden't sinner 'at nivver went to t' kurk, bit oft to t' public hoose;
'at I gat drunk an' sweàr an' dud a deal mair things I wad hev to repent on
befwore I deet, or else I wad gang tull a pleàce 'at needn't be mention't. 1
dunnet think 'at that's enny mak o' prayin'! Does t'è think thoo can send for
that methody chap, 'at leeves up t' broo yonder? They say 'at he pretends a
bit o' prayin'."

"I dar say I can," ses Betty; an' she went an' sent t' sarvent lad off to tell
him to come.

When he'd cum't an' gone ageàn, Betty went in to t' room, an' sed,

"Noo, fadder, hoo ur ye noo? What, ye'll be better satisfy't this time, I
whop. Hes he deùn enny better for ye?"

"Nay!" ses t' auld fellow, "he was varra laal better nor t' priest. He mebby
wassen't just as plain wi' me; bit he jibe't an' went on wi' a wry feàce, an' was
varra lang windit. I knew weel eneùf what he was hintin' at. I'll nut hev him
cummin' ageàn, I'll gi' the' my word o' that."

"Wy!" ses Betty, "I dunnet know what's to be deùn, I's seùr."

A few days efter that, when auld Gwordie was gitten to be sa' wake he
could hardly raise his-sel up i' bed, two iv his auld neighbours, Tom Benson
an' Jossy Jopson, com in to see him. They sat an' crack't on a while, an' when
they gat up to gang, Jossy went oot furst, while Tom stay't behint to say a
few mair words to t' auld chap, as they'd lang been friends.

"What," sed he, "ye'll varra likely hev settle't ye'r affairs, an' meàd aw reet?"

"Aye, aye!" ses Gwordie, "I gitten aw that deùn, an' theer nobbut ya thing
'at bodders me enny."

"What's that?" sed Tom.

"Wy," sed auld Gwordie, "thowt theer sud ha' been some prayin' afwore I
deet. I've hed beàth t' priest an' that methody fellow, an' nowder o' them dud
me a bit o' good. What does t'è think? Can thoo pray enny, Tom?"

"Nay, be divvel't!" ses Tom, "I can pray nin. Bit as ye say, I think theer
sud be some prayin', teù. We'll see what Jossy ses, if he can deù owt that way.
Here, Jossy, come back," shootit Tom.

"Can t'è pray enny? If thoo can, thoo mun pray wi' auld Gwordie."

"Wy!" ses Jossy, "I's neah girt fist at it, bit as it's a keàse o' necessity I'll deù t' best I can."

An' wi' that he com to t' bedside an' kneel't doon an' began;

"Lord hev marcy on auld Gwordie Thompson, an' help him to git better. Let him leeve menny an' menny a year yet. Send him good crops on t' moor, an' fine wedder to git them. Keep his wheys fra takkin' t' redwatter, an'---an'----"

When he'd gitten that far, auld Gwordie rais't his-sel up i' bed, an' shootit wi' aw t' bit strength he hed left,

"Howay wi' the', Jossy! Howay wi' the'! Hod on! Thoo fews t' best iv oot I've hard yet. Ods wons! theer some sense I' sec prayin' as that. Carry on, min!—carry on!"

Bit t' exertion o' raisin' his sel up, an' shootin', an' ya thing or anudder, snap't t' laal bit slender threed 'at was left; an' t' poor auld man sank back iv his bed, an' nivver spak mair: an' that was t' end o' auld Gwordie Thompson.

### *Lantie's Prayer*

Tom, Gwordie, an' Lantie war quarrymen three,
As lish, listy deelsmen as ivver ye'd see;
As streight, ivvery yan, as a poplar tree,
An' t' least o' them five feet elebben inch hee:
  Aw healthy an' strang,
  As June days ur lang;
  Stoot, stalwart, an' reet,
  Wi' hands fit for feet,
Their feet lang an' broad, an' weel splay't.
  Rare guardsmen for t' queen,
  Sec chaps wad hev been:
  If nobbut they'd yance
  Gien t' soldiers a chance,
They waddent in t' deàl lang hev been.

It chanc't on yà fine summer day,

'At Tom an' Gwordie teùk their way,

To t' toon, where they still gat their pay,—

What theer they wantit, I can't say:

    They'd mainly stop,

    An' tak a drop;

    An' sometimes they

    Wad sup away,

Till they war gaily fu':

    At times they'd rear,

    An' rip an' sweer;

    An' say they'd feight

    Owt o' their weight;

They kick't up menny a row.


Hooivver, it happen't on that summer day,

A pint just apiece they'd, an' than turn't away;

It's dootful, bit t' reason was mappen 'at they

War hard up, an' riddy for t' fortneth pay;

Whedder that was, or wassent, t' keàse,

They trailen went up t' market pleàce;

An' when they saw a weel kent feàce,

    They gev a frindly nod.

    Bit when ameàst to t' cross they gat,

    They saw a crood aw geàpen at

    A man, 'at steùd withoot his hat,

    An' sed he com fra God;

    To tell what sin,

    They aw war in;

    An' he was sent

    To bid repent,

Aw t' drucken, roysterin', sweerin' crew;

    An' than he sed,

    'At t' lives they led,

They needent try,

For to deny,

For aw their wicked ways he knew.


He preach't an' palaver't a full 'oor or mair,

A full 'oor that crood steùd to lissen an' stare;

Some whisper't an' sed it was hardly fair,

To shew aw their sneakin' tricks, neàked an' bare;

While udders a penneth o' snaps duddent care,

Who knew what they dud, or hoo, when, or where?

   Tom an' Gwordie steùd like t' rest,

   An' thowt 'twas varra queer,

   Hoo t' preacher chap hed known sa' weel,

   'At they wad beàth be theer.

   For paddy hints anew he'd gien,

   An' ivvery time they leùk't, they'd seen

   Him glowerin' at them wi' beàth een,

   Ower t' heids iv aw 'at steùd atween.

    Withoot a doot,

    He'd fund it oot,

    By heùk or creùk,

    Or auld black beùk,—

'At when they com to t' pays,

    Hoo oft it was,

    They spent their brass,

    An' drank an' fowt,

    An' aidle't nowt,

   For mebbe twea 't three days.


Ses Gwordie to Tom, as they went heàm that neet,

"This fuddlin' an' royin' whenivver we meet,

An' spendin' oor quarry-pay, cannot be reet;

For t' futer I mean to hev nowt to deù wi' 't;"

An' wi' Gwordie's opinion Tom quite agreet.

"An' Gwordie," ses Tom, "fra this varra day,

I mean to gang on in a different way;

I's gantè begin to keep swober an' pray,

I dunnet care what enny body may say;"

An' Gwordie agreet, for he duddent say nay.

Tom, Gwordie, an' Lantie that summer neet sat,

Their pipes to smeùk, efter their suppers they gat;

When up Lantie spak, an' sharply sed, "What

Maks ye sa' dull an' sa' sulky an' flat!"

Ses Tom, "We're convertit, theer neah doot o' that!"

Ses Lantie, "Is I gantè eat my auld hat!"

An' than wi' lang an' solemn feàces,

They telt him aw their desperate keàses;

    An' hoo their sins,

    As sharp as whins,

    Or auld dry thorns,

    Or uncut corns,

War stangin' through their flesh an' beàns.

    Bit Lantie laugh't,

    An' jaw't an' chafft,

    An' sed, he thowt,

    'Twad end in nowt,

Bit empty talk an' hollow greàns.


Lang feàces Tom an' Gwordie hed

That neet, when off they went to bed;

An' whisperin', teàn to t' tudder sed,

They waddent off ageàn be led;

They'd just gang on an' persevere,

An' tak their pay, an' heàmwards steer,

Withoot a drop their hearts to cheer,

Neah matter who mud laugh an' jeer.

    They thowt without

    A grain o' doot,

'At Lantie was

A stupid ass;

An' neet an' day,

They beàth wad pray,

'At sometime he

His fawts mud see,

An', like theirsels, convertit be.


Some twelve months efter, on a day,

(Time's fleein' still, an' willent stay,)

Oor heroes gat a parlish flay;

Hoo dud it happen! This was t' way:

They wrowt in a level 'at ran under t' fell,

A canny few fathoms, hoo far I can't tell.

Well, ya efterneùn they war sittin' an' smeùkin',

An' at yan anudder through t' dim leet war leùkin';

When aw on a sudden,

A prop (nut a good un,)

Through t' middle on 't brak,

Wi' a thunderin' crack,

An' doon wi' a smash,

An' a terrible crash,

Ten yards o' reùf fell;

An' awful to tell,

Quite block't up their passage fra under that fell.

Tom gev a scar't like, lowish shoot;

While Gwordie glop't an' glower't aboot;

An' Lantie sweàr his pipe was oot,

An' aw his 'bacca deùn.

Bit when he spy't aroond aw t' pleàce,

He saw it was a desperate keàse:

He let doon a bit langer feàce,

An' rayder chang't his teùn.

Ye know Tom an' Gwordie war beàth weel convertit;

While Lantie, poor fellow, was sadly pervertit!

For while they war mournin' for him as a sinner,

He was thinkin' o' laal else bit t' want of his dinner.

He grummelin' sed,

Aw t' grub they hed,

Was just a bite o' cheese an' bread;

They'd browt for t' bait,

An' noo their fate,

Wad be for dinner lang to wait.

"Ye see, lads," ses Gwordie, "we cannot git oot,

Away i' this bye-pleàce, neah body aboot,

To hear us, hooivver we yoller an' shoot:

I think we may

Kneel doon an' pray,

What d'ye say?

I's seur I see neah udder way.

I think if we,

(I mean us three,)

To that wad 'gree,

We mebbe mud deliver't be."


Noo, Lantie was glumpy, an' waddent submit,

As if in his oan mind some plan on he'd hit,

'At he o' that ratten-trap oot on could git;

Bit what he was thinkin' he nivver let wi't.

What! Gwordie an' Tommy gat terribly flurry't,

An' Lantie to kneel doon they pester't an' worry't;

Bit Lantie sed gruffly, he waddent be hurry't,

If he wantit to say owt, he durst say he could;

An' mappen git on wi't as weel as they dud.

An' if he was fworc't to pray, well than he mud,

He'd pray if he thowt it wad deù enny good.

At last he kneel't doon in a neùk,

An' three lang draughts o' air he teùk;

An' next he twin't an' screw't his feàce,

To git it into t' proper pleàce.

An' than, ses he,

"Oh Lord! help me,

My way to see,

Yance mair to git my liberty.

I'd scworn like them two chaps to be,

Creàvin' for ivvery thing they see:

They pray for this, they beg for t' tudder,

Furst ya thing an' than anudder;

Bit I declare, an' faith it's true,

I nivver pray't for owt till noo;

An' if ye'll let me oot o' here,

I'll nivver pray ageàn, I sweer!"


## Auld Gwordie an' his coo

Auld Gwordie was a tailyer,

   An' Nelly was his wife;

Aw t' neighbours sed, they nobbut led

   A dog an' cat-like life.

Auld Gwordie use' to brutches mak,

   For fwok beàth far an' near;

Bit Nelly still contriv't an' schem't,

   'At t' brutches she mud weer!

They hed a coo 'at went on t' rwoads,
    An' pastur't on t' dyke back;
She'd just a white snip on her feàce,
    Aw t' rest o' t'coo was black.
Her age was – nay, I cannot tell;
    Theer was neàh way to know;
Some t' wrinkles coont on t' horns, bit than
    She hed neah horns at aw.


Ses Gwordie, "Cowey's up i' years,
    I think we'd better try
To sell her off at t' furst May fair,
    An' than a younger buy.
I think I'll tak her up to t' fair."
    "Thou'll tak her up!" ses Nell;
"Whats t' use o' sendin' thee to t' fair?
    I think I'll gang mysel."


What, teàn wad gang, an' t' tudder wad,
    An' menny a fratch they hed;
They fratch't aboot it aw t' day lang,
    An' oft they fratch't i' bed.
Till t' fair-day com an' Gwordie sed,
    "I'll t' brutches weer for yance!"
"Wy, weer them – an' be hang't!" ses Nell,
    "Be off an' tak thy chance!"


Clean wesh't, an' shav't, an' in his best,
    To t' air off Gwordie set;
Wi' cowey marchin' on afwore,
    An' Nell at heàm i' t' pet.
Ses Gwordie tull his-sel', ses he,
    As he went on to t' fair:
"I'll sell her dear, an' buy yan cheap,
    An' than I needent care."

Bit Gwordie hed forgitten quite,
    Or else he nivver knew,
'At when a bargin's to be meàd,
    Theer always mun be two.
An' when he gat to t' fair that day,
    As luck wad hev't to be,
A wag frae Gursmer, ripe for fun,
    Poor Gwordie chanc't to see.

Ses he to yan just like his-sel',
    "A jolly brek we'll hev."
An' off he went, an' bowt t' auld coo;
    Just six pund ten he gev.
He paid his brass, an' dreàv her off
    To some back yard i' t' toon;
Ses he to t' mate, "We'll sell her back,
    I'll bet the' hofe a croon.

"We'll black her feàce, an' crop her tail,
    An' tak her back to t' fair;
To Gwordie thoo mun sell her back,
    An' ax eight pund or mair."
Twas deùn ameast as seun as sed,
    For seùr as we're alive,
Auld Gwordie bowt his oan coo back,
    An' paid doon eight pund five.

Off heàm he set, an' thowt aw t' way,
    Hoo he wad brag auld Nell;
An' tell her hoo he'd deùn as weel
    As she could deùn her-sel'.
Bit when he landit up to t' dooar,
    T' furst words auld Nelly spak,
Were, "What, ye hevvent selt her, than?
    Hoo is't ye browt her back?

"Browt what?" ses Gwordie. "Wy, t' auld coo!
    A feùl may see it's t' seàm."
"By gock!" ses Gwordic, "it caps owt;
    I thowt she kent t' way heàm."
Ses Nell, "I knew hoo it wad be;
    It's weel eneùf at thoo
Gat back thysel', an' duddent bring
    A jackass for a coo!"


## *Robin's Love*


They needent come, wi' flatterin' tongue,
    An' wheedlin' suggar't words to me;
My plightit faith I' geen to yan,
    An' he his promise pledg't to me.

To tempt my pride they needent come,
    Wi' promis't gold an' dresses fine;
Wi' Robin's love I's weel content,
    He sed he'd be content wi' mine.

What's aw their gold an' gear to me,
    If I mun false to Robin prove?
What signify their dresses fine,
    If I mun part wi' Robin's love?

A cottage low, wi' reùf o' straw,
    Wad me content, wi' Robin theer;
Bit oh! a palace e'er sa' fine,
    An' wantin' him wad be ower dear!

I cannot brek my plightit faith;

    I cannot fra my Robin turn;

What good wad riches deù, if I'd

    Heart brokken aw my life to mourn?


Than tempt me nut, for worthless wealth

    Can nivver me fra Robin part:

Aw t' gold i' t' Indies cannot buy

    T' love iv a faithful woman's heart !


## She's weddit an' weel


"She's weddit an' weel!" ses Betty to Jane;

"Submittit at last; bit t' maislin wad fain

    Hev teàn laal Bob Wilson for love."

"Bit, Betty," ses Jane, "theer sometimes, I guess,

When t' money's far mair, 'at t' cumforts ur less;

    It's t' eatin' 'at t' puddin 'ill prove."


Ses Betty to Jane, "Oor Fanny's aw reet!

I's seùr she's been lucky, an' fawn on her feet;

    Weel fedder't her nest is for life."

"Bit, Betty," ses Jane, "If love was away,

She nivver dud warse nor she dud, o' that day

    'At they meàd her an' unlovin' wife."


"Love willent full t' meàl-kist," ses Betty to Jane,

"Nor finnd fwok a shelter fra t' coald wind an' rain

    Nor mak t' pot o' Sunday to boil."

"Bit, Betty," ses Jane, "Love's a wonderful thing,

It gars sorrow laugh, an' grim poverty sing,

    An' maks leeter t' hardest o' toil."

Ses Betty to Jane, "I've hard auld fwok say,
When poverty com, love wad still flee away,
   An' nivver ageàn wad come theer."
"Oh! Betty," ses Jane, "Love desarvin' o' t' neàm,
Through plenty an' poortith ivver is t' seàm;
   Misforten maks t' object mair dear."

"Land an' money hes Gwordie!" ses Betty to Jane,
"Oor Fanny's deùn weel sek a husband to gain;
   She'll nivver know sorrow or care."
"Oh! Betty," ses Jane, "Theer fwok 'at I know,
Wi' money eneùf, bit neah cumfort at aw,—
   For mickle thoo knows wad hev mair."

Ses Betty to Jane, "He's this, an' he's that;
A hoose whoar she need nobbut hing up her hat."
   Ses Jane, "It's aw true, I dar say;
It comes to t' seàm thing, whativver thoo ses,
I'll know what he is, an' nut what he hes,
   When I give a dowter away."

## Angling

When toilin' on life's dusty track,
   Tir't nature will protest,
An' sternly bids you pause awhile,
   Your muddle't brains to rest.
Neah better way can ye your steps,
   For recreation turn,
Than fishin' rod in t' hand, to roam,
   By river, lake, or burn.

Away fra business carkin' cares,
    Fra t' endless hum o' men;
Away to some sweet ripplin' lake,
    Or some wild rocky glen;
Whoar nature, pleas't to see your feàce,
    Wi' liberal hand an' kind,
Will to your body gie back health,
    An' vigour to your mind.

Delightful 'tis to wander on,
    By some clear eddyin' stream;
To fish awhile, an' rust awhile,
    To meditate an' dream.
Whoar t' craggy fells, o' ayder side,
    To t' cloods their heids uprear;
An' nut a soond bit t' watterfaws,
    Or t' sang o' burds, ye hear.

Care nowt for Johnson's surly growl,
    Nor Byron's puzzent sneer;
Bit honest Isaac Walton tak,
    For aw he's quaint an' queer.
An' when wi' floggin' t' stream, you're tire't,
    Sit doon on some crag neùk,
An' see hoo nater corresponds,
    Wi' that auld fashin't beùk.

Ga threed some gorge, whoar two fells meet,
    An' t' boilin' fleùd is seen
Come lowpin' doon, faw efter faw,
    Ower hingin' crags atween.
Your bait drop in, just here an' theer,
    I' some bit whyet neùk;
An', mebbe, when a troot ye land,
    Ye'll see 't drop off your heùk!

Doon, doon t' broo side it jumpin' gangs,
    In t' watter wi' a splash;
Ye meàst may hear t' fish say, "Ye gat
    Your labour for your fash."
"Come, nivver mind," I hear ye say,
    "Fret nin for that 'at's gone;
It's t' chances, whedder won or lost,
    'At leads yan on an' on."

Or in some low an' holmy deàl,
    Whoar t' pool runs deep an' slow;
Wi' stiddy aim an' watchful eye,
    Your salmon flees to throw.
What better spwort could mortal hev,
    What mair excitement wish—
When boilin' up, a blash! a pull!
    Ye've hoald o' t' king o' fish!

Away it gangs, noo up, noo doon,
    Noo sulkin' willent stur;
Than off ageàn like t' wind, it gars
    Your line frae t' wheel to whurr!
Noo, nearer up to t' bank it comes;
    You calculate its size;
An' hoo exultant, when at last,
    You gaff an' land your prize!

Some for adventer mountains climm,
    Where ivverlastin' snow
Unmeltit is, when t' burnin' sun
    Is scorchin' t' plains below.
Some for excitement follow t' hoonds,
    An' ride neck-breck or nowt;
Nor when t' view halloo soonds, do they
    To danger give a thowt.

Some like to range, wi' dog an' gun,
    Ower stubble field an' moor;
While some at cricket, bools, or quoits,
    'Ill spend a leisure 'oor.
Bit gie me fishin' rod an' creel,
    An' varra seùn, I'll be
Away whoar nowt bit fell an' field,
    An' wood an' stream I'll see.

### Johnny an' his fat Buck

At Lyulph's tooer, auld Johnny leev't;
    Park keeper lang was he;
An honester or heartier chap,
    Yan needent wish to see.

When Norfolk' duke, to t' tooer com doon,
    A week or two to spend;
Reet prood was Johnny, on his wants
    An' wishes to attend.

Sometimes to Peerath toon he went,
    Provisions for to buy;
Sometimes to Ullswatter for fish,
    His teàble to supply.

Ya time, (as t' stwory gangs,) t' auld duke,
    A feast was gaan to hev;
An' orders for a good fat buck,
    'Mang t' rest o' things, he gev.

His fire-lock auld, wi' buck-shot charg'd,
    Auld John set off breest hee,
Up t' park; an' as he went, he hum't,
    "This day a stag mun dee."

An' seùr eneùf, a buck was shot,
    An' hoistit off to t' tooer:
T' auld duke, when he knew it was theer,
    Come oot an' leùk't it ower.

Says he, "You've got a fine one, John."
    Says Johnny, "aye, bit, dar!
Ye'r grace, that yan I aim't at, was
    A finer buck, by far!"

### *He hedden't a word to say*

Shy Willie lov't young Maggy Blain;
    An' oft he sigh't an' thowt,
If he could nobbut win her love,
    To wish for he'd hev nowt.
An' oft wi' pensive, lingerin' steps,
    He'd wander on that way;
Bit when fair Maggy Blain he met,
    He heddent a word to say.

Hoo lang he suffer'd, an' hoo sair,
    Nin knew bit his oan sel';
He thowt, when Maggy next he met,
    His secret he wad tell.
Lang speeches he meàd up i' bed,
    An' thowt them ower by day;
Bit still when he'd a chance to speak,
    He heddent a word to say.

An' when a chance was lost, he'd say,
    "A cloonish gowk was I!
When next sweet Maggy Blain I meet,
    To tell my teàl I'll try:
I'll tell her hoo I've love't her lang,
    An' ax for aye or nay:"
Bit when they met, 'twas always t' seàm,
    He heddent a word to say!

When Maggy saw his sheepish leùks,
    She gently led him on;
Till sheepish leùks an' bashfulness,
    War awtogidder gone.
An' when as lovin' man an' wife,
    Lang years hed slip't away;
They oft wad jwoke an' talk o' when
    He heddent a word to say!

### Irrepressible O.P.

*An humble imitation of a poem in the "Biglow Papers".*

Whoarivver yan happens to gang or to be,
Yan allus incoonters that silly O.P.:
It's mebby aw reet, bit it seems varra queer,
'At happen what will, he sud allus be theer:
    Oh, dear me! I nivver dud see
Sec a bore i' my life, as that horrid O.P.!

If a party o' weddiners gangs past, ye'll see,
Wi' a rose in his button wholl, smilin' O.P.;
If it's a funeral ye chance to be at,
O.P. 'ill be theer, wi' a crape on his hat;
    Oh, dear me! I nivver dud see
Sec a bore in my life, as that horrid O.P.!

If ye gang tull a teetotal meetin', ye're seùr
To meet wi' O.P., takken tickets at t' dooar;
An' if tull a clippin' ye happen to gang,
Ye'll hear fra O.P. recitation or sang.
    Oh, dear me! I nivver dud see
Sec a bore i' my life, as that horrid O.P.!

If ye oppen an album, wy, t' furst feàce ye see,
Is t' hairy phisog o' that silly O.P.!
An' barrin' subscription lists, t' list wad be queer,
Wi' a lang row o' neàms, if O.P. wassent theer.
    Oh, dear me! I nivver dud see
Sec a bore i' my life as that silly O.P.!

If a meetin' theer be, whativver aboot,
O.P. 'ill still mannish to poke in his snoot;
An' if it's a meetin', religion to talk,
He'll be don't in his sober religious cloke.
    Oh, dear me! I nivver dud see
Sec a bore in my life as that horrid O.P.!

He's blue or he's yellow, he's black or he's white,
To suit times an' chances to git sup or bite;
O' jibin' an' snirtin' unconscious he'll sit;
If fwok laugh at his daftness, he thinks 'at it's wit!
    Oh, dear me! I nivver dud see
Sec a bore in my life, as that horrid O.P.!

## *Nathan's Coortin'*

Greit Nathan went cwortin' to Maggie at t' Yews,
An' cuddent believe she wad ivver refuse;
Bit Maggie was saucy, and threw up her heid,
An' sed, "Will I hev thee? Aye, likely, indeed!"

Says Nathan, "Thoo'll nivver deù better, I think;"
An' leùk't varra wise, as he gev her a wink;
Says Maggie, "Wy, mebbe I mayn't, what than?
I care laal for that; bit I will if I can."

Says Nathan, "I've two nags, an' sebben good kye;
A nice stock o' sheep, an' some money, forby."
Says Maggie, "I whop it'll nut be my luck,
To wed wi' a middin' for t' seàk o' t' lock muck."

Says he, "What! Thoo's saucy; I think thoo's to bleàm;
Thoo'll leùk through thy fingers an' miss a good heàm."
Sars Maggie, "Just lissen, I'll nut tell a lee;
Theer laal fawt i' t' heàm, if 't wassent for thee!"

Says he, "If thoo means it, I think I'll be off;
Thoo'd better be takken noo when thoo hes t' loff!"
"Ay, likely," says Maggie; "what, mebbe I hed,
Bit fwok sud be cwortit befwore they sud wed!"

Says Nathan, "If cwortin' thoo wants, thoo sal hev't;
Thoo just spak i' time, for I'd varra nar left."
Says she, "Thoo may try a bit langer, an' than,
I mebbe may like the'—I will if I can!"

## Billy Spedding

*Billy Spedding was at school with John Richardson and worked as a porter at Penrith Station. He told Richardson the story of throwing a stone at Joe and Mally Gill's game cock and killing it—and letting "a laal nasty terrier" take the blame. Ed.*

AMONG the group of boys who were my playmates and contemporaries at school, (a group long since widely scattered by the relentless hand of time,) there was one familiarly known by the name of Billy Speddy.

In the far off memory pictures which the mind will occasionally conjure up, one does not see Billy sitting on the front form, or standing near the head of his class in the school-room, or as the captain and leader of the games in the play-ground; but he is conspicuously noticeable all the same. One may see him, always in the background, either standing on one leg on a bench, or in a far corner, peeping over the edge of his book, instead of at the pages, or in some out of the way nook of the playground, bullying and taking the marbles from some little boy about half his own size.

Billy, however, though a regular scapegrace at school, and as full of mean and contemptible tricks as he well could, grew up to be, as far as I have heard, a respectable member of the community.

Many years after he had left school, I met with him at the Penrith railway station, where he was then employed as a porter, and having to wait a considerable time for a train, I had a long chat with him about school-boy days and other kindred subjects.

Among other things, Billy told me the following story, which I made a mental note of at the time; and though he was not celebrated for veracity, in his boyish days, the tale is so thoroughly characteristic of him as I knew him, that I have very little doubt but it was mainly true.

Said Billy, "It's varra queer, I've thowt sometimes, 'at some fwok when they git a thing into their heids, if it be ivver sa' far wrang, hoo they'll stick teù't, an' twist an' twine ivvery thing else to fit it, an' imagine things, till they quite think 'at udder fwok sud believe't as weel.

"Aboot t' time we're talkin' on, when I went to t' scheùl, I use' to caw ivvery day, mwornin' an' neet, 'at auld Joe Gill's, to ax what o'clock it was.

Thoo kent auld Joe an' auld Mally weel eneùf? Thoo knows, auld Mally was a parlish body for hens; she keep't aboot hofe a scwore iv as fine ghem hens as ivver yan saw, an' a ghem cock; bit t' cock wassent hur oan. It beleng't to yan auld Mawson. What thoo kent him weel eneùf, teù? Thoo knows he follow't cock-feightin', an' it was yan 'at he'd carry't to auld Mally's to walk.

"Well, ya neet I was gaan heàm fra t' scheul, an' aw t' hens an' t' cock war in a field doon below t' rwoad. What! I was like t' meàst o' lads, full eneùf o' mischief, likely, an' I thowt I wad hev a shot into 'mang them wi' a steàn, nivver thinkin' 'at I wad hit enny o' them, or mair likely nivver thinkin' owt aboot it, whedder I wad or nut. Be that as it wad, I threw yan, an' as bad luck wad hev't, it hat t' cock reet ower t' heid, an' knock't it ower.

"By goy! it just gev a flap or two wi' t' wings on 't, an' nivver stur't mair. Thoo may be seùr I duddent caw to see what o'clock it was that neet; bit I think auld Joe an' Mally war nowder o' them at heàm, for as l was gaan by to t' scheùl t' next mwornin', they'd nobbut just fund it. Auld Joe was just cummin' oot o' t' door wi' t' deid cock under his arm; an' ses he, as seùn as he saw me,

"'That laal nasty tarrier at t' tudder hoose hes worry't auld Mawson' fine ghem cock. I dunnet know what I'll be to deù. I's just gaan to see.'

"Thoo may be seùr I was nin sworry to hear 'at t' poor tarrier hed gitten t' bleàm; an' as auld Mawson leev't nut far fra t' scheul, an' was a gay rough cheely, I march't off wi' auld Joe, an' thowt I wad hear what he sed. When we gat nut far fra t' pleàce, we met t' auld chap, an' as seùn as auld Joe saw him, he sed,

"'Theer a varra bàd job happen't. I dunnet know what mun be deùn. Yon laal nasty dog o' t' tudder fwok's hes worry't t' cock.'

"Mawson, thoo knows, was an ower t' Raise chap, an' he talk't ower t' Raise mak o' talk, an' ses he,

"'Od zounds! bit I'll wirry't if I git hald on 't! Ya thing or anudder 's gaantè destroy o' t' things 'at I hev! Theear' some unlucky divvels o' lads 'at gang wi' summet fra me ivvery week end. First they went wi' a duck, than they went wi' a goose: they'll be gaan wi' t' cow an' t' cuddy next. They wad ha' geàn wi' them lang sen, bit they cudden't conseàll them. Ye may tak t' cock yam ageàn, an' boil t' pot wi' 't: it's aw 'at ye'll git fort' walk on 't.'

"An', seah, auld Joe set off back wi' his cock under his arm, an' I went on to t' scheùl.

"When I went heàm at neet, I thowt to mysel', as they nivver suspectit 'at I'd hed owt to deù wi' killin' t' cock, I mud venter to caw an' ax what o'clock it was. Auld Mally was sittin' knittin' as she mainly what was; an' t' hens war pickin' aboot aw t' fleùr ower, bit theer was neah cock to be seen. Efter she'd tell me it was hofe efter fower o'clock, I venter't to say,

"What do ye think it hed been t' tarrier 'at kilt t' cock?"

'Theer' nut a bit o' doot on't," ses she, "a laal nasty urchin. It hed bitten 't aw ower. I poot it this efterneun, an' it heddnt a free bit on' t. It was aw bites ower.' "I dursent tell t' auld thing, or else I knew 'at t' dog hed nivver been nar't: for it was just kilt wi' a steàn ower t' heid on 't, as I telt ye befwore."

### *Auld Will Rutson' Machine*

*William Ritson of Wasdale Head, who died not long since, was well known to most of the tourists who went over Sty Head Pass, for nearly half a century. His house being a port of call or resting place which pedestrians almost without exception availed themselves of; and being a most original and note-worthy character, he managed to scrape an acquaintance with most of them. Young fellows sometimes attempted to draw fun out of him, but old Will always managed to put them down most effectually. The following lines are founded on an incident of the kind, and are literally true. Ed.*

> Auld Will was famous at a crack;
>> An' thowt 'at nin could tell,
> A better teàl or bigger lee,
>> Nor he could deù his-sel'.

> Ya day, a stuck-up chap com in,
>> 'At thowt auld Will to jeer;
> He sed he'd been to Manchester,
>> An' telt what he'd seen theer.

Aboot their butchin' swine, he talk't,
    Three hundred in a day;
An' yan could druss them off, as fast,
    As two could tak away.

Says Will, "It's wonderful, neah doot,
    Sec butchin' feats thoo's seen;
Bit in that granary loft, oot theer,
    We hev a queer machine:

"Thoo sees t' auld sewe, on t' midden theer?
    I'll bet a pund, an' win,
If thoo'll just tak her to t' machine,
    An' pop her nicely in,

"An' give 't three turns aboot, she'll come
    Oot bacon, nicely dry't!
Anudder turn, an' t' hams 'ill be
    Weel boil't, an' t' flicks weel fry't!

"Weel meàd aw t' sossiges 'ill be,
    Just by a turn o' t' crank!
An' t' brussels, min', 'ill come oot, teù,
    Good brushes riddy shank't!"

T' chap glowered at Will, an' than he sed,
    "Oh! what a horrid lee!"
Says Will, "Does thoo think I'd be bang't,
    Wi' sec a thing as thee?"

## *The Snow*

It com doon as whisht an' as deftly as death,
O' soond nut a murmur, o' air nut a breath;
Flake reàcin' wi' flake. Oh! 'twas bonny to see
Hoo it cuvver't up moontain, an' valley, an' tree.
Doon, doon it com floatin', sa' white an' sa clear,
Ivvery twig, ivvery leaf, hed its burden to beàr;
Ivvery dyke, ivvery hoose, ivvery rough cobble wo',
Hed its blossom, its reùf, or its copin' o' snow.
Doon, doon it com' floatin' sa' swiftly an' leet,
Seùn t' landscape was white as a tribble bleach't sheet;
An' t' grund 'at was leàtly sa' starv't like an' bare,
Was lapt in a mantle, a feùt thick or mair.

Their coald stores exhaustit, t' leet cloods floatit by,
An' pure white as t' earth was, as deep blue was t' sky;
Far sooth Sol appeared, majestic an' breet,
His rays wake an' slantin', an' guiltless o' heat,
Threw ower that white picter a splendour an' sheen,
'At twice in a life-time can rarely be seen.
Ivvery crag, ivvery dyke, ivvery snow-leàden tree,
Was an object worth gaan a lang journey to see;
Neah art, tho' by t' cleverest artist, could show
A picter sa' grand as that landscape o' snow.

T' grim demon o' winter, wi' envy hofe craz'd,
To see sec a scene i' December-uprais't
A fierce wind fra t' north, 'at whissel't an' rwoar't,
An' dreàv t' snow i' blinndin' cloods dancin' afwore 't.
Fra t' fells into t' valleys, doon whurlin' it went,
It fand ivvery crack, ivvery crevice, an' rent;
Through t' mortarless wo's; in auld hooses, it's sed,
Fwok waken't to finnd theirsels snown up i' bed.

While creelin' by t' fences for shelter, t' poor sheep,
In t' snowdrifts war hap't up, aye, ivver sa' deep;
For days an' days efter, t' auld shipperds wad post
Off wi' t' cwollies, to hunt up odd sheep 'at war lost;
An' some nivver fund war till spring, when leàte on
They frozen turn't oot efter t' last snow was gone!

## Nan's Secret

"It's a secret," says Nan, an' she whisper't quite low;
"I waddent for t' warld enny body sud know;
Tom Gill, low be't spokken, wad fain coddle me;
Bit say nowt; I waddent tell mortal bit thee.

"He com t' tudder neet, an' at my window tap't:
To know who it was for a while I was cap't;
Seah, I peekel't an' watch't, till his feace I could see;
Bit say nowt; I waddent tell mortal bit thee.

"Ses I, 'Tom, what wants t'è?' ses he, 'Let me in!'
Thinks I, that's a rayder blunt way to begin:
It's trew as I's here, I'll nut tell a lee,
Bit say nowt; I waddent tell mortal bit thee.

"Ses I, 'Thoo's a capper to come i' that way;
An' say-let me in: is that aw thoo's to say?'
Ses he, 'I'll say mair when thoo sits o' my knee:'
Bit say nowt; I waddent tell mortal bit thee.

"Lord! when he gat in, he hed plenty to say;
He thowt he wad wed me, I just wish he may.
He duddent just promise't, bit sed he wad see;
Bit say nowt; I waddent tell mortal bit thee."

I sed to mysel', as I went on my way,

It's a secret, an' nivver a word I mun say;

To tell owt, a sham an disgreàce it wad be,

When she sed, 'at she waddent tell mortal bit me!


Bit seùn I fand oot, when oor lasses I saw,

'At she'd tel't them t' seàm teàl as a secret an' aw;

An' than, what, I fand it was nobbut a lee,

When she sed, 'at she waddent tell mortal bit me!


## *The Final Parting*

Nay! git the' geàn, thoo durty slut;

    A fair disgreace thoo is!

I saw the' wi' thur varra een,

    Cock up thy neb to his!

An', noo, thoo comes wi' smilin' feàce,

    Just as if nowt hed been;

An' fain wad flaatch me up ageàn,

    As if I heddent seen.


Nay! nivver mair I'll trust the' noo,

    Lang time I've hard eneùf;

Bit ageàn aw 'at fwok could say,

    My trustin' love was preùf:

Bit what I saw, I can believe;

    Sa', nivver, nivver mair,

Will thoo deceive me wi' a smile,

    Or wi' thy speeches fair.

It's laal use noo to think o' t' past,
    Or talk what mud ha' been;
What happy years we hed i' store,
    If nowt hed come't atween.
Thoo's hed thy choice o' him or me;
    To beàth a smile thoo gev;
Bit aw thy schemin' noo mun end,
    For beàth thoo cannot hev.

Nay! dunnet say anudder word—
    For nut a word I'll hear!
Theer was a time when aw thoo sed,
    Was music in my ear!
Bit, noo, that music 's oot o' teùn;
    That voice hes lost its charm;
I saw the' smirk i' Jemmy's feàce,
    An' hod by Jemmy's arm!

### Keat Craal

I kent an' auld woman, Keàt Craal was her neàm;
An auld-fashin't body, beàth wrinkle't an' leàm
She sed, she was canny an' active when young;
Bit, Lord, she was alter'd! aw'd fail'd bit her tongue.

Her mem'ry was good: she'd tell whoar an' when,
Owt strange hed teàn pleàce, for three-scwore year an' ten;
Ses she, "I' this warld I've seen some queer scrowes;
An' langer yan bides in't an' queerer it growes.

"When I was a young lass aboot sebenteen,
Nowt smarter was Peerath an' Carel a tween;
Whoarivver I went—to dance, market, or fair,
I allus hed sweethearts, far mair nor my share.

"I flirtit wi' this, an' I flirtit wi' t' tudder,
Till sometimes aboot me, they'd feight yan anudder;
An' oft for a brek when teàn tudder they'd bang,
I'd slipe wi' anudder, an' wid him wad gang!

"Oh! man, aboot harvest sec jwokes we oft hed,
When whinbobs an' hollins we pot into bed;
An' than we wad lissen hoo t' shearers wad shoot,
When they pop't into bed, bit far sharper pop't oot!

"Beside bein' canny, reet weel I could sing,
An' aw t' lads i' t' toonship I hed in a string;
Just when I was twenty, it's trew, I declare—
My choice I could hed iv a dozen or mair.

"They talk't hoo they lov't me, an' aw sec as that;
Bit nowt bit a laugh an' sneck-possets they gat:
Till yan an' anudder began to tail off,
An' at five-an'-twenty, I'd nin sa much loff.

"At thirty, I fand through my fingers I'd leuk't,
An' was riddy to jump at t' furst finger 'at creuk't:
Oor Tommy was daftish, an' feckless, teù;
Bit when he wad hev me—Lord! what could I deù?"

## *Soavin' Time*

'Twas someway on i' soavin' time,
    An' frosty, I remember;
Fwok soav't far leàter than nor noo,
    Sometimes quite through November;
'At Gwordie Cwoats, an' Scott, an' me,
    Oor suppers when we'd gitten,
A walk wad tak, to streight oor legs,
    'At cravvick't war wi' sitten'.

Fra Girsmere quite up t' Raise we clam,
    An' warm't oorsels wi' walkin';
An' menny a laugh we gat at Scott,
    For he dud t' main o' t' talkin'.
A walk he sed wad deù us good;
    Says I, "We'll gang to t' top, than;"
When just wi' that a voice we hard,
    'At sed, "Wilt'e come op, than?"

For full a minute, mebby mair,
    We steùd stock still an' lissent;
Says I, "It's farder up on t' rwoad;"
    Says Scott, "Nay, nay, it issent!"
An' pointin' wi' his hand, says he,
    "T' soond com fra ower theer;
Nut far fra t' intack boddem, min,
    Or else my lug's a leear."

"Come op!" we hard ageàn or lang;
An' Scott was nut mistakken:
'Cross t' field we went, an' theer we fand,
What 'twas 'at t' row was makken,
A man an' horse war theer; an' t' feùl
A hog-wholl[43] through hed croppen;
An' t' bridle rine he poo't an' poo't,
An' theer he was, "Come op-pen'!"

"Ho! Ho!" says Scott, "What hev we here?
    What chance hes browt ye hidder?"
Says t' man, "I cuddent tell ye that,
    I's maizelt awtogidder;
I've wander't roond an' roond that field,
    Bit finnd a way oot, cuddent;
I think I nivver com thro' here"—
    Says Scott, "I's seùr t' nag duddent!"

We browt them beàth away to t' yat,
    An' when oot theer he'd gitten,
An' fand his-sel yance mair on t' rwoad,
    Astride o' t' galloway sitten:
He thank't us ower an' ower ageàn;
    An' than to 'sceàpe Scott's banter,
He gev his nag a sharpish switch,
    An' set off in a canter.

---

43  A "hog-wholl" is a hole about two feet high by eighteen inches wide, through the bottom
    of a stone fence, for the sheep to pass from one field to another.

## *What Matter?*

Hut, min! what matter? She's nobbut a woman;
   Brek nin o' thy heart aboot that.
Theer' good fish i' t' sea, min, as ivver com oot on't;
   When thoo's elder, thoo'll finnd oot what's what.

When next thoo leets on her be quite independent;
   Keep whusselin' Rory o' More;
To shew 'at thoo's merry, an' cares laal aboot her—
   Thoo'll seùn put her intul a stoor.

Some women gang allus by t' reùls o' contrary;
   If thoo whinges an' begs, thoo may whinge;
Bit if thoo puts on a fine "What care I," swagger,
   They'll turn roond an' follow an' cringe.

If t' warst come to t' warst, an' thoo happens to lwose her;
   T' warst 'ill mappen be t' best i' t' lang end.
If she dussent want the', thoo's better withoot her;
   O' that thoo may seàfly depend.

Seàh keep up thy spirits, an' sing rompti-addity!
   Ya laugh's worth a hundred greàns.
She's nobbut a woman, min, care nowt aboot her;
   Theer' plenty mair left when she's geàn!

## *Oor Betty*

Oor Betty's allus wawin', wawin'
　　Theer' summet ivver gangin' wrang;
Nowt in this warld, o' that I's sarten,
　　Wad keep her fra her wawin' lang!

Oor Betty's allus scrattin', scrattin'
　　Eneùf she thinks she'll nivver git;
Fra seùn i' t' mworn to leàt i' t' ibnin',
　　Sceàrce a minute will she sit.

Oor Betty's allus scrubbin', scrubbin'
　　Aye scoorin', rubbin', dustin' still;
T' wark she does, i' nowt bit cleanin',
　　Teà hofe o' t' younger mak wad kill.

Oor Betty's yan amang a thoosand;
　　An' efter aw 's been sed an' deùn,
Theer' nobbut oddens better leùkin',
　　When deck't up i' t' efterneùn.

Oor Betty's yabble, an' she's willin',
　　To help a neighbour in a strait;
An' ivver riddy when she's wantit,—
　　Ifs an' ans she duzzent wait.

Oor Betty's ran o' t' best in England,
　　Let t' udder come fra whoar she will;
For whedder wawin', scrattin', scrubbin',
　　Her heart 'ill be i' t' reet pleàce still.

## *Grummelin' Farmers*

Fwok talk aboot grummelin' farmers,
    An' thrum ower an auld cuckoo shoot;
Bit few ivver think or consider,
    Hoo much they've to grummel aboot.
Theer rents heigh eneùf to begin wi',
    For t' landlwords ur raisin' them still;
An' what is ther' for 't, bit to gi' them 't;
    If ye dunnet, somebody will.

Theer ur cesses an' taxes iv aw maks;
    T' collecters ur nivver away;
Yer hand 's nivver oot o' yer pocket;
    Theer nowt for 't bit grummel an' pay.
Fwok talk aboot t' balance at t' bankers;
    Oh! man, but they're sadly wrang;
Ye mak bits o' brass, theer neàh doot on't,
    Bit whativver ye meàd it wad gang.

Theer bills fra coo-doctors an' blacksmiths,
    They're wantin' their money o' t' day;
An' sarvents, industrious or lazy,
    Ye hev them their wages to pay.
An', than, ye hev losses an' crosses;
    Ye'r sheep dee i' t' seekness or t' sowt:
If milk coo or nag chance to torfet,
    Anudder 'ill hev to be bowt.

Theer flees to demolish ye'r turnips;
    Theer grubs aw ye'r havver to eat;
An' crops 'at ye thowt sud be heavy,
    'Ill come off bit stragglet an' leet.
What varmint theer fashes a farmer,
    Theer nowt bit a farmer 'at knows;
Theer wissels, an' foomarts, an' foxes,
    An' rabbits, an' pheasants, an' crows.

An, than, theer cross wedder to feight wi';
    It's coàld when it sud ha' been het;
An' i' spring oft when gurse sud be growin',
    It's dry when it sud ha' been wet.
Wet wedder 'ill oft come i' hay-time,
    When t' men for a month are just hir't;
Ye may wish for fine wedder, an' wish for't
    An' oft hev to wish till ye'r tir't.

It's nobbut a few things I've mention't,
    'At bodder poor farmers at times;
Udder plagues I could neàm withoot number,
    They'd hod oot far langer nor t' rhymes.
Bit plenty I've telt, I've a nwotion,
    Befwore aw my rhymes ur run oot;
To show fwok 'at farmers 'at grummel,
    Hev plenty to grummel aboot.

### The Hobthrush

I' them auld times, lang lang sen,—when ivvery lonely pleàce amang t' fells
hed it' oan boggle or ghost, when auld women an' black cats war nivver
seàfe o' bein' droo't or burn't for witches, an' when here an' theer i' some oot
o' t' way pleàces hobthrushes dud aw maks o' queer pranks an' unpossible

feats,—theer leev't up aside Watendleth tarn an auld crusty tyke iv a farmer they caw't Jos Harry. He was yan o' them cantankarous, cankert, crusty auld fellows yan sometimes leets on noo a days, for they're nut quite o' deid yet. Yan 'at neàh body could talk teù five minutes without hevven an argiment aboot summet or anudder. If ye'd sed tull him, "It's a fine day;" he wad mebby ha' sed, "Who sed it wassent?" If ye'd axt him hoo he was, t' answer as like as nut wad ha' been, "Does 't mak enny odds to the'?"

Hooivver, it was sec an oot o' t' way pleàce whoar he leev't at, theer wassent menny fwok he could git a fratch wi', an' for that reason he nivver miss't an opportunity when he hed a chance.

At that time just ower t' fell fra t' Watendleth, in a wood abeùn t' Rostwhate, fwok sed theer leev't a hobthrush. I could nivver larn what shap it was, or what colour or what size, or owt aboot it; bit yan use' to hear o' some parlish feats it hed deùn i' Borrowdale an' udder deàls as weel.

Sometimes in a mwornin' when fwok gat up they fand a field o' gurse mown, or a field o' hay they left oot t' neet afwore aw hoose't, or mappen aw their lock o' havver thresh't an' deetit. It was a teptious kind iv a thing teù, for if fwok gat t' wrang way on 't, it wassent to tell t' mischeeves it wad ha' deùn them. Sometimes when fwok hed hoose't hay aw t' day, an' thowt they'd meàd a good darrick, they wad ha' fund it aw oot in t' field ageàn t' next mwornin'! Or, mebby, when they gat up in a mwornin' aw their kye wad ha' been milk't, an' aw maks o' tricks o' that kind it gat t' bleàme on. Neah doot it wad be varra convenient for enny illdispwos't body, 'at wantit to deù a spiteful action, to hev t' hubthrush to lig t' bleàme on.

Auld Jos waddent oan 'at he believ't owt aboot enny hobthrushes, an' wad ha' flire't an' laugh't at fwok when they war tellin' ower what it dud; bit he believ't it aw t' seàm. It was nobbut for t' seàke o' contradiction he sed he duddent.

He hed a sarvant lass they caw't Mary Wilkinson, 'at was t' best match for him iv enny body ivver he leet on; for whativver he sed tull her she allus gev him as good as he sent. She was a girt strappen, lish hussy, an' was flate o' nowt. She wad ha' carry't a girt heavy sheet-full o' hay up t' fell breest, or clip't a sheep oot o' t' whicks, or soav't yan as weel as enny man in owder Watendleth or Borrowdale.

It happen't ya hay-time 'at t' wedder was varra shoory, as it oft is amang t' fells, an' Jos hed a gay lock o' gurse doon, an' that meàde him crosser nor ivver, if that was possible. Ya week it rain't ivvery day till Setterday, an' that day was darkish till ameàst neùn, an' than it clear't oot, an' was a regular whurler. Fwok gat aw into t' hoose 'at ivver they'd brokken, an' a lock o' them wish't they'd venter't mair.

Auld Jos gat a good slipe in as weel as t' rest, bit he hed ya field i' girt cock, they caw't Farclwose, 'at they duddent brek; an' when t' day gat oot sa' fine, it was ower leàt to scail't, an' seah it wad ha' been as weel to say nowt aboot it. Bit that wassent Jos's way. He went on grummelin' aw t' efterneùn. Aboot ivvery ten minutes it was, "I wish t' Farclwose hed been brokken." T' lass dud nowt bit laugh at him, an' tell't him she thowt they war deùin' ivver sa finely; they war gitten a good slipe in, an' he'd better mak hissel content. Hooivver, he grummel't on as lang as ivver he was up, an' went grummelin' to bed. T' last thing Mary hard when he turn't t' stairs landin' was, "I wish we'd nobbut brokken t' Farclwose!"

As seùn as they'd aw gone to bed bit t' lass, an' aw was whyet, what dud she deù bit slip oot, an' away to t' Farclwose, an' faw to wark an' skail oot ivvery haycock in t' field. She than com heam ageàn, slip't whyetly in an' to bed withoot ennybody seein' her.

T' next mwornin' it was rainin' pell mell. When auld Jos com doon his furst words war,

"I wish, to the lord, we'd brokken that Farclwose yesterday."

Mary laugh't in her sleeve, bit sed nowt. It pot on till aboot mid fworneùn, when Jos com in leùkin' varra scar't like, an' sed,

"What! t' hobthrush's been in oor Farclwose yesterneet."

"T' hobthrush!" ses Mary. "I thowt, maister, ye duddent believe i' hobthrushes?"

"Wy! I know nowt aboot it," ses he, "I know 'at t' hay's aw spread oot, an' it 'ill be as wet as if it hed been trail't through t' beck."

"Aye!" ses Mary, "that's like eneùf. It sometimes happens when fwok grummel when they've neah kashon to grummel, they git rayder mair nor they bargin't for."

## *Ill-gien Gossips*

Plague on that slanderin' tongue,'at still
Is whisperin' o' its neighbours' ill;
   An' blast that ill teùn't ear,
'At deif to aw 'at's good an' pure,
'Ill oppen like a swine-hull deùr,
   A filthy teàl to hear!

Blear't be that jandic't, squintin' eye,
'At bad intention still can spy,
   A neighbour's ways amang:
It's like a Jack-wi'-t'-lantern leet,
'At hings ower durty spots at neet,
   Daft travellers leadin' wrang!

Ill luck to t' brazzent, shamless feace,
'At smirks an' smiles when some disgreàce
   Hings ower a hapless soul:
That feàce 'at laughs at udder's ill,
Bit when yan weel succeeds, 'ill still
   Wi' envious malice scowl!

Ill faw that wretch 'at cannot feel,
Exaltin' thrill for udder's weel,
   Nor pang for udder's woe.
Lap't up in his bit worthless sel',
Neah cheerful stwory he can tell,
   Neah kindly feelin' know.

May he, despis't by young an' auld,

Be whidderin' left i' t' storm an' coàld,

   Like wretch 'neath popish ban.

A kindly word he nivver sed;

A kindly thowt he nivver hed;

   For his poor fellow-man,


## *T' fleet o' Time*


Days, weeks, an' months gang glidin' by,

Like cloods across a summer sky;

They come, an' meàst afwore we know,

They're gone ageàn like April snow.


Fair Spring, wi' laughin' feàce, we see,

I' green don up field, bush, an' tree;

Bit sceàrce we've time, "Hoo sweet!" to say,

Till Summer's here, an' Spring's away.


Prood Summer marchin' by 's noo seen,

Cled in a robe o' darker green;

Bit aw t' fine trimmin's hardly on,

Till Autumn comes, an' Summer's gone.


Fields, woods, an' trees we than behold,

I' purple, orange, green an' gold;

Bit Winter seùn wi' vengeful spite,

Maks t' trees aw bare, an' t' fields aw white.


Thus season follows season roond,

Like speeks o' wheels, noo up noo doon;

An' we, midge like, awhile hod on,

Bit seùn drop off, oor bit time gone.

Sen we war barnes, withoot a care,
Like plants i' Spring, young, fresh, an' fair;
To leùk back seems like yesterday,
An' noo we're growin' auld an' grey.

A few mair turns o' t' wheel, an' than,
Oor hoalds 'ill slacken, yan by yan;
An' we'll be left by t' side o' t' way,
For time 'ill nowder stop nor stay.

### Sec wark aboot a man

O loavin' days! sec wark theer is,
    An' aw just ower a man;
Theer hofe a dozen, which for which,
    To git him if they can.

Theer Betty cocks her cap an' smirks,
    An' thinks his wife to be;
Lord, bless me weel! hoo daft fwok ur;
    He'll wed nin, nay, nut he!

Theer Sally, teù, an auld daft thing;
    Yan thowt mair sense she hed.
She's forty, noo, if she's a day;
    An' wi' a lad wad wed.

An' than theer Aggie—ha! ha! ha!
    She cocks her wedder e'e;
An' ses, "Just wait a bit, an' than,
    Thoo'll mebby summet see."

Theer twea-three mair I willent neàm,
    An' they're aw just as bad;
What is t'er at him, bless me weel!
    To mak fwok aw gang mad!

I met him t' tudder neet mysel',
    He sed nowt much amiss;
He talk't some nonsense aboot love,
    An' fain wad hed a kiss.

What mair he sed, an' what I sed,
    Yan issent ty't to tell;
I think, if I my cards play reet,
    I'll mappen win mysel.

## Dick Watson

Yance on a time a man theer leev't,
'At oft wi' jealous thowts was griev't,
    Dick Watson was his neàm.
His wife was Betty, and for t' life
They leev't o' bickerin' an' strife,
    They teàn wad t' tudder bleàm.

A roysterin' butcher went that way,
'At oft to Betty things wad say,
    'At rile't auld Watson sair.
Reet savage war his leùks, an' soor,
While Betty steùd an' gaff't at t' dooer,
    An' nivver seem't to care.

'Twas on ya coàld November neet,
They coorin' sat by t' fire o' peet,
　　While t' reek ower t' hearth dud puff.
When Betty fain a crack wad hev,
While nowt for answer Watson gev,
　　Bit an' ill-nater't gruff.

At last up steùd Dick, brant an' streight,
An' leukin' fra his biggest height,
　　Sed, "If thoo wants a crack,
Put on thy hat an' cloak, an' gang
Whoar thoo's been hingin' efter lang,—
　　Ga off to Abram Jack."

"Reason!" ses Betty, "reason, man!
Just reason, Watson, if thoo can—
　　An' think hoo kind he's been!
For years oor swines he's kilt for nowt;
An' aw oor coaves an' fat sheep bowt,
　　An' t' best o' prices gien."

"What can yan reason, dus t'è think?"
Ses Dick; "Yan cannot git a glass o' drink,
　　Bit! wok mun laugh an' hint.
Beside, I've seen an' hard mysel',
Eneùf 'at I wad scworn to tell,—
　　Theer is neah reason in't.

"I'll tell the' what I's gaan to deù;
Tak nwotish, for I mean it, teù;
　　Seàh, thoo may let him know.
If ivver he comes here ageàn,
I'll shut him deid as cobble steàn,
　　As l wad shut a crow!"

Just then ootside a soond—thump! thump!
Meàd Watson start, an' Betty jump,
   While beàth their mooths geàp't wide.
Thump! thump! ageàn. Ses Dick," He's theer:
Talk o' the divvel, he'll appear:
   I'll shut him! Stand aside!"

Fra t' chimley boak his gun he teùk,
An' bleùdy murder in his leùk,
   Oot into t' neet he stryàd.
An' than to owder see or hear,
If Abram Jack was sneaken theer,
   He like a statue steùd.

Through t' murky darkness seùn he saw,
A heid peep ower t' low garden wo',
   An' than pop oot o' seet.
Ses Watson, "If thoo be a man,
Tell what thoo's wantin', if thoo can,
   At this deid time o' neet!"

Ageàn t' heid peep't, bit nivver spak;
Ageàn Dick Watson silence brak;
   Ses he, "Speak, or I'll shut!
I'll send through't hofe an oonce o' leid,
If up ageàn thy turnip heid,
   Abeùn that wo' thoo'll put!"

Than slowly up com t' heid ageàn—
A flash, a crack, an awful greàn,
   Through t' neet's still darkness ran!
In Watson rush't through t' oppen dooer,
An' white as sheet steùd up on t' flure,
   Ses he, I've shot a man!

"'Twas Abram's voice, a deep base greàn!
Oh! hed I letten him aleàn!

Whativver mun be deùn?
Oh! Betty, thoo mun stick to me,
An', like a cleg, I'll stick to thee;

An' we by t' leet o' t' meùn,

"Will tak him oor oan fields across,
An' hap him up i' Rontry moss,

Doon in a peetpot deep:
Whoar mappen nivver he'll be fund,
Till thee an' me be under t' grund,

If we oor secret keep!"

Says Betty, "Nay, thoo cannot 'sceàp;
Aboot thy neck thoo'll git a reàp;

Thoo'll hing on t' gallows tree!
Thoo's teàn thy oan ill-temper't way;
Thoo for thy feùlishness mun pay;

Thoo'll hang! an' that thoo'll see!"

"Oh! Betty, Betty, come away!
Sec dreedful things thoo munnet say!

To hide him let us gang!
Forgie me this time, if thoo will,
An' what thoo bids me, I'll deù still,

Let it be reet or wrang!"

"Wy, wy," ses Betty, "if I mun,
Put oot o' seet that nasty gun,

An' git thysel' a speàd:
We'll tak him off to t' moss at yance,
An' than to 'sceàp thoo'll hev a chance,—

A bonny job thoo's meàd!

"Bit, furst let's see if he be deid;
If nut, a speàd thoo willent need;
   A doctor we mun hev."
Beàth went togidder, till they gat
To t' pleàce whoar t' heid was peepin' at,
   An' ower a scar't leùk gev!

When Betty t' bleedin' carcase saw,
'At lifeless laid ootside o't wo'—
   Says she, "Ods wons! Od rot!
Thoo silly, newdlin', jealous ass,
Thoo's nut hofe wise, nor nivver was—
   Oor oan poor coo thoo's shot!

"Thoo silly feùl! it's like thy sense!
T' auld coo was stannin' under t' fence,
   An' rubbin' wi' her heid:
An' when it com to t' top o' t' wo',
Thoo thowt 'twas Abram Jack thoo saw,
   An's geàn an' shot her deid!"

## *Spring's Mistak*

Grim Winter soond was sleepin'
   Clwose up by Scawfell-man;
When Spring oot slyly peepin',
   Her wark o' love began.
She cuvver'd t' fields wi' greenness,
   Invitit t' burds to sing;
An' they, pleas't an' delightit,
   Meàd woods an' groves aw ring.

Breet crocuses an' snowdrops,
    On garden beds war seen;
An' daisies white war scatter't,
    Ower t' fields so fresh an' green.
Some trees push't oot their blossoms,
    An' primroses upsprang;
Bit t' auld esh pollard shak't its heid,
    An' sed 'at Spring was wrang.

Beàth burds an' flures fell laughin',
    To hear t' auld knarl'd thing;
Mair buds prepar't for burstin',
    Mair burds began to sing.
Bit t' pollard, neàk't an' leafless,
    Still grummelin' seem't to say,—
Young things 'at will be silly,
    Mun for their daftness pay.

Just tell them owt 'at suits them,
    They're riddy to believe't;
If t' treùth wad nobbut grieve them,
    They'd rayder be deceiv't.
Tell them 'at Winter's sleepin',
    They'll laugh at what ye say;
Bit aw their silly jeerin'
    'Ill nut mak March be May.

Wi' that sec sweels o' laughin',
    Brast oat o' ivvery side;
An' spread ower hills an' valleys,
    'Cross t' country far an' wide.
Burds, trees, an' flures aw join't in't,
    Fra t' biggest, aye, to t' least;
Till t' echo fra Helvellyn,
    Rang far up Scawfell breest.

At last grim Winter snworin',
 Up in a snow-druft theer,
Sprang up an' thunner't madly,
 "What's aw this din I hear?
Shut up your buds an' blossoms,
 Your seasons larn to know;
Keen frost, gang stop their silly pranks;
 Blow fiercely east wind, blow!"

Seùn t' burds war sad an' silent,
 An' t' flures their heids low hung:
Bit t' pollard growl't oot gruffly,
 "I telt you Spring was wrang.
When t' best o' frinds advise ye,
 Ye'll hev your awn daft way;
As if a sunny mwornin'
 Wad mak March into May!"

### Auld Cursmas

Spring, summer, an' autumn war here an' ur gone,
An' winter, coàld winter, ageàn hes com on;
Poor robin's at t' window to watch for his crumbs,
An' mittens ur laatit for fingers an' thumbs.
Noo cheerful auld Cursmas is on us yance mair,
Wi' his lang snowy beard an' his thin silver hair;
An' a smile on his feàce, as merry as when
Oor greit, greit granfadders war nobbut young men.
He ses, (as he hotches his shooders,) ses he,
"Ye'r yule logs git riddy, I's cummin', ye see;
Ye'r misseltoe bunches on t' mid-ceilin's hing;
Ye'r laurels an' hollies wi' red berries bring.

I's cummin', I's cummin', auld wives beàk ye'r pies;

Some big uns, some laal uns, some ivvery size;

Ye'r frinds 'ill be cummin' expectin' to meet,

A reet hearty welcome their cummin' to greet;

Ye fwok 'at hev plenty, bring oot ye'r good cheer;

An' doff off ye'r churlishness noo when I's here.

Put a smile on ye'r feàces, an' banish yer cares;

Forgit aw ye'r seàvin', ye'r banks, an' ye'r shares!

Just think hoo ye've prosper't sen I was here last;

An' shew yoursels grateful for aw blessin's past;

Ye've hed luck i' handfuls, an' joy i' full weight,

While some hev hed laal bit a toil an' a feight.

Just oppen ye'r hearts an' ye'r hands for a while—

Ye hev't in ye'r power to mak poverty smile;

An' t' greitest o' blessin's I bring i' my train,

Is t' sympathy shewn to poor misery an' pain.

Help that misery to lessen, an' than nivver fear,

Ye'll hev what I wish ye—a Happy New Year!


## *Political Economy*


TOM.        What thinks t'e Dick aboot aw thur strikes, an' turnoots, an' lockoots, an' things 'at t' papers ur full on ivvery week? What's this warld gantè git teù efter a bit, I wonder; theer use to be nowt o' t' mak when thee an' me war young.

DICK.        Neah, neah! fifty or sixty years hev meàde a girt change i' t' way o' carryin' on, an' I think t' meàst part o' things ur chang't for t' better. Theer' some fwok 'ill maunder on an' talk aboot good auld times, an' hoo fwok use to deù lang sen; bit I think theer' nut yan in a thoosand 'at ur alive noo, 'at wad care to leeve as they leev't, an don as they don't, or deù a deal o' things as they dud three scwore year sen.

TOM.        Mebby nut: bit hoo aboot thur trades unions, an' strikes, an' sec like—ur they aw for good? Ur they aw improvements, thinks t'e?

DICK.          Theer issent a bit o' doot bit trades unions hev deùn a deal
o' good to wark-fwok, i' t'way o' gitten them better wages, shorter 'oors, an'
sec like; an' strikes, for aw they cause a deal o' distress, an' deù ill eneùf t' time
they last ur like war an' some udder bad things, necessary evils, mebby. Thoo
sees, when t' men think 'at they sud hev mair wage, an' t' maisters doon't
want to gi' them't, an' beàth sides think they're reet, an' beàth git stupid, it
ends wi' a strike, an' beàth parties mebby throw twice as mickle oot o' their
pockets as owt they war disputin' aboot.

TOM.          Thoo talks aboot necessary evils, an' theer seems to be
laal doot bit they're varra girt evils; bit for my part I cannot see 'at they're
necessary at aw. Theer nivver use to be owt o' t' kind lang sen. Wark-fwok
dud withoot them than. What's t reason they cannot deù withoot them noo?

DICK.          They dud withoot them, we know; an' they dud withoot a
lot o' mair things 'at they hev noo. Thoo knows 'at they use to be treatit like
dogs, while they leev't like pigs. It use to be 'at if a fellow waddent work as
lang 'oors, an' for as laal a wage as a maister thowt fit, he mud gang whoar he
like't: an' if, as it oft happen't, he duddent know what way to gang to mend
his-sel, he hed to grub away fra leet to dark for a canny laal. Thoo knows
them lines by Bobby Burns:—

> See yonder poor, o'erlabour'd wight,
> So abject, mean, and vile,
> Who begs a brother of the earth
> To give him leave to toil:
> And see his lordly fellow worm
> The poor petition spurn,
> Unmindful, though a weeping wife,
> And helpless offspring mourn.

That's t' way 'at labourin' fwok war situatit i' Burns' time, aboot fower scwore
year sen. A deàl o' that's alter't noo, an' t' rest 'ill be alter't i' time, I've laal
fear, when worken fwok hev gitten to thinkin' for theirsels, an' understandin'
things better.

TOM.　　　What wad t' e gang farder yet? It seems to me 'at things hev geàn ower far noo, for wages ur gitten to sec a pitch, an' t' 'oors 'at they work for them sa' short, 'at if they alter much mair i' t' seàm direction, t' men 'ill git to be maisters, an' t' maisters 'ill hev to be t' men.

DICK.　　　Thoo needent be a bit flate o' that. Money's t' girt reùler i' this warld, an' them 'at hev it 'ill allus be t' maisters, as lang as t' warld stands. When theer a strike, an' t' maisters give in, it's nut because they're fworc't teù't, it's because they see 'at they're mair oot o' pocket ivvery week wi' aw their mills an' machinery stannin' idle, nor they wad be if they paid t' men t' advance o' wages 'at they wantit.

TOM.　　　Bit I see 'at theer some o' thur newspaper fellows 'at think fwok sud aw be equal, 'at theer sud be neah upper, an' middle, an' lower classes, 'at yan's as good as anudder, an' 'at aw fwok through t' country sud be iv a height. What does thoo think aboot that?

DICK.　　　I'll tell the' what I think. I think theer' a laal bit o' treùth in't, an' a girt deàl o' balderdash. Fwok ur aw meàd i' t' seàm way, o' t' seàm mak o' stuff, an' for aw they hevvent aw t' seàm gifts an' ability to larn gien, if they war aw browt up i' t' seàm way, an' aw hed t' seàm chances, theer' some 'at wad be gayly nar t' top o' tree 'at ur nut far fra t' boddom noo. I hevvent a grain o' doot bit theer' as good men i' in ivvery respect to be pick't oot iv a gedd'rin' o' five or six hundred workin' men as theer is oot o' t' seàm number in a Queen's drawin'-room, where nowt bit t' nobs ur alloo't to gang. What than! that doesn't bring us a bit nearer bein' equal. Neah body 'at hed as mickle sense as my dog wad ivver talk sec rubbish as that.

TOM.　　　What, if t' heigher an' t' lower classes ur aw meàd o' t' seàm way, o' t' seàm mak o' stuff, an' hev t' seàm talents gien to them, I cannot see enny reason 'at teàn sud be sa mickle abeùn t' tudder. Can thoo?

DICK.　　　Aye, reasons plenty to satisfy me 'at it issent possible 'at aw fwok ivver can be equal in enny country. I' t' furst pleàce, as I sed befwore, t' rich fwok 'ill allus be ower t' poor fwok, as lang as t' warld lasts, because money 'ill allus buy power, an' respect, an' ameàst ivvery thing else 'at sets ya body abeùn anudder. I' t' second pleàce, theer 'ill allus be rich an' poor fwok, as lang as theer' seàvers an' spenders, misers an' waistrels, generous fwok an' shabby fwok, cunnin' fwok an' simple fwok, honest fwok an' rogues, wise fwok an' feùls. I'll admit 'at a good, wise, an' clever man, let him be ivver sa' poor, is better in ivvery way nor a rich man 'at's nut particularly owder clever or good; bit t' rich fellow will be a lang way abeùn t' poor fellow for aw that. If a man be ivver sa' clever, he mun use his cleverness to git money befwore he mun expect to hev much owder power or influence amang fwok. An' than t' best reason iv aw 'at fwok cannot be equal is, 'at they nivver try; bit i'steed o' that, aw t' fwok i' t' warld ur reàmen t' best they can to git yan abeùn anudder. It's i' t' varra nater o' things, an' it's t' nater o' t' beast 'at maks t' hair growe. We needent gang up to lords an' dukes, an' doon to tramps an' beggars, to see hoo fwok set theirsels up yan abeùn anudder. Cannot we see eneùf on 't i' ivvery parish an' neighbourhood? Furst, theer' t' set wi' their three or fower hundred a year a piece, 'at can leeve a kind o' independent, an' hev "squire" set on t' back o' their letters. If they or their wives or dowters ivver mix amang t' farmers or tradesfwok, they tak good care to mak them understand hoo far they've condescendit, an' sec an' honour they've deùn them. Next theer' t' farmers, an' tradesmen, an' their wives an' dowters, wad a deal o' them throw up their nwoses, an' put on a leùk as if they'd been suppin' vinegar, if they war to gang tull a party, an' fand two or three sarvants or laberin' fwok invitit to tak tea wi' them. An' if yan gangs lower still to 'mang a lot o' sarvants, theer 'ill be upper sarvants, an' middle sarvants, an' under sarvants, an' they'll be yan lworden't ower anudder t' best they can. I hevvent a bit o' doot i' my awn mind, bit if theer war just three fwok left in a country, theer wad be t' maister, t' heid sarvent, an' t' slush.

TOM.          What's t' meanin' o' aw this noise aboot liberty, equality, an' fraternity, 'at they mak i' France? I see 'at theer' some i' this country bodderen' aboot it an' aw. If it be as thoo ses, 'at fwok cannot aw be equal, what's t' use o' talkin' sa' much aboot it?

DICK.          Thoo cuddent tak a better example nor France to preùve 'at fwok cannot aw be equal in enny country, for they've talk't aboot it noo for abeùn a hundred year, an' mair they talk an' farder they seem to git away fra 't.

TOM.          By jing! They've deùn mair ner talk sometimes. I was readin' t' tudder day aboot t' French revolution 'at began i' sebbenteen hundred an' eighty-nine; an' a bonny time it was amang them for menny a year efter.

What! they beheidit t' king, an' t' queen, an' hundreds o' girt fwok beside, an' teuk what they hed, an' dud as they like't wi' 't. Yan mud ha' thowt 'at when they hed o' things to bits, 'at they mud ha' meàd aw fwok equal than if ivver it could ha' been deùn.

DICK.     Enny feùl may poo things doon, thoo knows, bit it taks a chap 'at hes some skill to put them up ageàn. Enny girt lumpheid could poo oor clock to bits; bit if he dud it in t' crazy way 'at they poo't things to bits i' France, it wad tak a clever fellow to put it togidder ageàn; for varra likely t' better hofe o' t' wheels wad be smash't. Beside that, by t' accoonts 'at I've read aboot t' revolution o' eighty-nine; an' menny a revolution they've hed i' France sen that—they nivver try't to mak things equal, bit war allus feighten whilk o' them mud hev t' meàst say, an' tryin' yan to crow ower anudder; an' if thoo taks nwotish, it allus happen't 'at them fellows 'at meàd meàst noise aboot liberty an' equality, an' shootit t' loodest, "Doon wi' t' tyrants!" war allus t' biggest tyrants theirsels as seùn as ivver they gat t' upper hand. They may talk aboot equality as much as they like, an' turnt what side up they like, an' what side afwore, an' it 'ill allus amoont to t' seàm thing, an' they'll just be as far off 't as they war when Sampson was a laal lad.

TOM.     Theer' anudder thing I see i' t' papers: theer' some o' them speechifyen fellows think 'at t' land's gitten into far ower few hands, an' 'at it sud be dividit oot afresh amang mair fwok, an' into less bits. What thinks t'e aboot that?

DICK.     Aye, that's anudder silly nwotion, i' my opinion. I cannot see 'at land's enny different fra owt else 'at can be bowt an' selt. Yan may see advertisements o' land to sell ivvery week, an' enny body can buy't 'at hes money to pay for 't wi'; an' when a man hes bowt it an' pay't for 't, I can't see bit it's as much his awn, to deù what he likes wi', as t' hat I hev on my heid, or t' shoon I hev on my feet ur mine to weer, or give away, or deù what I like wi'.

TOM.     Bit they say 'at thur girt fwok tak far ower mickle o' t' land for their awn plesser an' amusement, makkin't into deer-parks, an' plessergrunds, an' sec like. I hardly think 'at that can be reet, when aw t' land i' t' country 'ill nut growe as much as 'ill feed t' fwok 'at ur in 't.

DICK.    It may seem nut at t' furst leùk; an' efter aw I think theer' nut sa menny fwok 'at wad vwote for aw t' plesser grunds, an' aw t' fine auld trees aboot t' gentlemen's hooses, bein' reùtit up, an' t' grund plantit wi' cabbige an' taties. We hear a deal aboot liberty, an' freedom, an' sec like, an' we wad grummel neah laal if theer was a law mead forbidden' us to plant in oor gardens a bit flure, or owt bit what yan could eat; an' yet that wad be just as reasonable as to forbid t' gentry to mak plesser grunds.

TOM.    What aboot thur girt deer-parks 'at they tell aboot than? I think it mun be a girt weàst to keep sec demains o' fine land, wi' nowt i' them bit them things 'at ur likely good for laal bit to leùk at.

DICK.    I fancy a deal o' t' fine demains o' land 'ill be laal bit craggy moors, an' grund 'at wad nivver pay for cultivaten if yan hed it for nowt, mebby; for I think 'at t' meàst part o' t' landlwords know t' vally o' land ower weel to let it lie idle if they thowt they could git enny rent for 't. At enny rate, I think 'at a man whedder he be a nobleman or a poor fellside statesman, if he hes land 'at's fairly an' honestly his awn, hes a parfet reet to put it to enny, or whativver use he hes a mind. I think 'at if a guvverment begins to meddle wi' sec things as them, they'll hev to deù away wi' aw useless things whativver. It wad be just as reasonable to forbid thee or me to keep a pet dog or a pet burd, as to forbid a gentleman to keep deer, for aw t' difference theer is i' t' two things is 'at t' gentleman can affword to keep deer, an' we can affword to keep nowt bigger ner a dog or a burd. They'll nin o' them leeve withoot meat; an' if theer be enny difference t' deer ur o' mair use, for they're eatable, an' a dog issent. T' treùth o' t' matter is, Tom, a deal o' thur fellows 'at mak speeches an' write in t' newspapers, ur wonderfully clever at stringen words togidder, an' makken them leùken sa plausable an' fine 'at it's neàh wonder if they deceive a deal o' fwok 'at willent bodder to think for thersels. If thoo'll tak yan o' their fine clues an' hev patience to reàvell't oot for theesel, thoo'll oft finnd at t' garn 'at aw t' fine wurds ur strung on 's nowt bit shoddy; an' when it's brokken at two or three pleàces, they're nowder summet ner nowt.

# SERIES 3 (1886)

### *A Grummel or a Grean!*

It's grummel! grummel! grummel!
   Fra mwornin' still till neet,
Fra ya week en' till t'tudder,
   Theer' nivver nowt 'at's reet:
Fra ya year en' till t' tudder,
   It's just a constant feight,
It's allus grummel! grummel!
   His feàce is nivver streight!

I nivver saw a smile on't
   'At stay'd till yan could speak;
By t' sunshine gits ower t' nwose on 't,
   T' clood comes on t' tudder cheek.
It's grummel! grummel! grummel!
   It's owder ower het,
Or else it's ower frosty,
   Or else it's owcr wet.

If t' sun shines het i' summer,
   Befwore a week's geàn ower,
Aw things 'ill be clean burn't up,
   Withoot theer comes a shooer.
An' if it rains i' hay-time,
   It's sek a desperat keàse,
T' rain-cloods ur nowt for blackness
   To t' cloods theer on his feàce.

It's allus grummel! grummel!

   Beàth oot o' dooers an' in;

At mwornin' when I waken

   He's riddy to begin,

To grummel! grummel! grummel!

   Till bedtime comes ageàn:

It's seldom 'at theer owt else,

   Withoot it be a greàn!


## What T' Wind sed


YA roughish neet, when t' wind was heigh,

   An' I laid warm an'snug i' bed,

I lissen't as it howl'd aroond,

   An' thowt I knew just what it sed.


It whissel't lood, an' seem't to say,

   "Just wait a bit till I git in:"

Says I, thoo'll mebby be misteàn,

   My cottage wo's ur nut sa thin.


I thowt it hard my words, for't com

   To t' window sash wi' sek a bang,

An' seem't to say, "I'll come in here:"

   Thinks I, thoo'll mebby finnd thoo's wrang.


At t' chimley top it rwoar'd oot next,

   An' seem't to say, "I'll come reet doon:"

Thinks I, auld wind, thoo's wrang ageàn,

   I hev na firepleàce in my room.

It madly shak't t' lowse sleàts on t' reùf,

    An' than awhile it went away;

Bit com back seùn, an' when it com,

    "I will be at the'!" it wad say.


At last it seem't to settle doon,

    Intul a low an' murmurin' sound,

I shut my eyes an' fell asleep,

    An' when I waken't aw was lownd.


## *Laal Jenny's say*


Thoo needn't come smirkin' an' leùkin' sa pleas't:

Bit noo, as thoo hes cum't, I'll git my mind eas't;

I cuddent ha' sleep't mickle, up or abed,

Till I'd seen the', an' telt the', an' hed my say sed.


I've hard aw aboot the'; aye, weel thoo may glower;

Thoo'll nut winnd me up as thoo's oft deùn befwore:

Oh! what hev I hard? What, I suddent believ't—

Bit quite lang eneùf, I've been blinn't an' deceiv't.


I' that fair feàce o' thine, nowt bit truth I cud see;

Bit noo theer' nowt in 't, bit deceit an' a le:

An' them whiskers sa fine, 'at my fancy yance teùk,

They're nobbut to hide thy ill sinister leùk.


Thoo needn't deny't, for thoo's guilty, na doot;

Thoo needn't mak't strange, an' ax what it's aboot:

For thoo knows weel eneùf, what a taistrel thoo's been;

Theer issent a warse here an' Carel atween.

Thoo gangs, slenkin' off, furst to yan, than anudder;
It matters nut much, whether t' dowter or t' mudder:
It's furst 'at comes handy, 'at's reet still for thee;
Bit thoo needn't come smirkin' an' kneppin' at me.

It's aw stuff an' nonsense! Aye, mebby it may;
Bit I'll tak the' contrary to what thoo may say:
Thoo's meàd it thy brag, 'at thoo welcome cud gang,
To enny i' t' deàl—bit thoo'll finnd thyseI wrang.

Thoo thinks 'at thoo's cunnin', an' lang i' bein' catch't;
Bit when thoo gits weddit, I whop tho'll be match't
Wi' an ill scoàdin' wife, 'at 'ill gi' the' thy pay,
An' cwoàm the' thy toppin oot ten times a day.

Thoo'd better be gaan, for I've noo sed my say;
Thoo's nut welcome here, sa thoo'd best bide away:
An' next when thoo brags o' thy sweethearts sa menny,
An' neàms them aw ower, thoo may leave oot laal Jenny.

### *A queerish mak iv a dream!*

I hed a dream, an' in my dream
    I thowt 'at I was deid,
A windin' sheet was roond me twin't,
    A neet cap on my heid;
An' I was in a coffin laid—
    Bit what meàd aw sa queer
Was, when I thowt 'at I was deid,
    I beàth could see an' hear!

I thowt 'at two priests hed come in,
    To tak me seàf away,
An' lock me up whoar I mud bide
    Till t' last greit judgment day.
Teàn hed a serpleth on as white
    As enny druft o' snow,
An' t'udder hed a silk goon on,
    As black as enny crow.

I saw them eye teàn tudder ower,
    When they com in at t' dooer,
An' thowt theer mud be summet wrang,
    They leùk't sa parlish soor;
At last teà priest to t' tudder sed,
    "That goon o'thine's quite wrang;
Is that black thing a likely dress
    For whoar we hev to gang?

"It's liker far for puttin' on
    To gang to t' pleàce below;
What! leùk at mine, hoo fine it is,
    As white as druftit snow:
Just gang thy ways reet heàm ageàn,
    An' throw that goon away,
An' put a serpleth on like mine—
    Thoo's just a parfet fly.

Ses t' udder priest, "I wadden't weer
    A popish thing like that;
Beside, thoo's gitten on thy heid
    A reg'lar Pusey hat:
Thoo's just gaen streight on t' rwoad to Rome,
    An' that's whoar thoo'll seùn be;
Thoo'll hev to tak them fallals off,
    If thoo wad gang wi' me!"

They sed a gay deal mair ner that,
    An' cross eneùf, an' aw;
An' argee't 'at they beàth war reet,
    An' sed they'd gang to t' law.
I thowt they fratch't an' argee't on
    Till it was var' nar neet;
Bit mair they fratch't an' less I knew
    Which priest was narrest reet.

An' warse ner that, when it grew dusk,
    I saw come sneakin'
Anudder chap, wi' lang black hair
    An' yellow wrinkel't skin,
A tail he held atween his legs,
    An' horns grew on his heid;
To tell me who that auld chap was,
    Theer wassent mickle need!

I saw t' auld thief cooer doon i' t' neùk
    I watch't his kneàvish leer,
An' guess't he aim't to slipe wi' me
    While t' priests war fratchin' theer.
He'd meàd his-sel cockseùr, na doot,
    'At seùn as it was dark,
He'd easy git me seàf away,
    While they fratch't ower the'r sarks.

Reet flate I was, bit cuddent shoot,
   My tongue was deid eneùf,
For aw my een could see quite plain
   Auld Clooty's cloven heùf.
At last some awful screech I meàd;
    "What's t' matter?" t' auld wife sed;
That roos't me up, an' fain I was
   'At I was seàf a-bed.


## T' Woefu' Partin'


FOR fifty year' o' ups an' doons
   They'd travvel'd side by side;
An' teàn to t' tudder still hed been
   A faithful frind an' guide.
Laal wonder 'twas when t' summons com,
   An' teàn was caw't away,
'At tudder mourn't sa bitterly,
   An' hardly care't to stay.


He leùk't far back through memory's e'e,
   For fifty year' an' mair;
When he was merry as a burd,
   An' she was young an' fair.
He thowt aboot that far off time,
   When they two met at furst:
Na wonder noo when she was gone,
   His heart was like to burst.

His thowts went wanderin' back to t' time
   When they two startit life;
When she hed nowt bit him to love,
   An' he luv'd bit his wife.
An' than when darlin's, yan by yan,
   War sent their love to share;
He knew 'at deeper grew their love,
   As greiter grew their care.


An' than he thowt hoo as they com,
   They went off yan by yan;
Till t' last was gone, an' they war left
   Just their two sel's ageàn.
An' they war groun beàth auld an' grey;
   An' 't wassent much they care't
For owt at t' warld could gi' them noo,
   As lang as beàth war spare't.


Bit deith hed caw't for teàn to gang,
   An' nin hur life could seàve;
An' sad it was to see t' auld man
   Stand totterin' by her greàv.
He teùk a last lang leùk, an' than
   He slowly turn't away,
An' murmur'd low, "I's fain to think,
   I hevvent lang to stay."

## *Tom Briggs*

Tom Briggs an' me war scheùlmates yance;
    Bit Tom's been lang away,
An's just cum't doon to see his frinds'—
    I met him t' tudder day.
He's just t' auld chap for aw the world,
    As when he went fra heàm;
A deàl wi' stinkin' pride git spoil't,
    Bit Tom bides allus t' seàm.


Ses I to Tom, "Reet fain I is—
    This minds yan o' lang sen;
Theer' some sa stuck up when they come,
    Auld frinds they dooent ken.
Hoo is't 'at thoo keeps free fra pride?
    Theer' some 'at boonce an' strut;
It maks me mad as a poo't swine,
    When they sec capers cut."


Ses Tom, "It's mebby want o' sense,
    Or, m'appen, want o' thowt;
Bit dunnet think 'at stinkin' pride
    Is aw fra Lunnen browt:
I've travel't England thro' an' thro',
    Fra teà end on't to t' tudder;
An' pride I fand at ivvery pleàce,
    I' ya shap or anudder.

"Fra lwords an' dukes, to tramps on t' rwoad,
    I nivver saw yan yet,
'At care't to bide in t' lower room
    When he could heigher git:
An' if thoo'll leùk aboot the' here,
    Thoo needn't leùk sa lang,
To see some fra the'r brudders turn,
    Wi' finer fwok to gang.


"Thoo munnet think 'at pride's confin't
    To him 'at struts an' brags;
Theer' pride 'at's whisht as enny moose,
    An' pride 'at's don't i' rags.
Theer' some, neàh doot, quite prood to think
    They're humbier far nor t' rest;
An' whoar theer' hoaf a duzzen rogues,
    Yan's prood to think he's t' best.


It's want o' thowt 'at maks us prood;
    If we could nobbut see
Oorsels as udders see us, barne,
    Sec things wad nivver be.
Bit while we're watchin' udder fwok,
    An' huntin' for a fawt,
We hev yan riddy catch't at heàm,
    If we could nobbut know't."

## *Thowts aboot t' War (1870)*

### BOB

Thoo's gitten t' paper—is t'er owt
   'At's fresh fra t' war to-day?
I hard they'd hed anudder feight,
   An' t' French hed run away.

### CHARLIE

They've hed anudder feight for seùr,
   A dreadful feight it's been;
A murderin' job, fra what I read,
   As ivver yet was seen.
An' t' French as good a threshin' gat,
   As ivver they've hed yet;
Bit run away they dudden't deù
   Because they cudden't git.

### BOB

If they war lick't, an' cudden't run,
   They likely mud give in;
Bit as I leùk, theer' laal i' t' odds,
   Whilk lwoses an' whilk wins.
Beàth sides hev thoosands kilt an' leàm't,
   An' varra much I doot,
'At owder side could tell yan what
   Aw t' feightin's been aboot.

## CHARLIE

That's true eneùf. I'll tell the', Bob,
    If two girt country cloons,
Like thee an' me, sud git on t' spree,
    An' knock teàn tudder doon;
We'd be caw't drukken blackguards, an'
    Afwore oor betters browt;
Bit mair they kill, an' mair they leàm,
    An' better men they're thowt.

I saw two lads in t' garden theer,
    Nut mair nor teàble height,
Aboot the'r marbles they'd fawn oot,
    An' nowt wad deù bit feight.
Teà lad—an' it was t' bigger, teù,
    Hed bully't lang an' sair,
When t' laal un threw his jacket off,
    An' sed he'd tak na mair.

He buckel't in, an' dreàv him back,
    Farder, an' farder still;
While t' girt un shootit, "If thoo does,
    I'll gi' the' 't, aye, I will!"

Bit t' laal un doon't him on his back,
    An' telt him to ax pardon;
Says t' tudder lad, "I nivver will,
    Till thoo gangs oot o' t' garden."
I thowt hoo like that was to t' French:
    They say they'll nivver 'gree,
Till t' Germans aw gang oot o' France,
    An' that they'll let them see.

BOB

If Buonaparte an' t' Prussian king,
    Like t' two laal lads i' t' garden,
Hed bray't teàn tudder's heids a bit,
    It matter't nut a fardin';
Bit when theer' tens o' thoosands kilt,
    An' thoosands cripples meàd,
I think if they've aw t' bleàm to bear,
    They'll hev a gey good leàd.

## *The Dialects of Cumberland and the Lake Country*

EVERY country, or at least every civilized country, has a standard or written language which is used both in speaking and writing by all educated natives; and all forms of speech used in particular districts of the same country, and differing in any material degree from the written language, are termed Dialect.

Any one who imagines that dialect consists of nothing more than corruptions of, and badly-spelt, English, makes a great mistake. The fact is, that the English dialects are much older than the English language as spoken at the present time, and so far from their being corruptions of, and departures from, the standard tongue, that tongue has in a great measure been derived from the dialects.

The language of the Britons before the Roman invasion was Celtic, and it does not appear to have been very much changed during the three or four hundred years of Roman occupation. A good many Roman words, no doubt, took root, several of which still remain in the language, but the ancient speech of the country continued much the same as it had been before.

During the next six centuries, however, owing to the continual incursions and settlement of so many different peoples, both German and Scandinavian, mostly speaking different languages or dialects, the speech of the island seems to have been completely changed, and the old Celtic tongue, as spoken by the ancient Britons, almost totally obliterated, except in the remote districts of Wales, Cornwall, and the north of Scotland. During the period named, there was scarcely a kingdom or tribe in the west of Europe, from the south of Germany to Iceland, but sent its quota of emigrants to Britain; and the consequence was, that a number of dialects came to be spoken in the island, differing more or less from each other.

As printing was not known for some centuries later, there are not many specimens extant of the scanty literature of that time; but the manuscripts which are in existence differ so much in character from each other, that it is more than probable that one which was written in one part of the island would not be understood in another. In the eighth century, according to Bede, there were five languages spoken in England, no one of which was quite uniform in itself, but each consisted of a group of dialects agreeing with each other in certain characteristics, just as the Cumberland and Westmorland may agree with each other at the present time.

The dialects which approach nearest in grammar and construction to standard English, are those of Huntingdon, Rutland, Northampton, and in Lincolnshire; and it seems to have been from a conglomeration of these dialects, as written by Wycliffe and Chaucer, that the English language first began to take a regular form.

Wycliffe died in 1385, and Chaucer in 1400, close on five centuries ago; and during all that long period, the language has gone on improving, and crystallizing as it were, discarding a word here, and picking up another there, until it has become what it now is—the most comprehensive and popular form of speech in the world. We may judge of the slow and gradual process which it has passed through, by comparing the writings of Wycliffe and Chaucer with those of Spenser and Shakespeare, who lived two centuries later, and whose language, though differing materially from the English of to-day, is much nearer to it than that of the older writers.

Some years ago, Charles Mackay published a volume entitled, *The Lost Beauties of the English Language*, which is simply a glossary of words which were formerly part of the English language but have now gone out of use. On looking it through, I made out a list of the words in it which are still in use in the Cumberland dialect, and on counting them over, I found that there were very nearly three hundred such. It would be too much to say that they are all beauties, but certainly they are many of them very expressive; and to me it seems doubtful whether the words substituted for some of them are improvements or not. To take one as a sample. There was a good old-fashioned word, "Flit," which meant to disappear suddenly; so that if a person disappeared, or got out of the way suddenly, he was said to have "flitted," but now it is fashionable to say, that he has skedaddled. I think the old word was much easier to say, or to write, and, moreover, was much more elegant.

One of the five languages, or groups of dialects, mentioned by Bede and other old writers, was the Northumbrian, consisting of the dialects spoken in the old Saxon kingdom of Northumbria, which, as its name implies, included that part of England north of the Humber. Some writers on the subject indeed, have included the south of Scotland in the same group of dialects Firth of Forth and the Clyde. However that might be, there can be no doubt about the Lake District dialects forming part of the old Northumbrian tongue. The Lake Country dialects would of course comprise those of Cumberland, Westmorland, and North Lancashire; and these, in common with all the Northumbrian dialects, though differing to some extent in vocabulary and pronunciation, have a general agreement in construction and grammar.

To those who have not paid much attention to dialects, and have only heard them spoken occasionally, it would almost seem a misuse of words to apply the term grammar to them at all; and if we meant the grammar of standard English, it would be so. But there are other grammars besides ordinary English ones.

When I published a volume of Cumberland Talk, a few years since, I made some allusion in the preface to the difficulty of writing the dialect properly, on account of the tendency of those who spoke it to disregard all the rules of grammar.

Dr. Murray, who has spent most of his life in studying languages and dialects, and who now stands very high as a linguist, wrote a friendly letter soon after to set me right on that subject, and in criticising the remark that I had made respecting those who spoke dialect disregarding the rules of grammar, asked the following questions. Which grammar? Portuguese or Hebrew? or Sanscrit? or Southern English? or Cumberland? What are the rules of grammar? How are they discovered? To the last question, he gave the answer: Simply by observing the tendencies or practices which those who speak it have, and registering them. He then went on to say: "Your error is, however, a very natural one, for all who write down their own dialect. They are ashamed of its most characteristic features, which they have in the nursery, and by the schoolmaster, been instructed to call bad grammar, and it has not yet dawned upon them that as a dialect has its own sounds and its own words, it has also its own way of putting its words together. I remember when I had the same weakness, and in my ignorance began also to set myself up as grammatical critic of my dialect, before I had ever investigated its grammar, or dreamed that it had one to investigate. But fortunately the light burst upon me when I began to read old northern literature, and was astonished to find that what I, poor ignorant and presumptuous being, was styling corruption, had been the rule of northern speech as far as I could trace it back." That was Dr. Murray's opinion.

He also gave me the following quotation, bearing on the same subject, from the writings of Prince Lucien Buonaparte, whom he styled the greatest of all dialect philologists. The Prince says: "Language is a natural production, living and growing, as much as a tree or a flower, and no natural development is to be called a corruption. The only corrupters of dialect that I know of, are the literary men who improve nature by writing them, not as they are, but according to their notions of what they ought to be, that is, in accordance with rules of grammar derived from other languages with which they may be acquainted, as though grammar were anything but a systematic statement of usage. What would be thought of the botanist who should mutilate his specimens of flowers and plants to improve their symmetry, or make them fit into prearranged artificial systems, instead of following nature, and drawing his laws and systems from her?"

It may be in the recollection of some, that about a quarter of a century ago Prince Lucien Buonaparte had the Song of Solomon rendered into twenty-two of the English dialects, which being afterwards published, form a useful reference for those who wish to examine and compare the different forms of speech. With all due deference, however, to so high an authority, it must be confessed that His Royal Highness was most unfortunate in his choice of a subject for his illustrations, the language of Solomon's Song being most unsuitable for rendering into dialect, the leading points of which are best shown in subjects more homely, and to some extent humorous.

The idea, however, of having one particular subject written in all the dialects of the country, was a good one, and the Buonapartean versions of the Song of Solomon are extremely useful for showing the grammatical construction of the different dialects. Any one, by comparing them, may, without much trouble, discover in what they agree and in what they differ. To make my meaning plainer, I will quote a couple of verses from the second chapter of the Cumbrian version, as rendered by William Dickinson, for the Prince.

The Bible version reads, "I am the rose of Sharon, and the lily of the valleys. As the lily among thorns, so is my love among the daughters." The dialect version is, "I's t' rwose o' Sharon, An' t' lily o' t' valleys. My leùvv wad leùkk amang t' rest, as a lily wad leùkk amang thorns."

It will be noticed that instead of saying, "I am the rose of Sharon," the Cumbrian says, "I's t' rose o' Sharon." "I's" means "I is." And Mr. Garnett, who is a great authority on dialects, tells us that although to say "I is" would be a gross violation of English grammar, it is in strict agreement with the usage of the Danes, who always say or write what is equivalent to "I is," "Thou is," "He is."

Another peculiarity of the Northern speech, as shown three times over in the former of the verses quoted, is the contraction of the definite article; thus, instead of saying, "I am the rose of Sharon, and the lily of the valleys," it is, "I's t' rose o' Sharon, an' t' lily o' t' valleys." In the same verse it will also be seen that the conjunction, "and," is shortened to an', and the preposition "of" to o'. "I's t' rose o' Sharon," not "of Sharon;" "an' t' lily o' t' valley," not "and the lily." There are several other points in the idiom which might be illustrated from these versions; but what I wish to draw your attention to just now is, that those which I have alluded to, as well as several others which I will note, are peculiar to and nearly general through all the Northern Dialects. Out of fourteen specimens of the Northern group, nine are "I's t' rose o' Sharon, an' t' lily o' t' valleys," and from my own knowledge of dialects, I am certain that two more ought to have been written in the same way.

In justification of this assertion, I will quote a short extract from a note by the Rev. J. C. Atkinson, editor of Mr. Peacock's Glossary of the Dialect of the Hundred of Lonsdale, in the County of Lancashire.

Mr. Atkinson writes, "Idiomatic vernacular is one thing, ordinary English in masquerade another; and, unfortunately, the latter is most frequently made to do duty in professing specimens of English dialects. No doubt the selection of Solomon's Song for conversion was unhappy, and added to the difficulties the translators would have to contend with in any effort of the kind; but still it is impossible to overlook the fact that more than one of the versions are open to grave objections."

Returning to the examination of the same specimens , and adding two more to the nine which read, "I's t' rose o' Sharon," we find eleven out of the fourteen in the Northern group to be uniform, while the remaining three, viz., South East Lancashire, and two of Yorkshire, together with Norfolk, Lincolnshire, Devon, and Cornwall, begin the verse with "I am," or something equivalent to it, as, "I'm" or "Awm." The four remaining specimens, viz., Somersetshire, Dorsetshire, Wiltshire, and Sussex are, "I be the rose of Sharon."

I stated before that there were many other peculiarities of idiom in the Northumbrian speech which might be shewn from the Buonapartean versions to be common to the whole district; but, to avoid repetition, I will endeavour to supply some more homely illustrations, which may probably serve as examples. There seems to be some inconsistency in the following. A person will say, "Tom an' Jack's gone for a helliday, an' they're cummin' back next week." You will notice that Tom and Jack is gone, but, they are coming back. There is a singular verb in the former part of the sentence, and a plural one in the latter. This seems quite irregular, but nevertheless it is a usage common to all dialect-speaking people in the Northern counties. Thus, one farmer will say to another, "Taties is cheap this year;" and the other will reply, "Aye, they ur, varra."

The next peculiarity of Northern grammar to be noticed is, that it has no genitive case. A person speaking dialect, instead of saying "William's wife's sister," would say, "Willie' wife' sister;" and instead of saying, "Robert's hat," would say, "Bob' hat."

The word "While" is frequently used in the dialect in the place of until. A person will say, "Wait here while I come back." This is a very old usage, as it occurs in Northumbrian Gospels, which are supposed to have been written at the beginning of the tenth century, or earlier. There in Matthew i. 24, is the passage, "And he knew her not while she brought forth her firstborn son."

In the Cumberland dialect, "While" is pronounced "Whell;" a person will say, "Wait whell I gitten my dinner."

The word "At," in the dialect, is put in the place of "To." Thus, a Cumbrian who has been repairing anything, will say, "I' deùn aw I can at it." There is still another way in which "At" is constantly used in the dialect, but it only seems to be an abbreviation of "That." An example may be given from Dr. Gibson's "Laal Dinah Grayson," where he says—There's nut mickle on her, we ken 'at good stuff Laps up i' laal bundles, an' she's laal eneùf.

There are many other idiomatic peculiarities belonging to the dialect which might be pointed out, but the few examples which I have given may serve, in some degree, to show how the Northern speech differs in its phraseology from ordinary English.

The vocabulary, or number of dialect words now in use in Cumberland is probably between three and four thousand. William Dickinson's Glossary consists of about five thousand words and phrases, while Robert Ferguson's has less than two thousand. As his main object, however, was to give the etymology of the dialect, Mr. Ferguson has left out the phrases and also the words which are derived from each other, and this may in some degree account for the difference The dialect vocabulary, therefore, compared with that found in any ordinary dictionary, is very meagre. Still, it must be borne in mind that nowhere is the speech made up of all dialect words.

Dr. Gibson's specimens come nearest to that spoken in Cumberland at the present time of any of the dialect works, and any one who will take the trouble to examine a page of Folk-Speech, will find that more than one-half the words are ordinary English, and spelt the same. A good many people who try to write dialect, seem to think that the only thing required is to spell the word in some absurd, outlandish way. They spell "cat" with a k, "specimen," with three s's and a z in it, and "physic" must begin with f. At the same time, words which really should be abbreviated into dialect, such as "and" and "the," they generally write in the usual way. 1 would simply observe that such writing is not dialect, but ordinary English made ridiculous.

Although Ferguson, Atkinson, and other writers on the subject may differ to some extent in the etymology of dialect words, there is a general agreement in their derivations which gives a considerable degree of trustworthiness to each of them. On comparing them together, it would seem that about thirty per cent of the dialect words of the northern counties are of Scandinavian origin; about eight per cent. Celtic; two-and-a-half to three per cent. Norman French; and the remainder Saxon and other Germanic roots.

There are certain classes of dialect words which differ in form from ordinary English words of the same meaning; and these, though many people would think them only modern corruptions, can be proved from very old authors to be genuine archaisms. For instance, the English prefix "be," is usually "a" in the dialect; thus, Before" is "Afore," or "Afwore." A person going from home for a few days will say, "I'll be back afwore t' week end." In like manner, "Behind" is "Ahind," or "Ahint," "Between" is "Atween," and "Beside" is "Aside." One person will say to another, "I'll sit doon aside the'." Another peculiarity is that several words which in English begin with "A" or "O," begin with "Y" in the dialect; for instance, "Acre" is "Yacker," "Ace" is "Yas," "Ale" is "Yal," and "Oak" is "Yak." The diphthong "oo" is changed in the dialect to something like "eu," so that "Boot" becomes "Beùt;" "Foot," "Feùt;" "Goose," Geùs;" "Fool," "Feùl;" and "School," "Scheùll."

Again, the English diphthong "oa" is pronounced as if there was a "'w" before it; thus, "Road" becomes "Rwoad; "Boat," "Bwoat;" "Coat," "Cwoat;" and "Goat," "Gwoat." In another class of words the "o" is changed differently. "Stone" becomes "Styàn;" "Bone," "Byàn;" "Gone" is "Geàn;" "Home," "Hyàm;" "Rope" is "Reàp." Also "Lame" is "Lyàm," and "Tame" is "Tyàm."

It must be admitted that many of the foregoing dialect words are very broad and uncouth, and in every way inferior to the English words which they represent; but there are others in the dialect vocabulary which are, as I noted before, very expressive, not at all rough, and for which there are no exact equivalents in ordinary English. I might point out scores of such, but as space is limited, I will take half a dozen almost at random, and endeavour to explain their uses. First, there is "Fash," which means "trouble." A person will say, "I cannot be fash't," or, "Yan's fairly fash't to deith." Then there is "Flaatch," which signifies to wheedle or coax. I once heard a girl who had quarrelled with her sweetheart, say, "Oh, nivver mind, I'll seùn flaatch him up ageàn."

"Gar" is another very expressive word, signifying to force, or compel. A woman will say to a child, "Thoo laal monkey, I'll gar the' gang to t'scheùl." The word "Lait" has two significations: the one is to seek, and the other to bring. A Cumbrian will say, "He's gaen to lait a lost sheep;" or, "He's gaen to lait t' kye in to milk," which are not lost at all. In many country places in the Lake district, when any one dies, two persons from every house within a certain well-defined boundary are invited to the funeral, and the houses within that circle are termed the "Laitin." "Lownd" is another good old Cumbrian word. When the atmosphere is perfectly still, and not a breath of air stirring, it is said to be "Clock lownd." In Dr. Gibson's Folk-Speech we read:—

Ther' cannot be anudder spot so private an' so sweet,
As Billy Watson' lonnin' iv a lownd summer neet.

The last word I will refer to in this class is "Mense," still common enough in country places, and which means something opposite to stinginess. If a woman is kind and hospitable in her own house, she is said to be "A rare menseful body;" while, if she is neither kind nor hospitable, she is said to be a "Menseless creeter." There is a very common saying in the dales, which is, "They've seàv't beàth their meat an' their mense," the meaning of which is, that when one party gives an invitation to another which is not accepted, they are thought to have saved their mense by giving the invitation, and their meat by the other party not accepting it.

I once heard two persons talking over their neighbours' affairs, when one of them remarked of a third person, that he was "Parlish greedy." "Aye," says the other, "Theer' three maks o' greedy. Theer' menseful greedy, an' theer' menseless greedy, an' theer' senseless greedy: an' he's menseless greedy." I think these three terms may be defined as follows: "Menseful greedy" applies to a person who is careful and saving, but who at the same time will not be mean or shabby in anything that he has to do. "Menseless greedy," on the contrary, would apply to a person who was thoroughly stingy, and would not, as the old saying is, "Part wi' t' reek off his keàl." And "Senseless greedy" may perhaps be taken to have the same meaning as the old English proverb, "Penny wise and pound foolish."

The principal difference in the dialects of the Lake Country, is not in the idioms or the vocabulary, but in the pronunciation, in which there is a considerable variety, and in some places a marked difference between two places only a very few miles apart. As might be expected, however, where the people mix together, towards the boundaries of particular districts, the pronunciation of many words becomes common to both sides of the dividing line. Thus, for instance, the people of Borrowdale and Wythburn pronounce many of their words in the same way as is done in Langdale and Grasmere, and quite differently from people who live four or five miles further north.

Many dialect words have the same pronunciation throughout the district, while others vary very considerably. As far as I can make out from Morris' and Peacock's Glossaries of the Dialect of North Lancashire, the pronunciation there does not differ so much from that of south Westmorland, as the latter does from the Cumbrian. A great many words which in the Cumberland dialect may be spelt with "ee," are pronounced differently on the other side of Dunmail Raise. I will give a few examples by way of illustrating the difference between what may be designated as the northern and southern divisions of the Lake District, taking the parallel of "Raise Gap" as the dividing line. Speaking of cattle, a Cumbrian calls them "Beese," a native of Westmorland, "Beeàse." In like manner, "Bread" is "Breeàd," "Head" is "Heeàd," "Dead" is "Deeàd," on the other side of Raise; while on this side we say "Breid," "Heid," and "Deid." A good many words, such as "Steal," "Meal," and "Peat," which in Cumberland are the same as ordinary English, are in Westmorland, "Steeàl," "Meeàl," "Peeàt," &c. There are also a great many words which in the Cumberland dialect have the sound of "o," which in Westmorland have that of "aa." The word "own," which is "oan" on this side, is "aan" on the other. A native of Ambleside will say, "He's gitten a son iv his aan now." The same word is also used in a different sense. A person meeting with an old acquaintance whom he has not seen for a while, will say, "What, ye nivver aan us now-a-days," meaning that he never calls to see them.

A very great number of words are pronounced in the southern district in the same way. "Old" is "Aald," "Blow" is "Blaa," "Cold" is "Caald," "Crow" is "Craa," and so on. "Waar," to spend money, seems to belong to this class. A Grasmere man said to his wife when she was going to Keswick, "Mind thou duzzent waar aw t' brass afoor thou gits yam." There are many other peculiarities of pronunciation in the southern division, such as "Itt" for "Eat." A north Lancashire man "Itts" his dinner; and when he is married, he says "He's getten wed't." The word "Foot" is pronounced in various ways in different parts of the district. On the low side of Skiddaw, down towards Wigton and Carlisle, they use the Border-Scottish, "Fit;" in the vales around Keswick it is "Feùt;" in Westmorland, "Fwoot;" and in North Lancashire, "Foote." "Christmas," which in the Cumberland dialect is "Cursmas," in Westmorland is "Kirsmas."

As I noticed before, there are many dialect words which are the same all over the Lake District. People speak of a "Feùt geàt," which means a footpath; and the tracks down the sides of the mountains which are still to be seen all over the district, are by old people termed "Sledd geàts," because they were formerly used for bringing the peats down on sledges from the table land on the tops of the fells. The same word, "Geàt," is sometimes used in a figurative sense, as when a person has spent his money in a way that has done harm instead of good, people say, "His brass is gone an ill geàt." Edwin Waugh, the Lancashire poet, in one of his songs uses the word in the sense of path. He says:—

> It's olez summer when the heart's content,
>     Tho' wintry winds may blow;
> An' theer's never a geeàt 'at's so kind to the foot,
>     As the geeàt one likes to go.

There is a good old word which used to be common in the district within my own recollection, but seldom heard now; it is "Jannic,'" which means fair or straightforward. Instead of saying, "That' not fair," they used to say,

"That issent jannic." Dr. Gibson makes a girl say to her recreant lover, after naming half-a-dozen girls he had been going after—

> Thoo says it's aw fun, an' sec fun may be fair,
>
> But it dussent seem jannic to me.

This word is of much more frequent use in Lancashire.

Very few Christian names in the district, either of males or females, are spoken in the same way they are written. In fact, there is hardly one but has two or three synonyms. It has long been a custom throughout England to form pet names by affixing a diminutive to the ordinary one, so that John becomes "Johnny;" Anne, "Annie;" Elizabeth, "Lizzie," and so on; but most of the nick-names used in country places are rather terms of contempt than endearment. Thus, John becomes "Jwohn," "Jwohnny," or "Jack;" George is "Gwordie;" Anne is "Nan;" Mary is "Moll," and so on. There is also a difference in the pronunciation of such names in different districts. In Westmorland John is "Jooan," and George is "Geordy."

The same observations will apply in a somewhat less degree to surnames, many of which have vernacular pronunciations. Thus, Richardson is "Richison," or "Rutson;" Fleming is "Flimmin;" Alcock is "Oak;" and Bristo is "Busto."

It would not be correct, however, to pass such names off as dialect, they being simply corruptions of common names, and in no sense archaic words.

There are many surnames in the northern counties which are not extremely old, and some the origin of which has been very curious, not to say ludicrous. I might give instances in our own district, but not to be invidious, I will relate an account which I came across, of how a surname originated in Wiltshire. In the Wiltshire dialect, "Born" is pronounced "Barn," and "So," "Zo," as if spelt with a Z. Well, there was a countryman there who had a twist in his neck, so that his head stood on one side. Coming home from market one day, when he had had too much drink, he fell from his horse and was unable to rise again. Some people coming past soon after and seeing that his head was to one side, thought that he had dislocated his neck with falling, and forthwith set to work to pull it right. The man cried out, "Barn-zo! Barn-zo, I tell ye!"

meaning that he was born so; and from that time he and his descendants, went by the name of "Barnzo."

The last point I will touch upon in connection with dialects, is the question which has sometimes been discussed of late years among the few who take an interest in the subject—whether under the altered circumstances with regard to education and the greater diffusion of literature, dialect will not go entirely out of use, and become altogether a thing of the past. For those who have only occasionally heard it spoken, and never made any enquiry into its origin and antecedents, it is very natural to suppose that it only requires a little more general education, and a little more intermixture of the people to be brought about, by the ever-increasing facilities for travelling, to stamp it entirely out of use.

However desirable such a consummation might be, I cannot in my own mind imagine a time when all the people will have come to speak fashionable English. The change will certainly never be brought about by the extension of elementary education. Those children who are sent away to boarding schools, and out of the way of home influences altogether, soon become accustomed to speak properly and may give up the use of their native dialect. But all those who attend country and village schools, and live at home, although they may be taught to pronounce their words correctly when reading, and never think of using a dialect word while in the school-room, are no sooner outside than it bursts out again as broad as ever. The reason is obvious enough. Their parents speak dialect; the servants speak dialect; and so does almost everyone they come in contact with, morning, noon, and night.

When young men leave the vales and go to London, or any of the large towns, they are generally obliged to submerge their dialect, and learn to speak proper English. They are liable to be jeered and made fun of by their shopmates whenever they let slip a provincialism, and as very few people like to be laughed at, it is requisite for them to be on their guard.

It has been said that there is no weapon so potent to correct a bad habit as ridicule; but unfortunately, in this case, as in many others, it cuts both ways. When children come home from school and attempt to speak properly, they are frequently laughed at by servants and others, and are thus driven back to their dialect by the very same means that the young men in a London warehouse are driven from it.

People who live in the dales and other outlying districts, cling to old habits and usages with remarkable tenacity, and it is difficult to convince them that there are other ways better than those they have always been used to. This is especially the case with regard to their way of speaking. They do not think that any mode of speech can be better than their own old dialect, which they understand so well, and in which they can express themselves so much better than they could in any other way. It is a mode of speech which has been used in the district almost without alteration or change for several centuries; and if, as some think, it should eventually disappear, we may venture to predict that it will die a very slow and lingering death.

I can look back myself for between fifty and sixty years, with a pretty correct memory of much that has happened during that period. It has been a half-century of wonderful progress and change. Indeed, I sometimes think that everything is changed, except our beautiful mountains, lakes, and valleys, and the old folk-speech that is spoken amongst the dalesmen of Cumberland, Westmorland, and North Lancashire.

# Miscellaneous items

### *Autumn*
(*West Cumberland Times*, 15 November 1879)

When quiet autumn with deft hand, anew
The landscape paints, in tints of every hue;
'Tis as some artist strange, of cunning hand,
With talent skill, and judgement at command,
Spread out his canvas, where in shades of green,
Fells, fields and meadows, trees and woods are seen.
Silent he stands and views the scene awhile,
With folded hands, and sweet, but pensive smile;
His bosom heaves with many a gentle sigh,
A tear unshed wells up in either eye.
And now, his looks half pleasure and half pain,
With magic touch he whitens fields of grain.
The beech tree branches, gracefully bent down,
He clothes in orange, ting'd with iron-brown;
Day after day, fresh colours rich, unfold,
Till every shade of crimson, pink and gold
By turns appear, and presently we see
Tints various, as are kinds of bush and tree.
A picture lovely now before us lies,
As ever charmed fastidious critics' eyes.
The artist, Autumn, stands with folded arms,
And contemplates awhile its wondrous charms;
But soon the calm his placid features leaves;
A strange, convulsive sob his bosom heaves;
His face, with frowns deformed, unlike the same,
A shivering ague shakes his palsy'd frame.
He stamps his feet, his body sways and bends,
While into shreds the landscape fair he rends,

And laughs with scornful laughter when he sees
Its scatter'd fragments dancing in the breeze.
Then from the scene he flies, and in his place
Stands howling Winter with his wrinkled face.

## *Preface to* Old Customs and Usages of the Lake District

*The following paper is a fascinating observation of the changes which evolve in communities and how some are more receptive than others to accept and adapt to these new customs. Written in the mid-nineteenth century, it is almost timeless in its relevance and may well evoke reminiscences from the reader. Richardson accepts these changes as "more in harmony with the ever improving and advancing state of society". Some regions are more open to them than others. He acknowledges that there was a time when now-obsolete customs were "in perfect keeping with the old-fashioned, uncultivated ways of the dwellers among the Cumbrian hills". This is the cultured, educated teacher speaking.*

*Some notable artefacts still exist as tourist attractions or souvenirs for twenty-first-century visitors. "Sweet butter" used at Christenings, and other less formal but recognized ceremonies, is sold as rum butter and made by many a sweet-tooth fan at home. Each type of gathering—wedding, funeral or whatever, drew residents from a different "Laatin" or radius of the venue. Recollecting the eighteenth century, Richardson describes how farming communities in Cumberland and Westmorland were socially more equitable and financially less viable and productive, compared with the days of subsequent landlord, farmer and tenant stratification. So, all shared in each other's celebrations with gusto, and notably at Christmas, with religious and secular occasions in equal measure. Work was suspended from Christmas Day until Twelfth Night except for stock feeding. Life allowed for nothing if not feasting, partying and dancing. Craft industries helped to keep the wolf from the door during winter months—was the word "diversification" in use then? Mechanization was to destroy this social fabric and bring about an emphasis on different customs especially for the New Year, Richardson evoking the sadness and inevitability of it all.*

*Readers may well recall Mayday celebrations at their junior school, or possibly at Oxbridge locations. The former involved maypole dancing, now experiencing a revival in many rural parts; a pagan, pre-Christian activity in honour of deities. Sports and dancing filled the remainder of the day. Were you unlucky (or proud?) enough to be chosen May Queen or May King?*

*Cumbrians, especially, may have personal experience of "Carling Sunday", the second Sunday before Easter, Passion Sunday. This ancient well-practiced custom, and a staple food of poor families at the end of winter in the previous centuries, seems, if my memory is correct, to have met its demise at the behest of the European Economic Community which decreed them,—boiled carlings in butter, optionally with vinegar—unsuitable for human consumption. So, unboiled, and without bread and butter, they continued as the staple food of racing pigeons and the like. We boys found them great for pea-shooter ammunition, even in church! Read the authentic background to their heyday in what promises to be a captivating read. Ed.*

This Paper was read at the Cockermouth and Keswick branches of, and published in, the Cumberland Association for the Advancement of Literature and Science, 6 November 1876. Ed. J. Clifton Ward.

In this age of cheap newspapers, when every occurrence of the least consequence is chronicled, and almost everyone reads the newspapers, it is to be presumed that most persons are perfectly well acquainted with the customs and usages of the present time, and therefore, the purpose of this essay is more particularly to notice some of the old customs of the district, which have either altogether passed, or are fast passing away. In a progressive country like our own, manners and customs are constantly changing. Old things are passing away, and new ones taking their places: these, in a generation or two, to be again superseded by others, more in harmony with the ever improving and advancing state of society.

The customs and usages of a country, or district, therefore, are always a true indication of the degree of civilization, or culture, to which the people of such country or district, have attained; and are usually those best suited to the condition, or circumstances, under which they exist. To this it may perhaps be objected, that customs when once firmly rooted among a people, continue to be observed long after the state of things under which they were established has passed away, and when they have become altogether unsuited to the altered state of society. But, if we look more closely into the matter, we will invariably find that in those remote districts, where old customs and superstitions linger longest. there also civilization and improvement are lagging behind, that there the majority of the people spend their leisure hours in talking a great deal about nothing, and that habits of reading and self-culture are the exception rather than the rule. In all cases, as soon as the mass of the people become sufficiently enlightened to see the absurdity and unsuitableness of an old custom, they let it drop quietly out of sight; and until that time arrives, no amount of persuasion, or even ridicule, will make them give it up. With respect to some of the old-world usages which in a somewhat modified form are still observed in rural districts, such for instance as eating, drinking, and smoking at funerals, there is very little doubt but that many of the more intelligent members of the community would be glad to give them up, but for a dislike of being thought singular, or stingy; and as soon as the majority has become enlightened enough to see them in the same light, they will be discontinued.

We will now proceed to notice a few of the customs formerly prevalent in the Lake country; and as many of them may no doubt appear incongruous, and ridiculous enough to us at the present time, the few foregoing observations may serve to remind us that, whatever we may think of them now, there was a time when they were in perfect keeping with the old-fashioned, uncultivated ways of the dwellers among the Cumbrian hills.

The three great epochs of life—Birth, Marriage, and Death—have in all ages been marked by particular customs and observances, varying according to the different ideas and beliefs of the people among whom they prevailed. Beginning with the Birth customs of the district, there was one in particular which belonged exclusively to the dales of Cumberland and Westmorland, viz.—the custom of making sweet-butter. As it is still occasionally made, there are probably few persons who live in the district who have not seen and tasted it; but if there should be any such here, it may be as well to explain, that it simply consists of soft sugar moistened with rum, and then mixed with an equal weight of melted butter. This mixture being well stirred together, is poured into a basin, and when cooled, is fit for use. It is eaten with bread, the thin oat-meal cake once so common in the district being accounted best for the purpose.

Down to a very recent date, it was an invariable custom, some weeks before a child was expected to be born, that a large china basin which was called the sweet-butter basin, (which was generally an heirloom in every family) was filled, to be in readiness; and as soon as the important event was safely over, this basin was brought out, and all in attendance invited to partake of its contents, the doctor being usually honoured with the first cut. It was afterwards offered, with oat-bread and ale, to every one without exception who called during the ensuing month. At the end of the month there was what was called an 'Old Wife do.' All the married women within a certain radius, which was termed the 'Laatin,' were invited to go and drink tea, eat sweet-butter, and rejoice with the mother for her safe deliverance. It was the custom, too, on that occasion for each guest to bring a gift—a pound of butter, a pound of sugar, or a shilling, was the usual offering.

There was also another curious custom connected with the old wife do's, which was termed "Stealing the Sweet-Butter." A number of young men of the neighbourhood, assembled in the evening, and waited outside the house, until the table was spread and the women all seated round it, when two or three of the boldest youths rushed in, and seized, or attempted to seize, the basin and carry it off to his companions; but as many of the old wives were prepared to make a desperate fight for it, it was frequently no easy matter to secure the prize and get out again; and it often happened that some silly pilgarlick was glad to escape minus his coat-tails, or perhaps some more important part of his habilaments. When they succeeded in getting the basin of sweet-butter, a basket of oat-bread was handed out to them, and they went to some neighbour's house to eat it, after which each put a few coppers into the empty basin and returned it to the owners.

Another curious custom connected with the old wife do's remains to be described. This was, "Jumping the Can." A large milking pail was placed on the middle of the floor, and in it was stuck a birch broom without the handle. Over this each of the women was expected to jump. It was no great height, and those who were young and active went over easily enough, but there were others who did not succeed so well, and that constituted the fun of the thing.

Only imagine the ladies of the present day, with their long trailing skirts and their tight aprons, attempting to jump over the can with the beesom stuck in it!

Passing from Birth, to Marriage customs, we may remark, that the bidden weddings and bridewains, so graphically described by some of the old Cumbrian writers, were altogether exceptional affairs, only happening now and then, and by no means general or customary. They seem to have been got up occasionally by persons who had an eye to the main chance, purely as money speculations, and never to have become common enough to deserve the name of a custom, so that we need not further allude to them here.

The common weddings, however, were usually celebrated by a good deal of sociality. There were generally ten or a dozen couples of young people, who went to church; and as the distance was frequently several miles, they travelled on horseback, there being then neither wheeled carriages nor roads suitable for them. There was always a public house not far from the church, where they put up their horses during the ceremony, and to which they adjourned after it was over, to drink health and happiness to the newly married couple. This having been done to the satisfaction of all parties, the horses were brought out, and all being fairly mounted, the word was given, and a race home took place, the prize being a ribbon to be presented to the winner by the bride. Mounted on their rough and shaggy farm horses (many of which carried double), a neck-break race of six or eight miles over such roads as they then had, was no joke, and many were the disasters which resulted. After a great deal of feasting, drinking, singing, and dancing, the last act at an old-fashioned wedding was throwing the stocking. The bride having retired, all the young women entered the room, and stood at the foot of the bed, when she sat up with her back towards them, and threw her left leg stocking over her shoulder, and the girl who chanced to be hit by it was supposed to be the next to be married.

The Funeral customs of the district, although, perhaps, still capable of improvement, have been greatly modified since the beginning of the present century. It was formerly the custom when a person died, and the body was laid out, to have watchers through the nights which intervened between the death and burial. These were always two of the nearest neighbours, who sat in an adjoining room, and went at stated intervals to snuff the candles, which were kept burning near the corpse, and to see that all was right.

The afternoon before the funeral, all the married women in the "Laatin" were invited to go to what was termed the winding, which meant the placing of the body in the coffin; but as this might be done in a few minutes, by two or three persons, the gathering was in reality a tea party, where, solemn though the occasion might be, a good deal of gossip was sure to be retailed. To the funeral itself, two were invited from every house in the "Laatin," which included a much larger circuit than the "Laatin" to the winding and these, with the friends from a distance, usually made a pretty large gathering. A substantial dinner was provided for all comers, as well as a supply of ale and spirits, and tobacco for those who chose to smoke. At the time appointed for starting to church, which was often about three o'clock, the coffin being brought outside the door and placed upon the bier, the mourners standing near, four verses of the sixteenth Psalm were sung. The way in which this was done rendered it a somewhat slow and monotonous proceeding.

A line at once was given out, in a peculiar sing-song tone, by the clerk, or sexton, and then sung by a few of those present, then another line, and so on through the four verses. The next step was termed lifting the corpse, when four men lifted the bier, shoulder height, and walked solemnly away towards the church, followed, first by the mourners, and then by other friends and neighbours. As the distance was often two or three miles, or even more, the bearers were relieved by fresh relays of men, at certain places on the route.

In the quaint old times of which we are speaking, they were very particular at funerals, about going the right way to church. From every hamlet or homestead, to the parish church, was a particular road, or path, called a corpse road, and so exact were they on these occasions, to keep upon that path, that in time of flood, a funeral party has been known to wade knee deep through the water, rather than deviate a few yards to the right or left. There was a general belief, which has partly come down to our own times, which in some degree accounts for the scrupulous exactness with which they kept upon these old established paths. It is a vulgar error of course, but there are old people yet living who will tell you that if a corpse on its way to church, is carried by a fresh way across the fields, that way becomes a public road for all time, not to be stopped by any thing short of an act of parliament, if by that. The ceremony over, and the body left in its last resting place, as many of the attendants as chose went back to the house, where each was presented with a small loaf of bread to take home. This was called arvel bread, and was originally given only to the poor, but afterwards came to be offered to all alike.

Turning to the periodical customs, or those observed at particular seasons of the year, we find that many such have disappeared within the memory of persons now living, and still more, if we go back another generation or so. In treating of these, it must not be supposed that they all belong exclusively to the district. The purely local customs are very few, and in looking into the matter, we find that many which have commonly been considered such, have had their counterparts in other places widely separated from each other. Most customs, however, have in each district, something quite local in the way of their being observed.

Very many of the old customs observed by our forefathers no doubt had their origin in some religious or superstitious belief. For instance, the customs once common in these counties of making bonfires at midsummer, and burning the Beltain, or Baalfires at Mayday, were no doubt relics of the fire worship which was universally practised among the Celts.

In like manner, the custom of visiting what were called holy wells, upon particular days, and waking the well, once much observed in Cumberland, most probably came from a belief in water spirits, a superstition which was a part of the Scandinavian mythology. There were several holy wells in the Lake District, at which annual meetings were once held.

Near Penrith were four such, which were visited in succession on the four Sundays of May, on which occasions drinking tents and confectionary stalls were erected, and various sports and diversions indulged in.

Whatever might have been the primary meaning, or origin of any particular custom, whether religious or otherwise, its annual observance always, in time, became supplemented by sports and rejoicings, frequently by athletic games, and in very many cases, these festivities were kept up and celebrated for hundreds of years after the first meaning and intention of the observance were altogether lost and forgotten. As a familiar example of this, we may take the Rushbearings, once so common in the north. Two or three hundred years ago, the country churches, and places of worship in the Lake District, were many of them little better than barns. They were open to the roof, with benches of the rudest description for seats, the floors being neither flagged nor boarded, but simply the bare earth, covered thickly over with rushes. On a particular day in each year, usually in autumn, the parishioners assembled, to take the old rushes out and carry new ones in; and this being completed, a special service was held, the intention of which was to bless, or consecrate the rushes, which had just been spread over the floor. In time, this became a festival, friends were invited from a distance, sports on the green were got up, and the day ended with drinking and dancing at the village inn. Now, it is probably more than a hundred and fifty years since any church floors have been strewed with rushes, and yet there are several places, such as Grasmere, Ambleside, Warcop, and others, where the festival has been observed annually, almost down to the present time. At some of them it is kept up still. The present practice at these gatherings is for the children to walk in procession round the village, bearing garlands and other floral devices, which they afterwards deposit in the church, where a service is then held, and although it may seem a curious mixing up of things sacred and profane, the day ends as of old, with athletic sports and a dance at the public-house.

Of all the seasons of the year, which were marked by our ancestors with particular observances, Christmas was perhaps the most noted. Religious both in origin and name, as it was, and although, after the lapse of many centuries, it retains all its sacred character and associations, there is no season of the year around which so many purely secular customs and festivities have clustered, and in no part of the island were Christmas customs formerly more observed than among the hills of Cumberland and Westmorland.

In order to understand the general hospitality which then prevailed, we must remember, that at the middle of the last century, society in the rural parts of Cumberland and Westmorland, was very differently constituted from what it is at present. Instead of there being Landlords, Farmers, and Labourers, which now form three distinct grades, the land was divided into a great number of small estates, each occupied by its owner and cultivated by himself and his family; so that the head of every house was landlord, farmer, and labourer, at the same time. Most of these holdings were so small, that with the then imperfect modes of cultivation, their produce was quite insufficient to support the families of their owners, who consequently had to eke out a living by hand-carding, spinning, and weaving the wool, shorn from their mountain flocks; an employment with which they occupied themselves during the long winter evenings; in wet weather, and at other vacant times. In a community so constituted, all were socially equal, and when there was any important event to be celebrated in a family, all the neighbours within a certain distance were invited to go, and partake of the hospitalities and join in the rejoicings of the occasion. Even the clergy assisted in the fieldwork, at busy seasons, and mixed freely with the people, in their sports and revellings. We learn from old authors, as well as from tradition, that on Christmas eve, all work was suspended, and with the exception of attending to the cattle, was not resumed until after the twelfth day.

During this fortnight the whirr of the spinning wheel was never heard, the looms were silent, and the flails hung idle in the barn while the people went from house to house, feasting, singing, dancing and card playing. Every dwelling was visited in turn, the Christmas pie, home-brewed ale, and ale possets without stint, were provided by every housewife.

Soon after the commencement of the present century, a great change took place in the district. When machinery came to be applied to manufactures, the trade all went into the towns, hand-carding, hand-spinning, and country weaving were thrown out of use, and the dalesmen found that the better half of their occupation was gone. In a few years many of the small holdings passed into other hands, and eventually, two or three, or even more of them were thrown together, and let as one farm. This change reduced two-thirds of the population to the condition of labourers, or farm servants, and the farmers and their families reckoning themselves a degree above these, left them out of their Christmas parties, and then it was that the Christmas merry-nights sprung up. These were held at the public-houses and served two purposes.

They were places of amusement for all who chose to go, and also annual benefits to the inn-keepers who made them. Some of them were simply gatherings at public-houses, where no stated charge was made but every one was at liberty to spend and drink what he chose. At others, each guest paid a shilling, or eighteenpence, for which they were supplied, in some cases, with supper, and in others with a basin of "Powsowdy," which was simply the old ale posset mixed with rum. As might be expected from the rough uncultivated manners of the people, the proceedings at these assemblies were often of the wildest description. There were dancing and singing, card playing, drinking and fighting. There was no etiquette, or ceremony there; every one made merry in the way he liked best, and did it in the most energetic manner. Anderson in describing the Bleckell merry night, tells us, that "The clogger o' Dalston" danced "Till the sweat it ran off at his varra chin end."

The mummers of Yorkshire, and the Christmas carol singers of other parts of England, had their counterpart in this district in the country fiddlers who on Christmas and New Year's eves, went about to every house, and after playing the "Hunt's up" wished the inmates a merry Christmas and a happy New year. In ancient times, it was the custom to herald in the New year with much pomp and ceremony but in these northern counties the Christmas festivities extending a week into the new year, there was no room for any special New Year rejoicings.

It was, however, the custom at some churches, for the bell-ringers to ring the old year out and the new one in; and it was also very common for young people to sit up on that night until the clock struck twelve, and then open the door to let the New year in. There was also a custom, very common on New Year's Day, in many villages of Cumberland, called Stanging which was highly characteristic of the days when the old parish constable was the sole guardian of the peace. A party of roughs assembled in the morning of the first of January, and continued throughout the day, to intercept all passengers, and extort from them a sort of black mail. If the person stopped was willing to pay sixpence or a shilling, he was suffered to go on his way without further molestation; but if not, he was hoisted by main force, shoulder height, upon a pole, and carried to the public-house, by which time he was generally ready enough to pay his ransom, when he was set at liberty. The money thus obtained was all spent at the village inn, during the same day and night.

Passing to Candlemas, the observances among our forefathers at that season, were more of a business than a festive character. It was the end of their financial year, when all accounts were settled. All interest on borrowed money then became due, and most of the farms and tenements were let to be entered upon at that time. In Westmorland and the north of Lancashire, it was the custom until lately for all tradesmen to give twelve month's credit, and no accounts were settled at any other time than Candlemas.

Coming next to Shrovetide, or the beginning of Lent, we find that most of the names and customs connected therewith have come down to us from Roman Catholic times. The name Lent is said to be derived from a term used by the Saxons. They called the spring Lengthentide, because then the days were lengthening. Shrovetide originally signified the time of confessing sins to a priest. The term was derived from the Saxon word shrive, to confess, and was applied to the first day of Lent, because on that day the people in every parish throughout England were obliged to confess their sins to the parish priest, each in his own parish church. In our own county, and perhaps some other parts of the north, the beginning of Lent was formerly called Fasten's even, because of its being the eve of the long Lenten fast. In the north of England, and especially in this county, the three days at the beginning of Lent have, time out of mind, been known as Collop Monday, Pancake Tuesday, and Ash Wednesday; and till lately, each was commemorated by a meal corresponding to the name. The two former evidently date from before the reformation. Under the Roman Catholic rule Monday in Shrove week was the last day on which people were permitted to eat meat until the end of Lent; and in consequence every one contrived to have it on that day, and hence it came to be called Collop Monday. Of the origin of making Pancakes on Shrove Tuesday, many widely different accounts have been given. The most obvious explanation seems to be, that the people being debarred the use of meat during the whole of Lent, eggs would be much used as a substitute; and the housewives of the time would, no doubt, for the sake of variety, contrive various ways of cooking them. They made them into pancakes and puddings, they mulled ale with them, and they dyed them into pace eggs for the children. Ash Wednesday is a remarkable example of the curious way in which, among dialect speaking people, words sometimes become corrupted both in pronunciation and meaning. It was called Ash Wednesday because, in early times, on that the second day of Lent, it was the custom for devout Christians to sprinkle themselves with ashes, in token of sorrow and humiliation. In later times, however, after the old religious observances were discontinued and forgotten, the day came to be called not Ash, but Hash Wednesday, and the country people commemorated it by having a hash to dinner on that day.

The second Sunday before Easter was formerly called Carling Sunday, and it was a very general custom, in the northern counties, on that day, to offer visitors peas, which had first been boiled, and afterwards fried in butter, and were called carlings. It was also common for people, on that day, to carry raw peas in their pockets, and to throw them at each other. The origin of this curious custom is very remote. For centuries before the introduction of the potatoe into England, and when grain was imported in very small quantities, if at all, pulse was one of the chief staples of food, and at that particular time in the spring, when the winter stores of the poor were all exhausted, it became a custom for charitable people to make a distribution, or dole, of peas, to the serfs, or carles, and hence it came to be called Carling Sunday. In some of the midland counties, doles of wheat are given out in the same manner.

The custom of Pace Egging, at Easter, common among children all over England and some parts of the continent, is still pretty generally observed in this district; while the more local ones of drinking mulled ale on Easter Sunday, and providing the children with new clothes for that day, are well nigh obsolete. The latter custom was once so general, that if any poor child was compelled to go out on that day, without wearing anything new, the other children thought that something terrible would happen to it. The practice of sending persons on foolish errands on the first of April, is so ancient, that its origin seems to be lost in obscurity. A great deal has been written by way of attempting to explain the meaning of this singular custom, but the accounts are so various, and all seem so purely conjectural, that no reliance can be placed upon them. In Cumberland, the same thing was practised on both the first of April and the first of May, the only difference being that the dupes at the one time were called "April Noddies," and at the other "May Geslins." Noddy, in the dialect, means one easily imposed on, and geslins are young geese, which are often hatched about the first of May.

There is strong evidence, both in some place names in the district, and particular phrases still used in the dialect, that the Mayday rejoicings once so popular in other parts of England, were common in the north. This very ancient festival was pagan in origin. It was a custom among the Britons, before they were converted to Christianity, to erect Maypoles adorned with flowers, and dance around them, in honour of their heathen deities. In the time of our Saxon ancestors, the festival was somewhat modified, but still retained its chief characteristics. The beginning of May was the time which the Saxons had chosen for the assembling of their "Folkmotes," or conventions of the people; and when the barons were absent at these ancient Parliaments, the inhabitants of each village gave themselves up to mirth and rejoicings. The feast was dedicated to Hertha, the goddess of peace and fertility, and all quarrels were to be laid aside during its continuance. On Mayday, the young people met upon the green around the richly decorated May poles, where they chose a village king, as he was called, who afterwards selected his queen. He wore an oaken, and she a hawthorn wreath, and together they gave Laws for the rustic sports, and bestowed the prizes upon the victors. After the Norman invasion, the May-day observances continued to be as popular as ever, and down to the time of the Commonwealth, every village had its May pole, where on the first of May in each year, the youths and maidens assembled, and having decorated the pole with garlands of flowers, they chose and crowned the May-queen, after which dancing on the green and various rural sports were kept up during the remainder of the day. In the time of Cromwell, the Puritans set them-selves against these rustic rejoicings, and, in obedience to an ordinance of the long Parliament, dated April 1644, all the May poles were taken down by the constables and churchwardens. After the Restoration the festival was partially resumed, but never again became so popular or general as before. Bourne tells us that, in his time, in the villages in the north of England, the children of both sexes were wont to rise a little after midnight on the morning of the first of May, and, accompanied with music and the blowing of horns, to walk to some neighbouring wood, where they broke down branches from the trees and adorned them with nosegays and crowns of flowers. This done, they returned homewards with their booty, about the time of sunrise, and decorated their doors and windows with the same. Alluding to the Restoration, we may remark in passing, that on the twenty-ninth of May, called Royal Oak Day, it was customary to carry about oak branches, in commemoration of Charles the Second's escape in the oak tree, after the battle of Worcester. In the old coaching and carrier cart days, the horses on that day used to be decorated with oaken twigs.

Coming next to Whitsuntide, if we endeavour to find out the meaning of the name, we become quite bewildered among the various explanations given by different authors. One writer tells us that it was "White Sunday," because in the early days of Christianity the converts who went to be baptised on the day of Pentecost, were all dressed in white. Another tells us that it took its name from a French word pronounced "Huiet," which meant eight, because beginning with Easter, Whit Sunday was the eighth Sunday. Another quaint old writer on the subject says that it was not Whit, but Wyt-Sunday, because at that time the disciples were endued by the Holy Spirit with wit and wisdom to teach and instruct the people in the Christian religion. Still another writer informs us that it was pagan in origin, and did not become identified with the Christian holiday of Pentecost till after the Norman Conquest, and that its original name was Wittentide, because it was the time when the Wittenagemote, or Saxon Parliament, assembled.

Whatever may have been its origin, or the derivation of its name, it is best known to Cumbrians as a hiring term for farm servants and the time at which, in conjunction with Martinmas, the statute fairs are held. It is difficult to understand why Whitsuntide should have been chosen for such a purpose, as, being a moveable feast, whilst Martinmas is fixed, it very rarely happens that the two divisions of the year are of the same length, and not unfrequently the winter half-year, as it is called, is thirty weeks, leaving the summer division only twenty-two. It was formerly the custom for all masters requiring servants, to attend some or other of these fairs, and there to hire such as seemed most suitable to them. The servants, male and female, stood promiscuously in the market place, with pieces of straw in their mouths, as badges of servitude, or signs that they were open to engagements; and the masters went among them in much the same manner as they might have done among a herd of cattle, out of which they wished to purchase two or three heifers, and their mode of choice was exactly the same, the judgment in both cases being guided by the physical appearance of the animal to be bought or hired. Having made a selection, and a bargain as to the amount of wages to be paid at the end of the next half-year, the master gave the servant a shilling, which was understood to make the agreement binding. This money was called "Yearls," probably from a custom once common, of hiring servants by the year; thus, when a master hired a servant for a year, and gave him the shilling, he was said to yearl him, or bind him for a year.

A great deal has from time to time been written and said of the half-yearly hirings, and at one time they possibly deserved all the odium which has been attached to them. However, to judge of them impartially, it will be necessary to go back some forty or fifty years, to a time when country servants were in a very different position from what they are at present. The wages they then got were less than a third of what they receive now; and when at the end of the half-year, they had paid their shoemaker's and tailor's bills, the few shillings which remained were too often squandered before the term was over. They then commenced another half-year of toil and drudgery, during which time they seldom left the farm, having neither the opportunity nor the means of going away in search of excitement or pleasure.

It would be difficult to imagine a rougher set of people than most of the farm servants were fifty or sixty years since. Thoroughly uncultivated in appearance and in manners, while at the same time many of them were overflowing with animal spirits and rollicking fun, which seldom found a free outlet at any other time, it is scarcely to be wondered at, if when they got to the fair, they threw off all restraint and rushed into every kind of excess. While, however, we are looking at this dark view of the subject, and cannot help lamenting such excesses, and the immorality which they undoubtedly sometimes led to, we must not forget that the picture had a bright side too. Among the poorer families, many of the members of which were out at service in different parts of the country, and who seldom or never met at any other time, the hiring day being the only opportunity they had to form a reunion during the six months, on that account was always looked forward to with the brightest anticipation. It was a kind of oasis in the desert of labour and servitude, where father, mother, sisters and brothers all met together to shake hands and exchange affectionate greetings, after a half-year's separation. The mother went shopping with her grown-up children, advising them how to lay out their wages to the best advantage, and in return, having her basket filled with fairings for herself and the children at home. The hiring fairs are still kept up to some extent, but are altogether modernized in character.

The march of improvement is nowhere more perceptible than among the agricultural servants of the northern counties. If in the manufacturing and mining districts high wages have led to reckless extravagance and intemperance, they have had the very opposite effect upon farm servants. When at the end of the half-year, they found that, after making their necessary purchases, they had a few pounds to spare, it was worthwhile to put them in the savings bank; and the very fact of their having an account there, led them into habits of sobriety and economy, and gave them feelings of independence and self-respect, which they had not had before. With few exceptions, too, they are now able to read and write; and availing themselves of the increased facilities for travelling, they go more from home, and are consequently as a class much better informed, and more civilized in every way. There are still, of course, specimens of the old boorish type to be found here and there, but they are getting fewer year by year, and will no doubt in time disappear altogether.

The midsummer rejoicings, once general throughout England, were partly kept up in the north, till the beginning of the present century. In Hutchinson's history of Cumberland, 1794, we learn that at Cumwhitten, the festival was then celebrated with bonfires and dancing; and Sullivan tells us, that the same custom was observed at Melmerby several years later still. At Michaelmas it was the custom among our forefathers to kill their cattle out of the pastures, for their winter provisions; and in October they brewed their ale for the ensuing year. There are other local customs, such as clippings, shepherds' feasts, and kurn suppers, which are still partly observed, and therefore do not require much explanation.

Forty or fifty years since, sheep shearing time, which extended over the second and third weeks of July, was quite a festive season among the vales. Every flock master made a clipping, to which he invited all his neighbours

and friends; and every housewife made a brewing of extra strong ale, called
clipping drink, for the occasion, and to it the dalesmen always did ample
justice before they went home. The shepherds' feasts do not date very far back,
being simply meetings of shepherds from the surrounding vales, which are
held at some particular inns. To these meetings, all the stray sheep picked up
on the mountains during the autumn are brought, and after being claimed
by their respective owners, a supper is provided by the host, and the evening
is spent in conviviality.

The kurn suppers of the district correspond to the harvest homes of other
parts of England, and the name is another example of the way in which words
sometimes become corrupted. It was originally called the "Corn winning,"
because it was a feast held by the country people when they had won, or
secured, their corn crops. It afterwards came to be called the "Kurn winning,"
and "Kurn" being the dialect word for churn, it became a custom for each
of the family and work-people to be regaled with a basin of cream, as a part
of the feast, and thus it became the kurn, or churn supper.

I will now conclude with a few brief remarks, which have suggested
themselves to me while investigating the subject. We are all prone to
retrospection. We look back with a sort of fond remembrance to the years
of childhood and youth, and affect to lament for the joys which are gone,
never to return. This feeling, however, when it comes to be analyzed, and
submitted to the test of critical examination, is found to be in a great
measure fallacious. If by any possibility we could have the choice, there are
probably very few of us who would elect to change the advantage which he
has, for the much lauded pleasures of youth. Would any of us be willing to
give up the endearments of our homes, our valued friends, the knowledge
and experience we have gained in all our battles with the world, and the
numerous other blessings we each of us have, for the sake of going back to
the frivolous pleasures of childhood and youth, which after all, were not the
unalloyed pleasures which we were apt to fancy then, when they are left a
few years behind. If we search our memories, we shall find that we all had
our troubles, our crosses, and our disappointments in youth, as well as now,
equal perhaps in number, if different in kind; and if we come to strike the
balance, it certainly ought to be in favour of what we are, and not what we

were. Now, it is just the same feeling which throws such a halo of romance around what are called the good old times, and it is equally false and fictitious in both cases. If we look back to the old times, by the light of history, we see little but a succession of wars, murders, and religious persecutions, with tyranny and oppression of every kind. We see the mass of the people of this country in a state of serfdom, or semi-slavery, most of them in the most abject poverty, and frequently dying by thousands of smallpox, famine, and the plague. In our own county, which perhaps retained more freedom and independence than any other part of England, there was for centuries very little security for either life or property, it being almost the constant theatre of Border raids, rapine, and robbery. If we judge of the old times from the manners and customs of the people, although we cannot help admiring the openhanded hospitality, and the jovial hilarity which characterized all their proceedings, we look in vain for any mixture of the intellectual element in any of their observances. Their celebrations were all, without exception, of the roistering, bacchanalian kind, and even their religious festivals were often mixed up with, or supplemented by, sports and revels.

If we contrast the state of things just described with that of the present, when the humblest individual among us has as much liberty and freedom at the noblest in the land; when any respectable cottager has a score of comforts and conveniences which, a hundred years since, the richest could not buy; when every township has its school, every household its newspaper, every village its library, and every town its mechanics' institute, its literary society, and numerous other facilities for improvement, it seems a curious misnomer to call those the good old times, in disparagement of these. However, having made this comparison, do not let us run away with the idea that the people of old times are deserving of all the blame, and we of all the praise. We must simply go back to the proposition with which we set out, viz.—the manners, customs, and institutions of former times were the best and only ones possible under the circumstances then existing, and we may make this addition to it; that, whereas our ancestors were rude and uncultivated because they had no means of culture or improvement; on the contrary, if any of us are contented to remain in the slough of ignorance and sensuality, we have ourselves alone to blame.

# STWORIES 'AT GANNY
# USE' TO TELL

*These Stwories were recounted to John Richardson by his mother-in-law, Mary Birkett, and retold by way of a series of fortnightly appearances in the* West Cumberland Times *of 1879–80. There is probably no record of the whole set, and I have included those that I have found in the newspaper archives.*

## *Untitled*
### (*West Cumberland Times*, 20 December 1879)

Ganny was aboot ninety-five when she deet, an' that 'ill be some eight or ten 'eer sen. If she'd been leeven' noo she wad 'a' been abèun a hundred. She had a terrible memory up to t' varra last, an' when she gat to talken' aboot auld times her tongue ran on an' was nivver like to stop. T' meàst iv her talk was aboot what 'ed happen't when she was young, or things 'at she'd hard fra fwok far oalder ner hersel', seah 'at her teàlls tak us back weel on tull a hundred 'ear, an' some o' them a gay bit mair ner that. Like aw elderly fwok she thowt neàh times like t' auld times, at ivvery change in t' way o' leevin' was for t' warse, an' 'at when hur an' a lock mair o' t' auld men war geàne, ivvery thing wad seùn gang to wreck an' reùin.

This dark sunless summer' just browt into me mind a crack at we hed, ya wet efterneùn aboot a dozen 'eer sen. It 'ed been varra wet wedder fur aboot three week, an' I sed to t'auld body, "Wy, ganny, dud ye ivver see sec a haytime as this afwore?"

"Aye, a dozen," says she, "I've seen aw maks o' haytimes. I've known some seasons 'at t' main o' t' hay was to git efter Michaelmas, as I've known 'eers when it was hofe on 't nivver gitten at aw, an' I've known summers 'at war as dry 'at theer was varra laal to git; an' fwok allas gat deùn some way or anudder. Bit, bless ya barn! I' my young days fwok thowt mair aboot a fine peat time ner they did aboot owder haytime or harvest: for if it com' a bad peat season theer was nowt bit starvation leuken' at yan aw through t' cummen winter."

"What," says I, "Hed ye nowt bit peat for fuel i' them days?"

"Fuel, be fiddle't!" says she, "speak English when thoo's talken to me. I dunnet know what this warld's gante git teù when yan's varra bit fireoldin mun hev a fine ootlandish neàme like that. I say fuel!

"Wy, wy," says I, "Hed ye nowt bit peats for fireoldin?"

"We gat a lot lock o' sticks amang hands sometimes," says she, "bit peats war t' main iv oor dependables an' a fine deal o' wark they heàdd, even when it was a fine season, let aleàne a wet un. T' meàst o' them war blown off t' tops o' t' heigh fells, an' efter that to turn, an' to double an' to work amang ivvery noo an ageàn for menny a week. When they gat fairly dry, we use' to tak t' nag up an' sled them t' the fell edge, whoar we owder stack't them, or pot into pleàce er meàd o' purpose caw't peat lodges. Fra theer they hed to be trail't doon by hand, an' that was t' hardest wark iv aw, for sleadgeàts war beàth rough and brant, an' t' trailer hed to carry t' empty sled up on his shooders ivvery time."

"It waddent be women's wark gitten peats?" says I, "men wad hev that to deù?"

"T' men fwok greàvv't them an' trail't them doon t' fell," says ganny, "bit t' women fwok dud aw t' rest. I mind when I was aboot sixteen an' leaven' a sarvant at Armboth, 'at oor sarvant man wa sent onto t' fell to greàvv peats, an' I hed to gang an' spreed for 'im. They cawt 'im Geordie Sewell; he was a girt strang fellow, an as big a govey as I've met wi' in aw my lang life. He was yan o' t' laziest chaps 'at ivver I saw, at enny time bit t' meal times, an' than he could 'a' deùn as mickle as enny two fwok. Wy, as I sed, we hed to gang to t' peat fell, an' tak oor dinners wi' us, an' as oor mistress was a menseful body, an' knew neàh laal wad sarra Gwordie an' me, t' basket was a gay good weight, an' t' girt lubbard waddent tak t' a yard, seàh at I hed to carry 't awt' way up t' breest an' onto t' fell, an a gay good sweat I gat wi' 't. When twelve o'clock com, we sat doon on a hill to git oor dinners, an' oppen't basket. I turn't oot twelve boilt eggs, some reùbarb keàke, havver breed an' cheese, an' I dar say some udder things beside. Well, Gwordie startit wi' t' eggs, and as fast as he could peel t' shells off them they disappear't; barn, they war nobbut bites apiece for 'im. Thinks I to mesel, "I'll just wark on till I see hoo menny o' them he'll eat; and seàh I teùk summet else, an' nivver let wit till he'd demolish't ten, an' was peelen' t' elebben't' when I thought to mesel, I'd better be takken' t' yan 'at was left afwore it went an aw; an' wi' tat, I just teùk 't an' gev't a tap ower a steànn, an', by geck, it was a rotten un. I just think I hear hoo that girt fellow goister't an' laugh't till yan mud 'a' hard 'im to Watendlath. Deary me! It's ameàst fower scwore 'eer sen that". I ast ganny if there was enny reùll, or law amang fwok i' them days aboot keepen' their awn pleàces on t' peat fells, or ivvery yan went an' greàvv 't whar they like't.

"Nay," says she, "ivverybody hev unlimited reet; theer was neàh law nor reùlls nowder. Whoar it was a good neighbourhood, fwok keep't their awn peat pots an' spreedin' grund year efter year, bit sometimes whoar theer war ill geàn, selfish fwok at war alles rievnen for t' best grund an' t' meàst on't, it natterally meàde bits o' disturbance noo an' than.

When I leevt at Patterdale, theer was a man 'at they cawt Jack Windless, 'at use' to git a deal o' peats off t' fell. He was nobbut a daftish sort iv a chap, bit he was yan o' them 'Tak care o' self' mak o' fwok, 'at if they can feed theirsels, dunnet care a fardin' who fails. He alles contriv't to begin greàvven' peats a week or ten days afwore ennybody else an' cuvvert up aw t' best o' t' grund, neh matter who'd hed it t' year afwore. Well, theer was anudder man i' Patterdale 'at they caw't Will Patrickson, as queer a feùll as ivver leev't. He'd nowt 'at was varra bad aboot 'im, bit he was keen o' playin' aw maks o' queer funny tricks an' pranks, whenivver he'd a chance. T' spring 'at I's tellin' aboot he'd teànn't inul his heed 'at he wad stop Jack Windlass o' gitten peats, an' wi' that intention he rais't a report 'at theer was a wildman leeven' in a cave on t' fell, 'at he eat nowt bit rowe mutton an' help't hissel tull a sheep whenivver he wantit yan. He was sed to be as black as a Hottentot, an nut to hev a wrap of owt on bit a sheepskin 'at he threw ower his shooders when he went oot. T' teàll, yance set upon, 't grew mair fretful ivvery time it was telt o'wer, tell a deal o' t' ........... mak o' fwok wad as seùn 'a thowt o' throwin' theirsels off Stybarrow Cragg into Ullswater as gaan on to t' fell. Jack Windless was in a varra bad way aboot it; he was ameàst as flate as enny body, an' yet he wantit to be t' furst on to t' peatfell, 'at he mud git t' best pleàce, an' efter a varat o' considerin' an' enquirin' he meàdd up his mind to venter ya Monday mornin'. Thar seàmm Monday, Will was drinken' at t' "Nell House," an' as seùn as he hard 'at Jack was geànn on to t' fell to greàvv peats, he sed 'By gay! Bit he'll nut greàvv lang, or my neàm's nut Will Patrickson!' Wi' that he set off, drunk as he was, to t' 'lenceunn' an borrow't a fleece o' woo' an' a lump o' wad 'at they use for markin' t' sheep, an' than he startit off up t' fell. When he gat oot o' seet iv aw t' houses he dofft his cwoat, double't up his shirt sleeves, an' black't his feace, arms an' hands wi wad, an' than oppen't oot his fleece o' woo' an' threw't ower his shooders like a clwoàk. I' that pickle he clam up an' went roond a bit to git ontull a hill aboot a hundred yerds fra whoàr he knew Jack wad be at wark. As he was gaan, it chanc't 'at he com across a part of a deed sheep 'at somebody's dogs 'ed been eaten', an' leùk't for a minute or seàh, bit when this thing meàdd a rush doon t' hill towarts 'im, he threw doon his speàdd, an' away he went across t' moss, down t' fell an' into t' hoose withoot yance leùken' behint 'im. Barn, he was as near freetent to deeth as maks neàh matter, for when they gat 'im to bed, it was weeks an' weeks afwore he gat up ageànn, owder to greàvv peats, or deù owt else." I thowt to mesel', an I said to ganny, "By gum! Theer's been some gay queer uns i' them days. Bit what fwok ur nut seàh fash't noo wi' gitten their fuel—their fireoldin. I mean, they've nowt to deù bit gang to t' station for cwoals when ivver they want them."

"Neah, neah," says she, "they can git them when they want them I dar' say, an' they may sarra whoar fwok hev nowt better, bit they're nobbut cwoals efter aw. Yan's forc't to put up wi' t' grime an' seùt as weel as yan can, like as yan hes to put up wi' a deal mair things, an' yan owt to be thankful for t' cumforts yan hes, bit things ur nut as they used to be when I was young. Bless ye barn, theers sometimes when I's sitten meùsen be mesel', I can see an auld fashin't chimley, weel stock't wi' logs an' shooders o' dry't mutton, a lang back't creùk hingen doon fra t' rannel boak, wi' a keàll pot at t' end on 't, boilen' ower a good peat fire; an', if ye'll believe me, I sometimes as far forgit mesel' as to begin lilten "Auld Robin Gray" or summet o' t' mak', bit t' furst sound o' me crack't voice breks t' spell, an' t' auld fashin't chimley, t' lang creùk, t'peat fire, an' t' good auld times ur geànn, like a gleam o' sunshine on a dark shoory day."

## Sec winters as they hed lang sen
(*West Cumberland Times*, 29 December 1879)

(Dialect, Threlkeld district)

Ya winter neet I happen't to say to Ganny, 'at it was freezin' varra hard, an'
was like for bein' a hard winter.

"Talk aboot hard winters," says she. "Bless yer heart, as fwok know nowt
what they're like noo, barn. Theer is neàh winters noo-a-days to what theer
use't to be yance. Sen I can think on, fwok thowt nowt iv a twenty week frost,
wi' thick snow aw t' time, an' by gock! they war warth cawin' snows than.
Mair ner yance i' my recollection ye mud a geàne oot and walk't for miles
across t' country on t' frozen snow, ower t' tops o' t' wos an' dykes at war
aw fairly hap' t up 'at ye cuddent tell where they war, for ye could see nowt
bit snow an mappen a row o' trees here an' theer. Barn, i' country pleàces
i' winter time, fwok nivver thowt o' gannin' to bed withoot first bringin' t'
speàdd into t' hoose an' setten' 't back o' t'doer, chancen' 'at they sud hev to
cut their way oot next mwornin. Meàst part o' t' auld country hooses war
built on by t' fell boddems an' hed nobbut ya doer 'at oppen't oot to t' fell
broo sooa 'at when it com a snowstorm, sec as use't to be lang sen, it oft
eneouf blew't in tell theer was a druft at full't up t' hollow atween t' hoose
riggin' an' t' fell side, an' than t' fwok had ta bide in tell t' neighbours com
an' cot them oot. Sometimes when a gay lock o' 't hooses was snown up it
was a day or two afwore some o' them war let oot, an' t' warst on 't was it oft
druftit up at neet aw 'at hed been oppen't oot durin' t' day."

It was afwore my time, but theer was a stwory, an' I dar say it was trew,
aboot two auld fwok an' a barn at war snown up in a hoose, someway up i'
Langdale, an' nivver saw dayleet for better nor three week. They leev't aboot
a mile and a hofe fra any neighbours, an' neàhbody hed miss't them or thowt
owt about them, an' be that means t' auld fwok war keep't in aw that time,
t'doer an' windows bein' aw druftit completely up. When at last somebody
dud gang an' mak a way in to them they war nivver mismazen theirsels. Auld
Jobby was thrang carden' an' Sally was spinnin' when neighbours inquir't,
"Hoo they'd mannish't sa lang i' t' dark?"

"Weel eneuf," says Sally. "We happen't to hev plenty to eat in t' hoose, an' plenty o' rash cannels for greasin'. Ye know oor Jobby's a fiddler, an ye see, when we war tir't o' cardin' an' spinnin', he teùk fiddle an' me my knittin', an' when we war tir't o' that, we went to bed, an' when we war hungry we gat up ageànn. We warren't gan te brek oor hearts aboot it, for we thowt if neàh body com to let us oot, it wad thow efter a bit mebby."

I said to Ganny, "at like eneùf theer wad oft be fwok starv't to deeth i' sec winters as them."

"Nut they," says she, "they were as hard as fell teàdds, barn. Fwok duddent pamper theirsels than as they deu noo. T' leevin hooses i' them days were not mickle better nor t' oot-bosses ur noo. Theer was nivver sec a thing as a ceil't room in any country hoose than, an' t' sleepin' rooms up t' stairs war aw open to t' reuff, an' t' sleatts hardly ivver hed any plaister on t' inside, to keepoot t' snow an' t' wind. Fwok use' to stop t' wholls up wi' moss as weel as they could, bit deù what they wad, when it come a girt blow o' snow, it use't to drive in 't aw directions, an many a time when yan waken't up iv a winter mwornin', t' top twilt on t' bed wad a been cuvver't wi' mappen eight or nine inch o' snow, an t' flute at t' bedside sec like."

I aks't Ganny hoo fwok mannish't to git any marketin, or owt to eat fra t' toons, when aw was snown up for sec lang times togidder? "Oh!", says she, "they wantit laal fra t' toons i' them times. As seùn as they gat their lock havver shworn an' into t' hoose, aboot October, they used to thresh 't oot, an tak 't to t' mill, an' hev't meàd into havver meal. If it was a fair crop it meàd as much as wad sarra for bread an' poddish till t' next October. When they gat their melder heàmm, t' wummen fwok hed a spell o' beakin' havver bread, at lastit three or fower days, an' sometimes langer. They mainly what beak't as mickle at yance as wad sarra t' family hofe a year, or there-a boots. T' remainder o' t' meal was put intul a girt knirst 'at they caw't t' meal ark, an they sometimes used to git in an' tread it doon wi' their feet to mak 't firm an' solid.

They'd neàh chimney pieces, nor fire grates, 'i their hooses, bit hearth fires, an' I've neàh doot bit ye've seen some o' t' greet auld fashin't chimleys 'at war shap't like a mill hoppe, whemmel't t' wrang side up, as wide as t' hoose end at t' boddem an' taperin' away till aboot a feut an' a hafe at t' top. I was gaan

to tell ye at t' boddem part o' them girt hoppen chimleys was used for dryen'
legs an' shooders o' mutton an' ye mud a' seen a scwore or two o' sec things
hingen i' yan o' them ameàst any time an' it was nowt uncommon to see a
heall sheep hung up to dry. Aboot Michaelmas two or three o' t' neighbours
wad a' join't i' killin' a coo, an' dividit t' beef amang them; an', seah ye see,
when they'd gitten their melder o' havver meal meàd, a good stock o' dry't
mutton i' t' chimley, a quarter o' beef i' t' pickle tub, an mebby a coo 'at gev
a sup o' milk, they war nin sa badly prepar't for a hard winter.

Theer was varra laal tea, coffee, or sugger use't i' them days, an' if they
hed a sup o' yal they always brew't it at heamm, seàh it was varra laal 't they
wantit fra t' market at enny time."

Says I to Ganny, "What, they wad hev a varra dull whiet time on't i'
winter time."

"Nut so dull as ye think on," says she. "Fwok war far mair neighbourly
than ner they ur noo. Barn, they'd nivver owt extra to dew whedder it was
kilen' a pig, twilten' a bedtwilt, or makken a lock o' Cursmas pies, bit t'
neighbours went to help yan anudder, an' than when t' wark was deùn,
theer was a good crack an' mebbe a gem at cards till bedtime. Bless ye, barn!
Aboot Cursmas theer was sec feastin' as nivver was seen. There was a feast at
ivvery hoose, an' ivverybody was invited to gang. Theer was neàh pickin' and
choosin' as theer is noo. Neàhbody 'Mead fish o' yan an' flesh iv anudder'
i' them days. Ye'll mebbie hev hard t' teall aboot auld Mally Watson, o'
Patterdale. It's a varra auld stwory, bit they sed it was trew eneùff".

"Theer was a woman deed, an' t'man 'at was sent to warn to t' funeral
hed likely hed mair glasses o' drink gien ner was good for his memory, an' t'
upshot on' t' was, 'at he forgot auld Mally awtogidder. What, it was thowt
sec a thing as nivver was deùn, 'at a body sud be left oot fra a funeral i' that
way; bit they cuddent aw mak auld Mally believe owt bit what it was deun
o' purpose. Awivver, she sed she duddent care, she wad be ebben wi' them
afwore lang, she was gante hev a funeral iv her awn an' she wad a' neàhbody
tult.

"Bit I see ye'rewanten to be off. Wia. Wia. Fwok mun leùk efter their bits
o' jobs. T' next time ye caw, I'll tell ye summet aboo their feastin' an' carryin'
on, an than ye'll hev some idea whedder they war an so varra dull or nut."

### Hoo Fwok use' to enjoy theirsels lang sen
(*West Cumberland Times*, 3 January 1880)

T' next time I caw't I remindit ganny iv her promise.

"Oh ay!" says she, "I can tell ye eneùff to satisfy ye 'at fwok war nin so dull in auld times, nowder i' winter ner neàh udder season.

"They use to start ten days or a fortneth afwore Cursmas to beàkk their pies; an' as I telt ye afwore, they yan went to help anudder. It was a gay jolly time was that, afwore Cursmas began. It was mainly t' lasses an' young wummen 'at went to help, an' than t' lads went at t' neet, not to help bit to hinder, an' to tak' t' lasses heàmm when they war deùnn.

"Aa man! what fun we had sometimes. When Cursmas ibben com aw t' woo-cards, spinnin' wheels, an' teùlls iv aw maks war sidit away, an' duren' that time fwok dud nowt bit gang aboot feasten'to t' neighbours' hooses, furst yan, an' than anudder.

"Theer was two Cursmas feasts at ivvery hoose, yan for young fwok an' yan for t'auld uns. Fwok wad caw them parties noo-a-days, bit theer was neàh parties than; fwok caw't things by their reet neàmms i' them times.

"Wy, as I telt ye afwore, fwok war aw axt, an' t' meàst o' them went, an' when they gat theer they meàdd theirsels merry an' cheerful yan wi' anudder. Theer was neàh primmin' an' turnin' up o' nwoses, bit Jack was as good as his maister an' Sally as good as her mistress. An' when t' supper was riddy, theer was neah 'Will ye take a little of this' or 'Do ye choose a litte o' that!' bit 'Noo, set to work, help yersels, an' need neàh biddin'. Theer's plenty iv ivverything, an' seàh mak' yersels at heàmm.' An' theer was plenty iv ivverything teù. Theer was sawt beef, dry't legs o' mutton, an' rostit geùse to begin wi'. An' let me tell ye, fwok needit neàh pressin', bit set to wark an' full't their bellies o' whativver they like't best. Neàh doot bit some eat mair nor udders, bit that meàdd neàh matter, fwok aw eat what they wad, an' hoo they wad, an' talk't as much as they wad, an' as a glass or two o' that strang heàmm-brew't yall seùn lowsent fwok's tongues, there was oft a gay change, I can tell ye.

"Efter t'supper was ower, an' t'things sidit away, theer was cardin', some playen' at whisk an' some at lant, some sang, an' udders talk't an' telt queer stwories. Aboot midneet they aw went heàmm an' to bed an' t' next neet war riddy for gaan to anudder hoose, an' ye may think 'at they'd a gay gangin' time on't afwore they gat aw roond.

"As muckle gangin' an' feastin' as theer was aboot Cursmas, ye munnet think 'at that was aw t' amusement they hed i' auld times. Bless ye, neàh, barn. T' Cursmas deùs war hardly ower till t' merry neets began.

"At ivvery public-hoose theer was an' auld fwok's an'a young fwok's merry neet, an' varra few fwok, withoot they war owder ailen' or varra auld, or had barns might gaan to them. Theer was oft a supper at t' auld fwok's deùs, an' t' shot was aboot three shillin' a couple, an efter supper theer was cardin', dancin', drinkin', an' singin' gaan on i' different parts o' t' hoose, an' fwok could choose whichivver suitit them best. Theer was oalus a fiddler present, an' t' auld wives war t' meàst part o' them stark't mad o' dancin', bit t' men war oft keener o' playin' at cards, an' sometimes t' wives wad a lot o' them gang to t' card teàbles, an' carry t' men out to t' dancin' room by fworce an' mak' them dance whedder they wad or nut.

"T' young fwok's merry neets war different. Theer was neàh supper at them. They use't to pay aboot a shillin' a piece, an' sometimes gat breed an' cheese an' yall, an' sometimes ivvery yan a basin o' powsardy. Theer wassent seàh mickle cardin' at them; they war mair for dancin'. Nut what fwok caw dancin' noo-a-days, whoar a lot o' fwok keep runnen' round an' roond like a lot o' laal barns laaken at 'roond about, roond about, magglety pie: an' caw that dancing! Oh dear me! I dunnet know what things 'ill git teù efter a while. Yan nivver sees a (giant step now-a-days). I wonder how far yan wad hev to gang afwore yan could finnd ennybody 'at could dance, 'Shuffle ower t' (buckle an' (******ty) patch.' Deary me! Sen I can think on fwok, know hoo to dance reels, jigs, an' hornpipes war aw 'at fwok ivver thowt o' dancin' when I was young, an' t' lads an' lasses could use their feet to some purpose, an' that's mair ner they can deù noo.

"Efter t' dance was ower, t' lads use' to get t' lasses heàmm, an' menny a cwoortship was begun at t' merry neets 'at mebby endit in a weddin' efter a while. Some 'at war theer war mebby auld sweethearts, an' went off, when t' dance war ower, like Darby and Joan. Sometimes it happen't 'at two lads war for t' seàmm lass, an' than theer wad 'a' been a feight, an' just as like as not a third chap for fun wad 'a' slipe't off wi'her when t' tudder two war squabblin' aboot her. An' than theer was oalus some poor things 'at cuddent git a chap at aw, but hed to gang heàmm by theirsels. Aw t' feastin' an' merry neets I've been tellin' ye aboot teùk pleàce ivvery year atween Cursmas and Cannelas, an'seah ye may think 'at their winters i' auld times war nin sae dull efter aw t' rattle.

"Bit they'd their jollifications at udder times o' year as weel.

"They'd their weddin's, their cursnins, their auld wife deùs, an their clippin's 'at war aw parlish girt deùs. An' them war nut aw. Theer war berry fairs, cheppel Sundays, auld wife Setturdays, an' hirin' days, some o' them keep't up yet in a feckless swort iv a way. Nowt like what they use' to be. Bit what can yan expect? Fwok ur larn't nowt noo-a-days, bit a deàl o' stinken' pride, tryin' wi*i?k can leùk t' heiyhest, an' don t' f?***

"I'll mebby tell ye sec weddin's an' auld wife deùs they use' to hev, an' some o' t' brecks 'at happen't a' some o' them, t' next time ye leùk to see me."

### Auld Fashin't Weddin's and Cursnin's
(*West Cumberland Times*, 17 January 1880)

Stay, it was summat aboot what sec weddin's they use to hev i' auld times 'at I was gante tell ye today, an' their auld wife deùs.

Sometimes theer use to be what war caw't "Bridewains" or "Bidden weddin's," an' they war parlish gedderin's them. It was when a couple wantit to git weddit, 'at heddent mickle to t' fwore-head, an' wantit to raise a lock o' brass to start life wi', 'at them deùs war meàdd.

They use to git a few o' t' neighbours to set off o' nag-back, an' ride, some ya way an' some annudder, to ivvery hoose for mappen a dozen or fifteen miles roond, to bid ivvery body to come to a boddy's weddin', on sec a day. They providit plenty for ivvery body to eat an' drink, an' gev a few prizes to spwort (for). Mappen a "*****" to trot for; a "(belt)" to wrussel for; a pair of "mittens" to run for an' mebbe an ounce o' bacco to girn for. What, fwok come i' droves fra aw quarters, auld an' young, rich an' poor. I've hard 'at theer war some times abeùn a thousand fwok at yan o' the bidden weddin's.

When t' weddin'ers gat back fra t' kurk, t' bride went out into t' fauld an' sat on a (copingstone) wi' a (powder) (dibbler)***** on her knee, an' ivvery body went an' put summet intult. Some a shillin', some hofe-a-crown, some a crown, an' some 'at were weel to deù mappen place in hofe-a-guinea or a guinea. When t' expenses o' aw' t' eatin' an' drinkin' was recken't up, there was always eneùff left to set t' new weddit couple up gradely eneùff t' hoosekeepin'.

It was nobbut noo an' than 'at a bidden weddin' teùk pleàce; but, winge barn! t' common weddin's war parlish deùn sometimes. When theer was gaan to be yan, theer was sec preparin' afwore-hand, sec brewin' an' beakin' an' keukin' 'at, bless ye barn, t' auld wives war as "thrang as thropwife," an' some o' them gat fairly moider't amang 't sometimes.

It was nowt uncommon, barn, for fifteen or twenty couples o' young fwok to gang to t' kurk at yan o' their ordinary weddin's, an' as they wad wed neàh body i' them days enny whoar bit in t' oald parish churches, a deal o' fwok hed to gang, mebby, ten or a dozen mile to git weddit. Theer war neàh carriage at that time, an' as it was oft ower far to walk, they use' to mainly-what-gang o' nag-back, two togidder on ya nag, t' men on a swort iv a saddle, an' t' woman behint 'im, on a thing 'at they caw't a "pillion seat."

A' seùn as they gat t' kurk, an' gat their jab deùn, an' war aw cannily moontit onto their nags ageànn, t' bride held up a bit o' blew ribbon an' whoivver war first heàmm was t' hav't. As seùn as they saw t' ribbon, off they set helter skelter through dub an' mire, up hill and down hill, on rwoads 'at fwok waddent caw gooduns noo, I can tell ye. It was nat seàh oft 'at they aw gat heàmm withoot some o' t' auld meers fwoalin' an' oft eneùf a meer wad fwoal twins.

What! Awivver, them 'at tummel't off gat theirsel's gaddert up ageànn after a bit an aw gat heàmm; some landed up reet enough, some aw muck an' some wi' sair behins, bit mainly what, aw riddy for their dinners an' gitten' that was t' next job they hed t' deù. Efter dinner theer was drinken as mickle asivver fwok hed a mind to (tumm'l) into them, an' as some war neàh way **** aboot takkin' on't, theer seùnn gat to be noisy wark, an' afwore neet theer was some gay larks, you may depend on't. Theer was aw kind of diversion gan on, I's warn ye, some war singin', some war dancin' and some fratchen', an' as it oft happens nooadays, them 'at gat drunk sarra't to mak fun fur them 'at keep't swober. Theer was a supper later on for them 'at was swober eneùff t' eat it, an' than mair drinkin' ageànn.

T' last thing at an auld fashint weddin' was puttin' t' bride to bed and throwin' t' stockin'! Awt' young lassie's at war theer hed to gang intet room, and as seùn at bride was i' bed she sat up wi' her feàce fra them an' threw her left leg stockin' ower her reet shooder into amang them, an' whoivver chanc't t' tak' it was sed to be next i' turn to be weddit. It was ya way o' tryen' their forten—ye know.

Anudder way was for ivvery yan o' t' lasses to put a bit o' bride-keak through t' weddin' ring, an' than put it under t' bowster when they went to bed, 'at they mud dream aboot t' men 'at they war to hev for husbands.

When auld Matthew Jopson was gante be weddit he (wantit) to be axt t' Kirk, an' seàh he wrote a letter to old Mr. Denton at was then t' vicar o' Crostet an' leev't at t' vicarage; an' as Matthew could contrive neàh way o' sendin' one they went and carry't it hissel'. It was atween nine and ten mile to gang and when he gat theer an' axt for t' vicar he was shown intul a room, an' presently Mr Denton com in.

Matthew gev a (poo) at his toppin,' an' says he, "Please sir, I browt ye a letter, bit as I's nobbut a varra bad writer, I think I'd better read ye 't; an' with that he poo't oot his letter, an' I dar say Mr. Denton (hotch't) an' laugh't when Matthew read,

"Please Mr Denton, will ye publish me an' Jane Watson o' Sunday fworeneùn if it suit ye?—Yours trewly, "MATTHEW JOPSON."

Theer was anudder man 'at I kent varra weel bit I hadn't better tell ye who it was, 'at when he steùdd up to be weddit an' t' parson axt 'im, "If he wad hev that woman for his weddit wife?" an' seàh he answer't "Aye! aye! to be seùr I'll hev 'er, I nivver mean't nowt else bit hevvin' 'er or else what cud I come here for?"

T' auld wife deùs at they hed whenivver they'd a barn bworn, war parlish jobs sometimes. Aw't weddit wummen within a sartan distance war axt to bring on a particular efterneùn to t' hoose whoar it happn't at; an' ivvery yan carry't a present o' some mak for t' sicek wife. Some teùk a pund o' butter, some a pund o' sugger, some an oonce o' tea an' udders gev 'er a shilling to

git what she like't wi' 't. Than they awl hed t' hev tea a' theer was (barn)-keàk
an' aw maks o' fine (stivery) keàks, an' when I tell ye 'at theer was oft eneùff
a lang way into t' teens o' auld wives, I dar say I needn't tell ye 'at theer was
plenty o' noise ower't.

Leàter on i' t'neet theer was a girt whacken' begin o' sweet butter set on t'
teàble, an' plenty o' havver bread an' cheese, an' yal, an' it was a custom 'at as
seùn as t'auld wives hed aw sitten doon aroond it, for a lot o' young fellows
i' t' neighbourhood, 'at hed been waitin' aboot, to rush in an' ga wi' t' basin
o' sweet butter if they cud git it.

Sometimes they gat it gaily easily, an' udder sometimes t' auld wives wad
a meàdd a disparet feight for 't.

(Whoa) barn! t' wummen fwok hed some spunk i' them times. They
waddent 'a' sitten' primmen' as they deù noo like as menny alabaster dolls
wi' starch't frocks on.

T' roughest "auld wife deù" 'at ivver I was at, war yan 'at was at t' fell-end,
rayder mair ner sixty (year) sen.

Theer was a lock o' auld wives theer 'at war detarmin't 'at lads suddent
hev t' butter if they cud hinder them; an' a few o' them dofft their caps, an'
rise't up their goons riddy for t' fray, an' my (song), a bonny row it was when
it dud start.

Theer was a chap they caw't Jack Hodgin 'at thowt a terrible deal iv hissel,
far mair I dar say ner anybody else thowt on 'im. He was nobbut a swort iv
a (hauflin), bit he use't to don terrible fine. He woarr fine starch't sark neeks
an' breests, an' gev his **** *** as ye nivver saw.

Wiah! That neet, as seùn as they rush't in for t' sweet butter, two or three o'
t' roughest o' t' auld wives went at Jack, "What for smack" an' if ye'll believe
me, they varra nar heàve ivvery wrap o' cleàss off t' back on 'im 'at he'd on,
an' nut content wi' that, they black't his feàce afwore they let 'im gang. Poor
Jack! It was lang er he hard t' last on't.

Efter sweet butter an' aw was sidit by, they set a milkin' can on t' middle
o' t' fleùr, an' stack a (birch) beesom in 't for t' auld wives to jump ower.

Theer was some fine spwort ower that, for they aw hed to try, an' some
jump ower, an' some jump it nut aw ways. That was t' finishin' off o' t' auld
wife deùs always, an' than they aw bundle't off heàmm.

Theer neàh "auld wie deùs" noo-adays, ner deùs o' any mak else 'at er good to owt. Fwok ur nowt like what they use't to be. What, ye're gaan? Wiah! whia! what, ye'll be cawen' ageànn some day an' ah'll tel ye summet mair. Barn, I like to talk aboot auld times.

## Auld fashint clippin's an' sec like
(*West Cumberland Times*, 31 January 1880)

T' NEXT time I cawt t' see Ganny, she sed she'd been thinken' ower what she'd been tellin' me aboot auld times when she was a young body; an' says she:—

I think I telt ye what sec stiven', an' feàstin', an' cardin theer was aboot Cursmas; sec merry neets we use to hev; an' sec rive-oots theer use to be at t' weddin's an' cursnin's. Bit ye munnet think 'at that was aw t' fun we use to hev.

Neah, barn! Theer was clippin' time 'at lastit abeùn a fortneth i' summer days, an' a gangen' time it was; an' theer use to be some gay yarks sometimes 'i' soavin' time; an' theer was kurn suppers an' "Chepple Sundays," an' hiren' days an' "Auld Wife Setterdays," an' "Tip Setterdays," an' menny udder stirrin's beside.

Ivvery body amang t' feels 'at hed a lock o' sheep, use to mak a girt clippin', an' ax aw their neighbours to gang, whedder they war enny use amang t' sheep er nut. T' greeter part o' t' wummen fwok an' barns went, as weel as t' men, an' theer was beàth tea an' supper meàdd for them aw, an' as mickle drink for t' men efter supper as ivver they'd a mind to teùmm into them. An', winge barn! t' clippin' drink 'at they use to mak' than was worth cawin' drink. It was brew't o' purpose, an' nut t' way 'at a varst o' t' ayl's meàdd noo, wi' a varra laal lock o' mawt an' a varra girt sup o' watter, bit we use to put a good lock o' mawt in at t' furst, an' nut content wi' that, efter it 'ed mass't awhile, we drain't it off an' teùmm't it onto fresh mawt, to mak 't stranger. Gockson, barn! when it 'ed been keep't awhile it was varra nar as strang as brandy, an' aboot twea glasses on't wad 'a' setten a body a singin' enny time.

On t' clippin' day, efter t' sheep war clipt an' turn't oot, t' supper ower an' sidit by, an' t' men fwok aw sitten aroond t' teàble, a girt clippin-jug full on 't was browt oot, er mebby two, yan at ayder end. "Luck to t' stock" was alles drucken furst, in a full bumper, 'an a full bumper o' that stuff gev a gay lock o' them a start seah 'at they wantit neah preasin' efter.

Theer used to be a deal o' sang singin' at clippin's, an' seùnn efter supper theer was oft some varra good songs an' varra weel sung, bit that was seùnn ower, for when they'd gitten a few glasses into them, they wad aw sing togidder, an aw make o' songs.

T' last thing at an auld fashint clippin' was drinkin' t' shipperds' health. To deù that, aw 'at could stand steùdd up on t' fleùrr in a roond ring, aw bit yan 'at steùdd in t' middle wit' t' jug new full't, an' a glass. When aw was riddy, he full't t' glass, an handit it to him 'at was to drink furst, an' than t' rest aw sang—

> The shepherd's health, and it shall go round, and it shall go round,
> And it shall go round, and it shall go round,
> The shepherd's health, and it shall go round,
>     Heigh ho! Heigh ho! Heigh ho!
> And he that doth this health deny,
> Before his face I him defy.
> He's fit for no good company,
> So let this health go round.

Him 'at hed t' glass than liftit it tull his lips an' drank, while they sang—

> Hold your canny cup to your chin,
> Open your mouth and let liquor run in,
> The more you drink the fuller your skin,
> So let it go merrily down.

If he mannish't to empty t' glass while they war singin' them fower lines, they sang—

I hold a crown it's all gone down,

It's all gone down, it's all gone down,

I hold a crown it's all gone down,

So fill it up again.

If he fail't to empty t' glass, while they war singin' t' fower lines 'at began "Hold your canny cup to your chin," he was fine't, an' that mean't at t' glass hed to be full't up ageànn, an' he'd to try till he did it. Lord bless me weel! sec uprwoars theer use to be sometimes ower drinken t' shipperd's health. Fwok war aw middlin' fresh afwore that come on, an' what wi' drinkin' an; singin' an' shootin', an' ya thing er anudder, it was varra nar eneùff to lift t' reùff of t' hoose an' afwore t' last they hoistit t' shipperd onta their shooders, an' he was lucky if he duddent git a brokken heed ower some o' t' auld yak boaks 'at reach't across t' room. When that was ower they brak up, an' fwok set off heàmm, some ya way an' some anudder, an' war aw riddy eneùff for anudder clippin' t' next day.

Dud ye ivver hear t' teàll about auld Joe Dodds an' Alfred Sargison's clippin'?

Auld Joe, an' his wife, auld Mary, war tweà nwotit characters, i' their way. They war elderly fwok when I kent them, an' hed a girt family, at war aw squander't, an' they war left just their two sels.

Auld Joe used to git a darrick o' threshin', er dykin', er fullin' muck, er owt o' that mak, enny way whoar he could, an' auld Mary went oot o' weshin' an' beakin' er owt she could git to deù.

Joe used to work for sixpence a day an' his meat, an' when I tell ye at he was keen o' beàth bacco an' drink, ye may be seùrr 'at auld Mary an' him war nobbut varra poor. T' auld lad wad a' shoot, an' deùnn varra nar enny mortal thing for a pint o' yal. He was a varra good whusseler, an' when he gat to t' public hoose fwok use to give 'im a pint for whusselen' a teùnn, an' theer he wad 'a' sitten wi' ya leg cross't ower t' tudder, drinken' pints o' yal, an' whusselen' till he wad 'a' fawn off t' chair ontet fleùrr, an' than they wad 'a' trail't 'im intul a corner an' left 'im liggen' theer, an' auld Joe wad 'a' whussel't away liggen' on his back i' t' corner till he fell asleep. He used to contrive by owder heùkk er creùkk to git to aw t' clippin's an' timmer-raisin's, or owt o' that mak, whoar theer was gante be enny drink to be hed; an' t' way 'at he hed to scheme to mannish't sometimes was varra divarten.' Auld Joe fwok, whoar they leev't, was nut varra nar neighbours to Alfred Sargison's, bit Joe use to gang to thresh sometimes; an' auld Mary to beàkk an' wesh, an' when t' clippin' was comen' on, auld Mary hed to gang to help to wesh t' dishes an' sec like, bit Joe was nut invitit to gang at aw. When t' time gat nearer an' nearer, an' neàh word com', t' auld fellow was like a fish oot o' watter, bit he was determin't nut to give 't up withoot tryen' some way er annudder, an' seàh when it gat t' last day he contriv't to meet Alfred, an' efter bidden' good mwornin' says auld Joe—"Theer been a terrible dispute at 'oor side o' t' hill, this last two er three days, an' neàh body bit yersel can decide it, Alfred; ye may as weel deù't noo."

"Varra weel," says Alfred, "if it be owt 'at I can settle I's varra willin'. What is t' dispute aboot?"

"Wey," says Joe, "some o' t' neighbours say at I's axt to your clippin', an' some o' them say I issent. Is I er nut?"

"To be seùrr ye ur," says Alfred.

An' seah auld Joe conquer't ageànn. Soavin' time use to be a parlish time in t' deàlls eno. Where they'd a gay few sheep, they hed to hire a lock o' soavers, for three week er a month mebby, an' when ther chanc't to be a lot o' them young fellows, they war up to aw mack o' antics, an' theer was some divvelment gaan on amang them always.

Bless ye, barn! if theer was sec rows noo, as a lot o' them rascallions wad a' sometimes meàdd i' soaavin' time, theer wad be sec wark wi' policemen an' justices as nivver was seen.

### *Auld Fashint Farmin'*
(*West Cumberland Times*, 14 February 1880)

When next I caw't to see Ganny, I remindit 'er iv 'er promise to tell me summet aboot their farmin' and mannishin' t' land lang sen, when she was young.

"Aye, aye," says she, "theer greet changes i' that mak o' wark sen I was a laal lass, an' nut aw for t' better owder. Theer a deàl o' fine machines an' things noo-a-days 'at they heddent than, bit t' fwok 'er seàh mickle fecklesser 'at I cannot bit think 'at things war deùnn just as weel, an mebbe better, i' auld times ner they ur noo.

"Lord 'a marcy! I wonder hoo fwok wad ivver git deùnn noo, if they hed to mannish an' work their wark wi' t' teùlls 'at they hed i' them times. Wy, t' lang an' t' short on 't is, it cuddent be deùnn at aw.

"Theer issent a boddy i' t' country, nowder man ner woman, 'at wad know hoo to begin owder to mak a truss o' hay, er to deet a lock o' corn widoot a machine, as they hed to deù than, an' in a varra few years mair theer 'ill be nowder soavers ner mowers. Theer mair ner hofe o' t' woman fwok noo 'at can nowder mak a stannin' pie ner beàkk a bit o' havver bread, ner muck a byre for that matter. Bit ahaagh! it's neàh use talkin'; fowk think theirsels far clivverer noo ner ivver they war befwore, and they're welcome to their opinion. I'll keep my awn.

"Some fifty-year afwore my time, I've hard my grandfadder say theer wassent sec a thing as a car, ner a wheel't thing o' enny mak, enny way o' t' heigh side o' Cummerland.

"T' hay aw hed to be meàdd into square bundles caw't trusses, an' carry't heàmm o' nagback. It tekk six reapps, three ayder way, to tie a truss o' hay, an' they always hed three sets, seàh 'at when t' man gat he wi' a truss, he weltit it off at t' hayloft deur, gat hoàld iv a set o' empty reàpps, jump ontet nag an gallop't back to t' field, whoar theer was annuder truss ready for 'im by he gat theer. Barn! They knew hoo to gang aboot their wark. Theer was neàh time lost, an' they could slipe a fine lot o' hay in i' that fashion on a fine day.

"When they wantit to carry a lock o' muck out into t' field, they hed what they caw't muck bots 'at hang yan o' ayder side o' t' nag, summet like t' crates, 'at ye've seen potters hev, hingen' o' ayder side iv a cuddy, to carry their pots in. T' muck hots hed lowse boddoms, just fassent in wi' a wood pin, seàh 'at when they gat to t' pleàce whoar they wantit to be, they'd nowt to deù bi poo t' pin oot, an' t' muck drop't oot ontet grund just at reet spot. T' way 'at they empty their cwoal trucks at t' station ye see, is neàh new invention; it's nobbut an imitation o' t' auld fashint muck hots

"Ivvery thing 'at was carry't fra ya pleàce tull anudder, i' them times, hed to be carry't o' nagback. As I telt ye afwore theer was neàh cars ner owt o' that mack, ner neàh rwoads 'at they could 'a geànn on if theer hed been enny. Theer was carriers 'at went atween t' toons, to carry goods on packhorses as they cawt them. Sometimes theer was ivver seàh many horses went togidder, ivvery yan wi' a contrivance on it back 'at they cawt a pack-saddle, an' t' leàdd was fassent onte that. It 'at went fworemost hed a bell fassent on 'at keep't tinklin' as it went, an' aw t' rest follow't yan efter anudder, an' i' that way they toil't away wi' their leàds, ower t' fells an' through t' deàlls, mile efter mile, on rwoads whoar theer was nobbut just room eneùff for yan to gan abreest.

"I've hard them say 'at Dan Crostet o' Wanthet gat t' furst car 'at ivver was abeùnn Keswick, an' it was thowt sec a curiosity 'at fwok com for miles ower t' fells to see 't, an' I mak neàh doot bit if t' seàmm car could be yok't up noo, i' t' seàmm fashin, it wad be thowt as greet a curiosity as it was than.

"T' furst 'at com up war what they cawt tummel-wheel't cars. T' wheels war nut spock't as they ur noo, bit meàdd solid an' fix't ontet assel-tree, an' that t' car-kist hed fower wood pins on t' underside for t' assel-tree to gang atween, seàh 'at it could be liftit ontet wheels, er off, es they like't, an' when they startit it forret, t' wheels an' t' assel-tree aw went roond togidder. Theer war varra little iron aboot them mak o' cars, nowder chairs ner (creùks) ner steàpples to yoke them wi', nowt bit a lock o' wood pins an' roàpps 'at they cawt hammerheads, an' if they happen to throw t' car over in a brantish field, t' wheels wad 'a' run away wi' t' assel-tree, an' left t' nag an' t' car liggen whoar it war.

"It was a mishap o' that mak 'at finnish't Dan Crostet earnin'. Oa account o' t' narrow rwoads an' gapsteeds, it was nobbut come varra odd jobs 'at they could use 't for, but Dan teùkk a fancy 'at if they could nobbut git it ontet top o' Wasthet Fell, it wad be t' finest thing 'at ivver was to fetch t' peats t'

"Auld geàtt heed" riddy for sleddin'. What, they teùkk 't up Wanthet Bank, an' away roond by Moosdale, an' I hardly know what geàtt, bi, awivver, they gat it up at last, an' aboot t' second er third carful, it gat whemmel't t' wrang side up, an' 't wheels an' t' asseltree went doon inte Wanthet crag an war nivver seen efter.

"Sen I can think on, t' farms in aw thur fell deàlls war nobbut aboot hofe t' size 'at they ur noo. Theer was far mair o' them, as ye may see be t' auld rewin't buildin's sticken' up an' doon on't fellsides whoarivver ye leùkk. Ivvery family, varra nar, leev't on it awn bit esteàtt, 'at consistit iv a heàmsteed be t' edge o' t' common, an' a few crofts an' parrocks roond it, 'at togidder, wi' what they could git off t' common, wad paster some hofe scwore o' brease, a nag, an' a hundred er tweà o' sheep.

"It was nobbut a bare leevin', an' when t' family was a gay girt un, they use' to eke oot wi' cardin an' spinnin' their lock o' woo', an' oft eneùff they hed a leàmm er tweà, an' wad 'a' woven 't as weel.

"They plew't as mickle ivvery year as wad growe them a lock o' havver to mak meal on, an' mappen a lock o' big to be meàdd inte mawt. They warrant fettle't up wi' plews an' geer es fwok ur noo, an' it was a gay job gitten' a bit o' ley turn't ower ye may depend on 't. As nut menny o' them keep't mair ner ya nag, they hed to help yan anudder i' plewin' time. It teùkk three nags an' fower fwok to plew ley. Theer was yan to hod t' stilts, yan to hod t' beam doon, an' two to caw t' plew.

"What's cawin' t' plew?" says I.

"What cawin' t' plew!" says Ganny, "It's leaden' t' nags, turnen' them in at t' ends, an' sec like. I caw't 't plew mesel menny a time, an' a varra unthanful berth it was ye may depend on't. If t' fur was creùkt, an' it wassent seah oft straight, t' cawers gat awt bleàmm. Sometimes when you war gan at full speed, t' plew sock wad mebby 'a' gone ageànn a yearthfast cobble an' spanghewt t' chap 'at was hedden' t' stilts, like a paddick: sometimes t' geer wad 'a' broken, an' sometimes ya mishap an' sometimes anudder, an' whativver went wrang it was always t' cawer 'at was i' t' fawt."

"Wy indeed," says I to Ganny, "theer is a wonderful improvement i' agriculter sen them times"

"Agrifiddlesticks!" says she, "ye're on wi' ye're fine neàmms ageànn.

"If it's enny improvement to hev fine dicksuary words to caw ivverything be, theer plenty on 't. Mannishen' a bit land mun be cawt agriculter: t' gripe, an' t' speàdd, an' t'scrat mun be cawt implements, an' a coo doctor a veterinary. Just think o' auld Jwohnny Walker o' Armboth, bein' cawt a veterinary; an' if yan was to gang by t' number o' beese an' nags 'at he cure't, he was mappen as weel desarven' of a fine neàmm as enny o' them. Jwohnny heddent a morsel o' pride: nut eneùff to keep 'im oot o' t' muck. He use' to gang to Keswick market ivvery Setterday, an' he went just as he was, withoot ivver owder washen' his feàce or changen' his cwoat, or owt o' that mak. He reàdd on an auld hollow back't white Galloway withoot owder saddle or bridle. Wi' just a helter on t' heed on 't, an' an empty sack in t' hollow iv it back to sit on, he use't to ride away till he gat to beside t' brick kilns on Keswick common, an' than he fassent t' helter shank roond t' galloway neck, an' turn't it lowse amang t' whins, to paster tell he com back fra t' market. I' that way he spare't payin' beàth t' turnpike yat an' t' wostler. He was varra careful was Jwhonny, an' indulg't hissel wi' nowt i' t' way o' luxerys bit a lock o' snuff, an' ower that he nivver went to t' expense iv a box, bit what he duddent carry on his top lip he hed in his weàstcwoat pocket.

"That wad nobbut be a queerish description iv a veterinary noo-a-days, wad it? Bit Jwhonny was a deàl thowt on iv his day, an' was lastit an' sent for menny a mile sometimes."

# OTHER WRITINGS

### The Old-Fashioned Foxhunter
#### (*West Cumberland Times*, 10 January 1880)

In the month of November, in the year seventy-two,
Three jolly foxhunters all kindly and true,
Rode forth to Blencathra thro' dub and thro' mire,
To take their diversions with Crozier the squire.
        Tally-ho! Hark away, &c.

He went to his kennel and took them within,
"On Monday," says Crozier, "our joys shall begin;"
Both horses and hounds how they'll race thro' the glen,
How they'll follow afoot, not forgetting old men.

When Monday was come, right early at morn,
John Crozier arose and he took down his horn;
He gave it a flourish so loud in the hall,
Each heard the glad summons and came at the call;

For a drag hit at morning is seldom so slow,
"Hark to Skiddaw!" says Crozier; "the scent he has now;"
And the sweet dappled darlings like music and rally,
They charmed every hill and they echoed each valley.

So when we came home we toasted the health
Of a man who ne'er varied for places or wealth!
With mirth and good humour did cheerfully sing
Success to John Crozier, and God save the King!

## *The Cumberland Dialect and the Bards who have written it*

As the Cumbrian is only one among a great number of dialects which are spoken in Britain, each of which differs more or less from the others in pronunciation and idiom, it perhaps may not be out of place, by way of introduction to the subject under consideration, to glance at the probable origin of the dialects in past times, and the causes of the slow but gradual disuse which they seem destined to fall into in the future.

No one who has thought at all on the subject can fail to see that the origin of so many different modes of speech in this country has been principally owing to the absence of a written language, and, in a less degree, to the imperfect means of communication which existed in primitive times between one district and another. It is little more than four hundred years since printing was first introduced into England, and although there might be printed books a few years sooner, and manuscripts some centuries earlier still, these, besides many of them being in Latin, were so extremely scarce and inaccessible that there could not be said to be any written language available to the common people, among whom the dialects originated, until towards the end of the fifteenth century.

Now, it is supposed that the first inhabitants of Britain were Celts, who crossed over from Denmark about five or six centuries before the Christian era; and, assuming this to be correct, there was a period of more than two thousand years during which the people of this island had no written language, and consequently no fixed standard of speech—a fact which is of itself quite sufficient to account for all the variations and irregularities which have prevailed.

Setting out with the assumption (which is by no means certain) that the first settlers all spoke the same language, or dialect, which would of course be Celtic, we can easily imagine how, in the course of time, when the coast where they had first established themselves became overpopulated, parties would wander off from the main body, and go in search of other favourable situations, where they would build their huts and form separate communities; how in these new settlements any word which by chance got a different pronunciation, or any new phrase or idiom started by one, would be imitated by the rest, learned by the children, and so perpetuated; how, other words and phrases would follow, and other colonies, branch off to other parts of the island. And when we reflect that Britain was then a vast wilderness, without roads or means of communication between the different settlements, we can easily understand that in the course of ages every district would have a community in a great measure isolated from the rest, with a dialect of its own. How these dialects were acted upon and modified in after ages by successive incursions of new comers from different parts of Europe is a subject beyond the range of this paper. No doubt many of them were almost entirely changed in their character, but that they were never totally obliterated is evidenced by the numerous Celtic words and roots which still remain in all of them. We may, however, observe that the dialects would not all be acted upon in an equal degree. For instance, in the southern parts of the island, where the German intruders were most numerous and longest established, the Anglo-Saxon would become the dominant tongue. In the Northern parts the Danish and Scandinavian element would prevail; while in the more inaccessible districts such as North Wales, the Celtic would remain almost unchanged.

As, therefore, there can be little doubt but that the great diversity of speech in this country arose, as has just been stated, from the absence of a written language, and the imperfect means of communication which formerly existed between one district and another, it would seem to follow as a natural sequence, that, these wants having been supplied, the dialects would quickly die out. How is it, then, it may be asked, that many of them and notably the Cumbrian, are nearly as vigorous as ever?

In replying to this question, and taking the Cumberland as the dialect with which we are best acquainted, we may observe that though books, periodicals, and newspapers, are now so plentiful and cheap as to be easily obtained by every one and although the means of travelling and postal communication have become almost perfect, the people who speak the dialect in the rural parts of the country have hitherto as a rule, neither read, written, nor travelled. There is, however, a marked change taking place in this respect. Newspapers and books are becoming far more common in country houses; and it is probable that as our dream of general education becomes gradually realized, old prejudices will be given up, old habits laid aside, and at some future time the rural inhabitants of Cumberland may perhaps converse together in the ordinary Queen's English. The intention of this paper, however, is rather to treat of the dialect as we find it, than to inquire into the changes it has undergone, or to speculate upon the length of time which may elapse before it is entirely laid aside. It will therefore be limited in a great measure to the two questions—"Where is the dialect spoken at the present time?" and "What are its chief distinctive characteristics?"

To the first question, "Where is the dialect spoken at present?" we may answer: It is spoken under one form or another over all the agricultural and pastoral districts of Cumberland, and by the common people in the towns as well, but only in its pure state towards the middle of the county, being mixed with other dialects around the outsides. This may be accounted for in the following manner. In former times, when England and Scotland were separate kingdoms, and almost constantly at war with each other, there was a strip of land, a few miles in breadth, stretching from Berwick, on the German Ocean, to the Solway Firth, which was called the debateable ground, being a sort of overlap of the boundary; and this land was claimed by both nations, but could not properly be said to belong to either. Now, something similar to this happens, wherever two districts meet in which different dialects are spoken. There is a sort of overlap, where the words and phrases have become so blended and intermixed, that the folk speech cannot be said to belong exclusively to either district. Hence, in that part of Cumberland bordering on Scotland, from the Cheviot Hills on the east, to Silloth on the west, the dialect is half Scottish. In the higher part of the dales, such as Borrowdale and Wythburn, which run up to the southern boundary of the county, it is mixed with that of Westmorland. In the east, towards Crossfell, it has many Northumbrian words; while in the west, of late years, since the iron manufacture has become so much developed, the Cumbrian, Irish, Welsh, Cornish, and other dialects, have become in some instances rather awkwardly jumbled together. It is, therefore, only in the central part of the county that the Cumberland dialect is spoken in its purity; and this central part may be defined as a tract of country surrounding the Skiddaw and Blencathra range of mountains, and extending about fifteen miles east and west from their base, and some five or six north and south.

To those persons who have always looked upon the dialect as something exceedingly vulgar and outlandish, it will no doubt appear paradoxical when we refer to its being spoken in its purity. It will therefore be as well to observe here that there is nothing necessarily vulgar about it. One may be vulgar either with or without it. There are some people excessively vulgar who do not speak the dialect, while there are others who use no other form of speech who have not a particle of vulgarity about them. They make quite as great a mistake who think that all dialect words are corruptions, or wrong pronunciations, of ordinary English. On the contrary, there can be little doubt but that a great many words now used in standard books, were formerly so used exactly in the form in which we now find them in the dialect, but have since been modified and altered to suit our modern ideas of speech. In proof of this, if we look into the writings of some old authors—books which, no doubt, were standard works at the time they were published—we find numbers of old words written in just the same way as they are now used in dialect writing; and it is quite possible that many old dames, who have spent all their lives up in the dales, could give a much more sensible explanation of some doubtful passages in Chaucer than many learned members of the Philological Society.

We will, however, proceed to point out a few of the peculiarities of vocalism and idiom which render the dialect so difficult to understand by persons not acquainted with it. One of the first things that will strike a stranger on hearing it is the way in which the double vowel or diphthongal sounds vary from the ordinary English. The proper diphthongal sound of "ou" or "ow" is changed to that of "oo": thus, house becomes "hoose"; cloud, "clood"; round, "roond"; and so with "ow," cow is "coo"; now, "noo"; how "hoo"; and so on. Then such words as have the "oo" sound in ordinary English require "eu" in the dialect: book is "beùk"; look, "leùk"; school, "scheùl"; and fool, "feùl." Again such words as in the English have the long "o" and "oa" sound, are sometimes pronounced in the dialect as if spelt with a "w," so that note is "nwote"; coat, "cwoat"; and boat, "bwoat"; but sometimes the long "o" is changed into the proper diphthongal sound of "ow," so that brought is "browt"; thought, "thowt," &c. The sound of the long "i," too, is often changed to that of "ee" and right is "reet"; light, "leet"; bright "breet"; and so on. The short "e" also is occasionally changed to the long "e," when head becomes "heed," and dead, "deed." Passing from the vowel sounds, we will proceed to notice some other peculiarities of pronunciation. In the dialect the termination "en" is invariably used instead of "ing"—thus writing is "writen';" walking, "walken';" working, "worken'," and so on. The dental sound of "th" is seldom heard in the dialect either—as: father is "fadder"; mother, "mudder"; and brother, "brudder"; twentieth is "twentit"; and thirtieth, "thirtit." Even in the article "the" the "th" is not sounded. Instead of saying "The master and the mistress," a Cumbrian says "T' maister an' t' mistress." "And" is always contracted to "an'," "thee" to "the'," and "with" to "wi':" thus, the sentence "I will go with thee," is shortened to "I'll ga wi' the'."

It will be seen from these few examples, that in the Cumbrian pronunciation there is a marked tendency to contract, or shorten the words, a tendency of which many more specimens might be given, such as "slape" for slippery; "flate" for frightened; "'pleen" for complain, and such like. The few words we have noted will, however, be sufficient to give a fair idea of the Cumbrian vocabulary, and therefore we will next glance at a few of its idiomatic peculiarities. Perhaps the most noticeable thing about the way in which the dialect is spoken, and its worst feature, is the total disregard which the speakers have for the rules of grammar. They use pronouns in the objective case instead of in the nominative; and singular verbs instead of plural ones in almost every sentence. Instead of saying "He and I are going," a Cumbrian says, "Him an' me 's gaan." They do not use the possessive case of proper nouns at all. Instead of saying "George's cow and Harry's horse," they say "Gwordie coo and Harry horse." Then they have an odd way of omitting the object of a sentence, and leaving it to be guessed at. They will say, "They're gante wesh," or "They're gante clip," without saying whether they are going to wash clothes, or the sheep, or themselves; or whether they are going to clip the sheep, or a hedge, or something else. The anecdote told by the butcher was an instance of this kind. A butcher went to a farmhouse to ask for his weekly order, when the old dame said to him, "Nay barn, we'll nut want enny this week, we're gante kill oorsels." That did not mean that they were all going to commit suicide, and so would not require any more meat, it simply meant that they were going to kill a sheep of their own. They sometimes confound quantity and numbers in a droll way, too. They will say, "A few poddish" or "A few broth," but they would laugh at you if you said a few water, or a few milk. Although these and other peculiarities of the idiom, which might be pointed out, render the dialect almost unintelligible to strangers, they are so perfectly familiar to those who speak it, that they do not hinder conversation in the least. Only give two or three Cumbrians some subject of dispute for instance, the merits or demerits of some particular horse or cow,—and they will argue the different points with as much energy, and as fluently, as if they had all the rules of Lindley Murray by heart. Indeed it is when listening to an argument or "fratch" as it is called, that one may pick up some of the broadest and richest specimens of the dialect. It will be seen, however, by all impartial critics that the irregularities that we have mentioned are simply corruptions and excrescences, which no more affect the real character of the dialect than the bad English of uneducated Londoners, or the coarse slang of the American rowdy affects that of the English language itself.

We will next notice some of the redeeming traits of the dialect. Chief among these are its conciseness and its expressiveness. We have already referred to the shortness of Cumbrian words and pointed out how monosyllables in the dialect are frequently synonymous with ordinary English words of two or three syllables; and when we consider that, besides this, many of the phrases, too, are extremely laconic, it is easy to understand that a Cumbrian requires far less time and breath to express his ideas to his neighbour than would be required to do it in Queen's English. Take for example, the questions, "Where are you going?" "What are you doing?" and "What is the matter?" It will be observed that each of these questions consists of five syllables, whereas, in the dialect they only require three each, thus, "Where's te gaan?" "What's te deùn?" and "What's t' matter?" Numerous examples of this kind might be given; but as the above will give an idea of our meaning, we will proceed to make a few observations on the expressiveness of the Cumbrian mode of speech. We cannot illustrate this part of the subject better than by giving a few specimens of the short saws with which the folkspeech of Cumberland abounds. Indeed, there is hardly a circumstance or incident in the lives of the dales people, but there is a figurative phrase of some kind applicable to it. Here are a few. If a person is thought foolish they will say, "He's nobbut hofe rock't," or "He's as thin as a cat lug." If one is slow in his movements, they say, "He'll gang farder i' two days ner yan." When an old courtship is renewed, they say, "Auld ke'all ur seùner warm't nor newens meàde." If a man marries for money, they say, "He's weddit t' middin for t' seàke o' t' muck." If a person is not to be depended upon, "He's not to ride a watter on." If an insignificant person has had a narrow escape, it is said "That 'at's nowt 's nivver i' danger." If a person is cross and cantankerous, "He's as creùk't as a tup horn." If one is sly and deceitful, they say, "Smooth water runs deep." We might go on quoting these old saws, but the few specimens given might serve to give some notion of their character, and though many of them may not be so very refined, we must at least admit that they are uncommonly expressive and much to the purpose.

Alluding, in a former part of this paper, to the corruptions and irregularities of speech which abounded among the dialect-speaking people of Cumberland, we remarked that such irregularities were no obstacle in the way of conversation, but to any one attempting to write in the dialect it is very different. In composition (even in the dialect,) a writer is obliged to pay some attention to the laws of grammar, and consequently is prevented from writing many of the most common and striking phrases exactly as they are spoken; and although the pronunciation may, as a general rule, be pretty clearly indicated by means of phonetic spelling, there are some words in use the sound of which it would be impossible to give a correct idea of on paper by any combination of letters.

It may perhaps be asked, "But what is the use of writing in the dialect at all? If people will write, why not write in ordinary English?" Well, perhaps it is fancy as much as anything. Tastes differ so much, that it is said there is no accounting for them. Talents differ very much, too. People who do write ordinary English have very different ideas. One writes prose, another poetry. One truth, another fiction. One songs, and another sermons. But there may also be utility in dialect-writing. If, as we surmised at the beginning, the Cumbrian mode of speech is destined to die out in the course of two or three generations, it may be desirable to preserve as many specimens of it as we can, from which our grandchildren and greatgrandchildren may see the rough and homely garb in which their forefathers were wont to clothe their ideas. And further, the peculiar manners, traits, and above all the humour of Cumbrians may be far more forcibly depicted in the dialect than in any other way. If any one wishes to know about the manners and customs of the people who lived in this county towards the latter end of the last and beginning of the present century, he will do well to read, not Nicholson and Burn's or Hutchinson's History of Cumberland, but the dialect writings of Anderson, Stagg, and others. From the songs and ballads of these writers, one may get a far better insight into the peculiar traits and rough manners of the Cumbrians of that time than from any other source whatever.

Our old border county has been peculiarly rich in native writers. Not to speak of Wordsworth and others, who have distinguished themselves in the higher walks of literature, Cumberland has never, for the last one hundred and fifty years, been without its dialect writers; many of whom have enjoyed a large amount of local popularity. The first who attempted to rhyme in the vernacular, (of whom we have any authentic record) was the Rev. Josiah Relph, of Sebergham, who died in 1743. He was followed in succession by Evan Clark, of Wigton; Miss Gilpin, of Scaleby Castle; Miss Blamire, of Thackwood; Blind Stagg, of Burgh-by-Sands; and Robert Anderson, of Carlisle. The last has been commonly styled the Cumberland Bard, and has been the most popular of all the dialect writers. Then, there were Mark Lonsdale, John Rayson, and Woodcock Graves; and there was Alexander Craig Gibson, who, I have no doubt, was personally known to some here present. There are still living Mr. William Dickinson and Miss Powley; so that we have a continuous chain, or succession, of dialect writers, stretching from Relph to the present time.

It may be that but few educated persons take much interest in the dialect. Nevertheless, if entered into without prejudice, or affectation, the study of it, as the study of most other things, may become very interesting. I have in my possession a letter which I received from the late Dr. Gibson, two or three years before his death, in which he styles it our "Grand old dialect;" and when we reflect that, to the people of Cumberland, it has for hundreds of years served every purpose for the interchange of their ideas; that they have ever found in it words and phrases which were amply sufficient to express every emotion of their minds; that in it they have told their joys and their griefs; their hopes and their fears; and that in it they have sung their loves and their sorrows, their sports and their rejoicings,—I think that if we do not go so far as Dr. Gibson, to style it our "Grand old dialect" we may, at least, respect and value it as an old and faithful servant.

(The CHAIRMAN afterwards observed that the author had alluded to writers in the Cumberland dialect past and present, but his modesty had not permitted him to tell them that he himself was one of the foremost dialect writers of the day. Mr. Richardson's book was one of the very best that had been issued, and was remarkably free from the errors that some of the writers in the dialect had fallen into. They were very much indebted to Mr Richardson for his paper.)

# APPENDIX

## John Richardson and the Cumberland Association for the Advancement of Literature and Science

John Richardson was a regular speaker at meetings of the Cumberland Association for the Advancement of Literature and Science in Keswick and Cockermouth. There are records of him presenting seven papers, though it appears that only three of them were selected for printing in the Association's Transactions. The three published are:

27 November 1875, "The Cumberland Dialect and the Bards who have written it", published in J. Cliton Ward (ed.), *Transactions of the Cumberland Association for the Advancement of Literature and Science*, Part 1 (Keswick: Printed by R. Bailey, Pt.1, 1875–6), pp. 50–8.

6 November 1876, "Old Customs and Usages", published in J. Clifton Ward (ed.), *Transactions of the Cumberland Association for the Advancement of Literature and Science*, Part 2 (Keswick: Printed by R. Bailey, 1876–7), pp. 107–24.

18 February 1884, "Dialects of Cumberland and the Lake District", published in Series 2 of *Cummerland Talk*.

Those unpublished, and with no record that I can find, are:

5 November 1877, "The Superstitions once Common in the Lake District"

2 December 1878, "Sports and Pastimes in the Lake Country"

2 February 1881, "Cumberland before the Union with Scotland"

5 December 1881, "Scottish Life and Character"

www.ingramcontent.com/pod-product-compliance
Lightning Source LLC
Chambersburg PA
CBHW051848090426
42811CB00034B/2262/J